3/11

D0500517

Restoring the
American Dream

Restoring the
American Dream

The Defining Voice in the Movement for Liberty

ROBERT RINGER

Foreword by

STEPHEN MOORE

WILEY

John Wiley & Sons, Inc.

Published by John Wiley & Sons, Inc., Hoboken, New Jersey.
Published simultaneously in Canada.

Portions of this book were originally published in 1980 by Fawcett.

For general information on our other products and services or for technical
support, please contact our Customer Care Department within the United States at
(800) 762-2974, outside the United States at (317) 572-3993 or fax (317) 572-4002.

Wiley also publishes its books in a variety of electronic formats. Some content that
appears in print may not be available in electronic books. For more information about
Wiley products, visit our web site at www.wiley.com.

ISBN 978-0-470-62762-4 (cloth); 978-0-470-89334-0 (ebk);
978-0-470-89335-7 (ebk); 978-0-470-89403-3 (ebk)

Printed in the United States of America

10 9 8 7 6 5 4 3 2 1

May all our children and grandchildren
experience the wonders of living
the American Dream.

Contents

Foreword

Restoring the American Dream requires a resurrection of free market capitalism and a rejection of Obamanomics and the slow but steady socialization of America. We have foolishly allowed the left in America to destroy the dream by undermining the fundamental principles of limited government on which prosperity is fostered.

Clearly, President Reagan understood the true meaning of the term *American Dream*, and he emphasized that understanding by saying that "government is not the solution to our problem; government *is* the problem." Unlike Jimmy Carter, he understood that high tax rates reduce people's incentive to produce.

With Reagan's emphasis on smaller government, lower taxes, and less regulation, the U.S. economy experienced the greatest sustained period of economic growth in its history. As explained in my book *The End of Prosperity* (coauthored by Arthur Laffer and Peter Tanous), the economic expansion under Reagan was "resilient and powerful because economic policy was radically realigned to reward risk taking and entrepreneurship and unleash the gale-wind forces of technology, information, and the new digital age."

While Ronald Reagan's ascendancy to the presidency was a great step forward for America, like so many things in life, his policies may have had an unintended negative consequence. The consequence I am referring to is that the success of Reaganomics may have caused Americans to become complacent about both prosperity and liberty.

Even though the explosion of high technology kept the economy robust throughout the 1980s and 1990s, something else was going on quietly behind the scenes: The progressive movement was licking its wounds from the Reagan Revolution and retooling its weapon of choice—gradualism—to slowly move the country to the left once again. And Americans seemed too busy enjoying their prosperity to even take notice.

As a result, over the past two decades America has quietly moved away from freedom and free markets and, at an increasingly accelerating pace, toward socialism. This acceleration has been especially rapid under the Obama administration, so much so that our elected representatives seem perfectly comfortable with ignoring the Constitution.

The power of gradualism is that each new generation comes to accept less and less freedom as a normal way of life, especially if children are fed false information by their teachers and the media. The once-mainstream media has become so out of touch—refusing to even cover stories unfavorable to the current administration—that it is now referred to by many as *the fringe media*. As to schools, more and more parents are becoming outraged by the purposeful disinformation that is being taught in their children's classrooms.

Thankfully, however, Americans are a resilient people who have a remarkable way of remembering, albeit sometimes waiting far longer than they should to do so, that liberty is an integral part of their heritage. For a majority of Americans, it's like riding a bicycle. Once experiencing the joys of liberty, they never forget it. It's in their blood. And never has this been so apparent than in the nationwide protest rallies that are becoming increasingly larger and bolder.

The silent majority has been awakened by an out-of-control and corrupt government. As I watched the tea parties and town hall protests begin to unfold, it occurred to me that *Restoring the American Dream* is far more relevant today than when it was first published in 1979. As a result of our current economic chaos and the cancerous corruption that has spread throughout government at all levels, I believe people are much more prepared to hear the sometimes uncomfortable truths that Robert Ringer sets forth in this book.

Much more so than in the late 1970s and early 1980s, readers can relate to his unwavering belief that government has no right to interfere in the lives of individuals who themselves do not violate the rights of others. They can relate to his view that government's only legitimate function is to protect the lives and property of its citizens, and that politicians are the employees of those citizens, not the other way around.

The Foreword to the original edition of *Restoring the American Dream* was written by the late William Simon, who served as Secretary of the Treasury under Presidents Nixon and Ford. Simon, a true patriot, once said, "There is only one social system that reflects the sovereignty of the individual: the free-market, or capitalist, system."

In his Foreword, Simon wrote, "I am in total agreement with the author that our greatest hope for the future lies in teaching the facts to our younger generations. If every high school and college student were to read this book, America's presently beclouded future would begin to shine brightly once more. It is essential that the young people of this country learn to respect the right of every man and woman to seek his or her happiness with minimal interference from the government."

I totally concur with William Simon on this point. High school and college students need to learn not only about the sanctity of freedom and property rights, but, as Robert Ringer so eloquently explains, that there is an inextricable connection between the two. Indeed, without property rights, no other rights are possible—a concept that is today foreign to many Americans.

All this is what prompted me, when Robert interviewed me for his Liberty Education Interview Series, to say, "I want to see a new edition of *Restoring the American Dream.* That was such a great book when you wrote it in the late 1970s. We need a new version of it today."

Little did I know when I spoke those words that Robert had been mulling around in his mind the possibility of revising and updating his classic work. To the extent that my words helped catalyze his decision to move forward with this undertaking, I am pleased, to say the least. And now, in a pleasant twist of fate, I am proud and honored to step into the shoes of William Simon and write the Foreword to this new edition of the original *New York Times* best seller, now titled *Restoring the American Dream: The Defining Voice in the Movement for Liberty.*

I am deeply concerned about the present direction in which our country is headed. I am concerned about the total disregard for the Constitution of the United States by so many of our politicians. I am concerned about the willingness—even eagerness—of our Congress and the new administration to dramatically increase the federal deficit, explode the national debt, and impose draconian regulations on business that can only worsen the economy and create more unemployment.

With this in mind, an important lesson that I hope you will take away from this book is that the survival of a democratic republic is possible only through a strong people and a weak government, not the other way around. I also hope you will understand why this principle is such an integral part of the task of restoring the American Dream.

Unfortunately, millions of Americans now believe that the American Dream is somehow tied to government favors and benefits, but they could not be more wrong. As Robert Ringer points out, the American Dream that our grandparents knew was about people, not government. It was about people declaring that they were above government. It was about individualism and the opportunity to achieve success without interference from others. Above all, the American Dream was about freedom.

It is my fervent hope that this book will help people throughout this great country of ours to better understand the real American Dream and motivate them to help restore it.

STEPHEN MOORE

Publisher's Note

The views expressed in this book are those of the author and do not necessarily represent the views of the publisher or any organization with which the author is or may have been associated. The publisher and the author make no representations or warranties with respect to the accuracy or completeness of the contents of this work and specifically disclaim all warranties, including without limitation warranties of fitness for a particular purpose. No warranty may be created or extended by sales or promotional materials. Neither the publisher nor the author shall be liable for damages arising herefrom. The fact that an organization or Website is referred to in this work as a citation and/or a potential source of further information does not mean that the author or the publisher endorses the information the organization or Website may provide or recommendations it may make. Further, readers should be aware that Internet Websites listed in this work may have changed or disappeared between when this work was written and when it is read.

It may be true . . . that you can't fool all the people all the time,
but you can fool enough of them to rule a large country.

— Will and Ariel Durant

Introduction

S ince the late 1980s, a surprising number of people have expressed to me their belief that *Restoring the American Dream*, originally published in 1979, was ahead of its time. They have offered a wide variety of reasons for their viewpoints, the three most common being those that follow.

First, when *Restoring the American Dream* was initially published, the average person was much less informed about economics, politics, and ideology—and, thus, far more naïve. But since the advent, then blossoming, of cable news and conservative talk radio, that has rapidly changed. Fox News did not even exist until 1996.

As a result, many of the ideas I expressed in the original edition of *Restoring the American Dream* that were considered by many to be extreme are now commonly discussed on radio and television, as well as in print media and on the Internet.

Second, until recently, progressives in Washington seemed content with gradually moving the United States to the left, slowly enough so as not to waken the average citizen out of his slumber. But since the progressives took control of all three branches of government in January 2009, all socialist hell has broken loose—and people are frantically looking for answers. I believe that many of the answers they are looking for are to be found between the covers of this book.

Third, just as progressives long ago appropriated the term *liberal* as a means to accomplish their ends, so, too, have they perverted the meaning of the term *American Dream* in an effort to pollute the minds of Americans. True liberalism believes in tolerance, but today those who call themselves liberals aim to *silence* all opposing views and take control of people's lives.

Likewise, today's liberals, who are really progressives—or, more properly, socialists—would have you believe that the American Dream was about increased government benefits and government-created "rights"— for example, the right to "free" healthcare, the right to a "decent" job at a "decent" wage, even the "right" to own a home.

But, in truth, the American Dream was about none of these things. Quite the opposite, in fact. The American Dream was about people knowing that they were above government. The American Dream was about individualism, self-responsibility, and freedom—including the freedom to succeed or fail on one's own according to his unique abilities and his willingness to work. Simply put, the American Dream meant that each individual possessed the God-given right to his life, his liberty, and the pursuit of his happiness.

For these reasons and more, I finally made the decision to undertake the challenging task of updating and revising this book. There is no question in my mind that the Constitutional usurpers in Washington have inadvertently made this the perfect time for us to begin the arduous task of restoring the American Dream. The time has come to reject the progressive's serpent-like notion that the American Dream is about receiving benefits and cradle-to-grave security from politicians.

It is my sincere hope that this updated version of my original work will resonate with many who, in 1979, were simply not ready to face up to the reality that Americans have steadily and increasingly been losing their liberty.

My Personal Evolution

The past 25 years have been an intellectual tug of war for me. Morally, my soul is still attached to the notion that the keystone of libertarianism—liberty—must be given a higher priority than all other objectives. The problem, however, is that this noblest of all objectives often collides with the most dominant aspect of secular life: reality.

Reality is synonymous with *truth*, and truth is unyielding. One can choose to ignore it, scorn it, or even curse it, but all to no avail. In the end, truth impassively stands its ground in the face of the most overpowering emotional, verbal, and intellectual onslaughts. Further, truth can be especially brutal to those who insist on worshipping at the Altar of Theory. This is because truth has a way of frustrating theory and, much like a mongoose circling a snake, ultimately wearing it down and devouring it.

More to the point, truth—or reality—seems to take special delight in thumbing its nose at theory and leaving purist libertarians frustrated in the process. So much so that the past three-and-a-half decades have brought about a personal and accelerating evolution that has brought me ever more rapidly to what I consider to be a more mature and realistic view of life.

I believe that this view has made it possible for me to see the world as it actually is rather than the way I would like it to be. Instead of seeing life as a black-and-white objectivist or unyielding, purist libertarian, I now view it through the eyes of a hybrid ideologue: theoretical libertarian/practical conservative, or, more simply put, libertarian-centered conservative.

A government's primary function—many would argue its only function—is to protect its citizens from aggression. More specifically, it is to protect their lives and property. In today's post–9/11 world, the overriding question is whether government can, in fact, succeed in protecting lives and property without restricting certain freedoms.

Unfortunately, aggression from brainwashed fanatics from other countries is not the most ominous threat to our country. Far more threatening is the enemy from within. Or, more properly, the enemies from within. I am referring to people in this country who are sworn enemies of the very heart and soul of Western civilization: a generally accepted code of civilized conduct. Plain and simple, no civilization can continue to exist, let alone flourish, without a moral foundation that is not only clearly understood, but also accepted and practiced by a large majority of its citizens.

To employ a parody, the barbarians are not at the gates; they are *inside* the gates. The enemies from within include a wide array of forces clearly intent on undermining all that is decent, pure, and civilized in Western culture. Make no mistake about it, the enemies of freedom and Western culture have no qualms about lying, deceiving, and, if necessary, using force to achieve their ends.

I should point out that I do not see this threatening situation so much as good versus evil, because the debate over good and evil—and, indeed, whether good and evil even exist—is an intellectual and religious hornet's nest. Rather, I see today's worldwide conflict as one between civilized and uncivilized people. Framing the problem in this fashion removes from the equation such emotive factors as religion, skin color, sex, and nationality.

Millions of Americans have bought into the lie that diversity is what makes our country great. But the truth is that diversity is not a strength; it's a weakness. This is so self-evident that I am tempted to posit it as an axiom. History makes it clear that diversity is not a good ingredient for keeping a civilization intact. Diversity has always proven to be a divider of people.

It is important to understand that diversity has nothing to do with skin color. It has to do with culture. There is a great cultural divide between those who revel in all that is repugnant to civilized people of goodwill and those who make a sincere attempt to abide by Western civilization's generally accepted code of conduct. The haters of Western culture are among the worst of the barbarians dwelling inside our gates, and it is clear that nothing short of a total destruction of our long-accepted mores will satisfy them. Because they are rebels without a moral cause, to attempt to reason with them is folly.

If the 9/11 factor and the internal decay of Western culture over the past 50 years have taught us anything, it is that the great paradox of democracy is alive and well. The paradox to which I am referring is that in order to preserve freedom, freedom must, to some extent, be restricted.

In theory, unlimited freedom is a good thing. No one believes this more than I do. It is, in fact, my ultimate fantasy. In reality, however, a society without a clearly defined social structure is not a civilized society. The lack of social organization opens the gates to barbarians whose main purpose in life is the spread of death, and encourages the barbarians from within to destroy what is left of the true American Dream.

This is where libertarian-centered conservatism comes in. It is an ideology that concedes, however reluctantly, that we live in an imperfect world inhabited by imperfect human beings. Thus, it is a pragmatic ideology that believes in adherence to the tenets of pure libertarianism to the fullest practical extent, but also believes in the use of force, when and where it is absolutely necessary, to not only protect the lives and property of citizens, but also preserve the traditional American code of conduct. Having said this, however, the overriding rule must always be: When in doubt, the nod should be given to liberty.

Just as democracy is not a perfect political system, neither is libertarian-centered conservatism a perfect philosophy. Restricting freedom is not a subject to be taken lightly. The age-old question of whose freedom, and how much freedom, should be restricted to protect lives, property, and Western civilization looms as large as ever.

The only thing we know for certain is that under today's democracies throughout the world, people are increasingly losing their freedoms, and they certainly are losing their once-cherished civilizations. Above all, the rights of producers and people who abide by the generally accepted code of conduct of Western civilization are increasingly being trampled by special-interest groups, nonproducers, and relativists who revel in sloth, vulgar behavior, theft, and violence.

If They Understood the Situation

When you first realize you possess the innate ability to reason, you have an inkling of what slaves throughout history must have felt when finally released from their shackles. Not that you think you're free. In fact, for the first time in your life you realize just how unfree you really are. But your mind is free—free from the enslavement of confusion, doubt, and irrational rhetoric.

"The noblest pleasure," said Leonardo, "is the joy of understanding." The pleasure of understanding produces a high that no artificial stimulant can provide. An indescribable exhilaration comes over you. You're so excited that you want to spread the word. For the first time, morality and ethics and virtue and love have meaning to you.

Then it begins: the sheer frustration. When you try to share your newfound ability to think rationally, people either stare blankly at you or return your words with abstract clichés.

You talk about liberty; they answer with incoherencies about social justice. You enthusiastically explain why everyone benefits from the virtues of individualism; they retort that your ideas are antiquated. You persist with the morality of mutually beneficial, non-coercive relationships; they shake their heads patronizingly and mumble about the need to control man's greed.

After a while, they wear you down. Your excitement fades and you get back to the realities of everyday life. Then, hopelessness sets in as you realize that *Atlas Shrugged* has arrived. The United States is strangling at the hands of a draconian, progressive government that grows more out of control each day.

Civil rights are routinely violated by the irrepressible Washington behemoth that is now reaching into every area of our lives at an accelerating pace. *Freedom* is only a convenience word used to justify a thousand different violations of freedom. Ayn Rand's warnings about the future are applicable to the present. As recent town hall attendees have discovered, ordinary citizens do not tell their elected officials what to do. Government tells them what to do—and backs it up with force.

Then, just when you're about to give up hope, you run smack into a rational individual in the least likely place. You can't believe it: He knows all about Natural Law and natural rights. He understands the difference between equality and freedom. He understands why laissez-faire capitalism improves the well-being of all people of goodwill. You pinch yourself and find, to your amazement, that you aren't dreaming. Reluctantly, you admit it: You're hooked again. You're excited.

These moments of enthusiasm come and go over the years as you bump into other oddballs who believe in man's right to be free, in his right to own his own life and pursue his own objectives so long as he does not violate the rights of others.

In his book *A Time for Truth*, William Simon described the hundreds of congressional hearings he was required to attend as Secretary of the Treasury, none of which accomplished anything positive. He cited personal accounts of Richard Nixon's and Gerald Ford's rationalizing away economically disastrous decisions in the hope that such appeasement might pull in more votes at election time.

Simon virtually stumbled into his post in government and, after viewing the horrors of Washington from the perspective of a lofty position in the hierarchy, he stumbled out as fast as he could, returning to his home in New Jersey, in his words, "a very frightened man."

But it's the very facts that Simon addressed—the maze of irrational government policies, the restrictions on freedom, the self-destructive regulation, and the depressing economic realities—that frustrated me. The problem of big government is *so* big that I was doubtful it could be reduced to comprehensible components in a single book and explained in such a way as to make the causes and consequences crystal clear to everyone. But these doubts represented a challenge I could not resist.

Amidst all of the incisive material in *A Time for Truth*, there is one statement by William Simon that stands out in my mind even today: "I am confident that the American people would demand massive reforms *if they understood the situation.*" [Italics added.]

For years, I believed that the majority of Americans did not, in fact, understand the situation (i.e., they did not understand that we were gradually winning our own enslavement by continually electing politicians who saw themselves as our rulers rather than our employees). This lack of understanding reached its zenith during the last presidential election when people voted for change without demanding to know exactly what kind of change was being proposed.

Many people feel that subjects such as inflation, unemployment, regulation, entitlements, and fiscal and monetary policy are mysterious and complex topics that can be understood only by intellectuals and politicians. And from the government's point of view, such a mindset is ideal. Why? Because, as Montaigne pointed out, "Men are most apt to believe what they least understand."

Over the years, I have found that the corollary to Montaigne's statement is also true (i.e., the better one understands government, the less he is inclined to believe anything politicians say). In my own case, the more I learned about the realities of government, the more I realized that I had thought it to be complicated only because I was accustomed to thinking in rational and logical terms. But logic and rationality are incompatible with government policies because such policies are based on a hopeless potpourri of contradictions, illogical premises, and irrational actions—all mixed together with a great deal of corruption.

The truth is that government is not really complicated at all when reduced to its simple components. All that is required to understand the effects of government on one's life is the willingness to reject beliefs that cannot stand the test of facts and logic. That part is up to the reader. My job is to cut through the intellectual aura surrounding government and explain, in simple terms, topics often thought to be complicated.

I am well aware that one runs the risk of criticism when he tries to simplify subjects jealously guarded by intellectuals. There is a snobbish element that prevails not only in literature, but also philosophy and political science. Quite simply, the public is not supposed to understand the complex workings of government. "Woe to him," said Will Durant, "who teaches men faster than they can learn."

It seems that the intent has been for the world of the intellectual and the world of the layman to remain forever separated. The socially progressive intellectual thrives on terms like *consumer price index;* the layman just wants to know why he can't purchase as much with the same dollars as last year. The socially progressive intellectual explains the economic intricacies of the gross national product; the layman just wants to know why he has to pay taxes to support services he neither wants nor uses, not to mention bailouts of major corporations. The socially progressive intellectual speaks in abstracts such as *the common good;* the layman just wants to know why no one seems to care about what's good for *him.*

I am a believer in Occam's Razor Principle (also known as the Principle of Parsimony), which states: Never multiply explanations or make them more complicated than necessary. An explanation should be as simple and direct as possible. Obviously, Occam's Razor Principle is not popular with people who earn their livings making simple problems appear complicated by creating crises that either do not or need not exist and by talking in abstractions.

I also feel duty bound, at the outset, to remind you that no system or philosophy is perfect because man himself is imperfect. That, however, does not lessen the value of knowledge and truth. This book does not pretend to be an end all, be all. My intent would be better described as giving the reader a broad insight into the evolution, operation, results, and future of government. And to best accomplish this, I have tried to avoid getting sidetracked by statistics and details that detract from one's understanding of the underlying philosophy of freedom. This underlying philosophy is the key to restoring the American Dream, and, unfortunately, it is a philosophy that I believe far too many Americans do not understand.

I seek the truth in this book fully recognizing that history has rarely made truth and popularity bedfellows. Obviously, to investigate the facts, basic premises and traditional thinking must be challenged. Often we are made to feel uncomfortable by reality. Words like *socialism* frighten us. We don't like to hear things that make us feel uncomfortable. We don't like our neatly structured notions to be disturbed. But preconceived, set-in-stone beliefs are incompatible with truth. People say they love truth, but, instead, they try to make true that which they love.

Perhaps it is right that "he that increaseth knowledge increaseth sorrow, and in much wisdom is much grief." Perhaps it is not so much that people do not understand as they do not want to understand. Perhaps that is what Aldous Huxley had in mind in *Brave New World* when Mustapha Mond, the supreme government power holder, said to the awed and confused Savage from the Indian reservation, "The optimum population is modeled on the iceberg—eight ninths below the water line, one ninth above."

"And they're happy below the water line?" asked the Savage.
"Happier than above it," replied Mustapha Mond.

Although I have great concern over the possibility that Huxley may have been right, I am writing this book based on a series of assumptions, assumptions with which Huxley probably would have disagreed. I am assuming that most men and women are basically good but are misled, which is why an understanding of the facts is so essential. I am assuming that most men and women, when armed with the truth, will act honestly and rationally. I am assuming that most men and women know, deep down, that using the government to extract wealth from their neighbors is morally wrong.

The orientation of this book is an appeal not only to man's decency, but also his rationality. It gives everyone the benefit of the doubt. It assumes that virtually everyone—union members, welfare recipients, businesspeople, private-sector workers, government employees—is a victim of one of man's greatest weaknesses: expedient, short-term thinking. This human failing motivates people to group themselves together to expedite the realization of their desires (i.e., to bring about quick, short-term solutions to their problems through government intervention). And it is precisely such action that perpetuates the cycle that has nearly destroyed the American Dream.

This book specifically rejects the destructive us-against-them philosophy. So long as people, in pursuit of their own well-being, see themselves as laborers versus management, blacks versus whites, environmentalists versus polluters, or liberals versus conservatives, to list but a few examples, this destructive cycle will not only continue, but worsen. The truth is that it's really all of us against the forces of expedient, short-term thinking, which politicians count on to control our lives.

Isaac Asimov, the renowned science fiction writer, once said that the danger in demanding special favors from government is that you risk the ultimate destruction of freedom and free enterprise, which necessarily means the destruction of your own special interest as well. Asimov emphasized his point by suggesting the following analogy: "If my right arm decided to stab my left arm to death, my right arm would die too." The success of this book will depend on how many people, after reading it, will understand that their own special interests will be destroyed in the long run if they think only in terms of expedient personal gain.

Many believe that we've already traveled too far down the road to socialism to reverse the trend. In the original edition of this book, I said I was a pessimist trying hard to be optimistic and that I gave Western civilization about one chance in a hundred of surviving. However, with more and more people now beginning to realize that the progressive usurpers of the Constitution in Washington are blatantly attempting to establish a dictatorship—and openly rebelling against them—I believe that the liberty–tyranny pendulum may be slowly swinging back in the direction of liberty.

In their zeal to get to their promised land of a totalitarian utopia (created, of course, by them), progressives may have made a mistake by pressing down too hard on the tyranny accelerator. As a result, they may have awakened a sleeping giant: Americans who place a greater value on their liberty than on government benefits. If so, this may be the perfect time to undertake the enormous challenge of picking up the pieces and begin rebuilding what was once the greatest civilization the world has ever known.

I hope this book will serve as a reminder to those who place the highest of all priorities on liberty that the fight against totalitarianism is a generational struggle. It is time to stand tall, lock arms, and work together to restore the *real* American Dream.

Restoring the American Dream

CHAPTER 1

In the Beginning

The certainty of higher taxes, the stress of trying to keep pace with inflation, the fear of unemployment, and the feeling of being stifled at every turn by draconian regulations are just a few of the government-related problems that have most people on the edge. But these items receive special attention only because their effects on our lives are so obvious. In reality, however, they barely allow us to glimpse the extent to which government is involved in practically everything we do.

Government actions affect your daily life from the moment you wake up in the morning. The clock radio that awakens you is subject to many consumer-protection regulations. The music set off by the alarm mechanism comes from a station able to broadcast only because it has been granted a special government license to do so. It must comply with the government's notion of good programming or run the risk of having its license being revoked.

After getting out of bed, you wash your face and brush your teeth with government-controlled water. The toothpaste you use has been approved by the government. The towel with which you dry your hands has met many government-imposed standards. And so it goes with your comb, your clothes, and almost everything else you use in the process of getting ready for the day.

Your day continues much the same: You drive to work on government-owned streets and highways, pay bills and send letters via the government-monopolized postal service, read newspaper accounts of government-released facts and figures on the state of the economy, and, when you finally enter the privacy of your home in the evening, you take into account the government's standards of morality (backed by law) regarding leisure activities.

It is ironic that even though people generally recognize at least the most visible manifestations of government's creeping infringements on their freedom, it is government to whom they turn for solutions.

1

If it is government to whom most people turn, then one of our objectives should be to find out if government really can, or should, be the solution to our problems. And that question can be properly answered only if we start at the beginning.

To understand how government first came into being—how and why men* initially came under the control of other men—and to appreciate what the creation of government has meant in terms of human freedom, it is essential to have an understanding of "Natural Law" and the nature of man.

Natural Law

Any philosophy—political, religious, or other—must begin with a premise, a foundation upon which to build its concepts. Therefore, inherent in every philosophy is the same type of first-cause question with which one is confronted when philosophizing about the nature of the universe. No matter how self-evident a concept may seem, no matter how axiomatic a person may claim it to be, the truthful philosopher is obliged to admit that the starting point of his philosophy is but an opinion.

The opinion the philosopher uses as his premise may be rational or irrational, popular or unpopular, strongly supported by evidence or based on little more than mysticism. But regardless of any of these factors, the initial premise of any philosophy can never be classified rightfully as anything other than an opinion.

The initial premise underlying the philosophies of libertarianism and true conservatism (hereafter referred to jointly as *libertarian-centered conservatism*) is that each individual owns his own life and therefore has the right to do anything he wishes with that life, so long as he does not forcibly interfere with the life of any other individual.† This forms the basis for what I shall hereafter refer to as Natural Law. Natural Law also may be properly thought of as the *law of nonaggression* (i.e., even though an individual possesses the right of self-choice, self-choice does not include the right to commit aggression against others).

---

*The terms *man* and *men*, as used in this book, are meant to include both genders, except where I have specifically referred to the male or female gender.

†For the sake of brevity throughout this book, I often will leave off what I call the *libertarian tag* when talking about Natural Law. By libertarian tag, I am referring to "so long as he does not forcibly interfere with the life of any other individual" (or similar qualifying statements of this kind). Therefore, whenever I make a statement such as "man has a right to do anything he pleases," the libertarian tag should be assumed.

Aggression may be thought of as the use or threat of force or fraud. Hence, from a Natural Law point of view, only one thing is against the law: aggression against others. When aggression occurs, man's rights are violated. It naturally follows that violence for any reason other than self-defense is a violation of Natural Law.

Thus, one of the basic tenets of this book is that liberty must be given a higher priority than all other objectives. Intellectually, one must either accept or reject the principle of Natural Law from the outset. It cannot be accepted initially on the basis of reason and then later be allowed to fall on an emotional whim.

In other words, Natural Law, like all principles, allows no room for compromise. Ayn Rand illuminated the moral impossibility of compromising on basic principles when she asked, "What would you regard as a 'compromise' between life and death? Or between truth and falsehood? Or between reason and irrationality?"

Natural Law, therefore, is a no-compromise principle. Whether one calls himself a libertarian, conservative, or libertarian-centered conservative, if a person claims to understand human freedom, but insists on certain exceptions to freedom, he is either admitting that he advocates the violation of Natural Law or demonstrating that he does not really understand the concept of Natural Law. One must remain steadfast to the moral belief that no matter how worthy the cause for which a person's rights are violated, the end never justifies the means. That is to say, no matter how moral or humane certain people may believe a cause to be, if its attainment requires a violation of the rights of even one individual, the end has been achieved through immoral action.

Therefore, while the needs and desires of certain individuals (whether they be the poor or any other vaguely defined group) may constitute a legitimate concern to many people, they nonetheless fall outside the scope of man's natural rights. This does not mean people should not be concerned about others; it does not mean they should not be sympathetic toward others; it does not mean they should not be helpful to others; it does not mean they should not be charitable toward others. What it does mean is that people do not have the right to force others to be concerned, sympathetic, helpful, or charitable toward others.

If Natural Law is to be meaningful, no part of any individual's life and efforts can belong to anyone else without that individual's voluntary consent. Any time an individual (or any group of individuals) takes authority over someone else's life without his consent, he is violating Natural Law. Therefore, the difference between Natural Law and government law is that Natural Law demands freedom, while government law demands that certain people obey the dictates of those in power.

Obviously, then, one individual cannot grant natural rights to another individual, because all human beings already possess these rights at birth. All individuals are born with equal natural rights. However, being born with equal rights does not mean people are born equal. That is, people have a right to be free to live their lives as they choose. An individual has a right to survival, a right to try to better his existence, a right to enjoy 100 percent of the fruits of his labor, a right to do as he pleases—a right to "life, liberty, and the pursuit of happiness."

Property Rights

It is a basic tenet of libertarian-centered conservatism that without property rights, no other rights are possible. Unfortunately, most people do not understand this fundamental concept. They view property only as inanimate matter, separate and apart from a person's life. They cannot seem to make the connection between the two. In fact, they are so connected that one is virtually an extension of the other.

Consider: John T. is told he is a free man. So, free to do as he pleases, he buys a plot of land. He mixes his energy and creativity with the soil and manages to grow profitable crops. A group of men, calling themselves the People's Protection Council, approach John and explain that he must give them $1,000 to help bear the costs incurred by them in protecting the people (including him).

John thanks them, but explains that he is not interested in being protected. Unfortunately, the representatives of the People's Protection Council don't believe it is John's choice to make. He is told he must pay the $1,000 fee or they will have no choice but to sell his property to obtain the funds (i.e., they will take his property by force and sell it to obtain the required $1,000).

Clearly, John's property rights have been violated, but that's not all. John's property is actually an extension of his body in that he has used his time, effort, and ability to create the crops that now grow on the land he purchased. Thus, if someone takes his property from him, they are also confiscating his time, effort, and ability.

How can one separate this man's life from his property? If you took everything a man owned, the fact is that he would not own his own life, because whenever he attempted to create something for his personal financial gain, the fruits of his labor could again be confiscated.

The same is true of purchasing property. The money used to make a purchase was earned presumably through the purchaser's efforts. That makes the money an extension of his life, and, therefore, the same would be true of anything purchased with that money. No matter what the circumstances, when a person's property rights are violated, his freedom is violated.

A libertarian-centered conservative, then, believes that no one has a right to any other person's property, which includes both his body and everything he owns. Once this concept is understood, it would be proper to say that, in reality, all crime is based on trespassing on the property of an owner.

When people make "humanitarian" statements about human rights being more important than property rights, they are, in a sense, correct. That's because human rights *include* property rights, as well as all other rights of man. A man has the right to dispose of his life and his property in any way he chooses, without interference from anyone else. By the same token, he has no right to dispose of any other person's life or property, no matter what his personal rationalizations may be.

As explained in *Fundamentals of Liberty*, there are only three possible ways to view property:

1. Anyone may take anyone else's property whenever he pleases.

2. Some people may take the property of other people whenever they please.

3. No one may ever take anyone else's property without his permission.

Later, when we address more specifically the functions of today's government, it will be important to keep these three alternatives in mind. It will also be important to remember that the true tests of ownership are whether you may do anything you desire with your own property and whether anyone may take any or all of your property from you.

Belief in Natural Law is what differentiates the libertarian-centered conservative from today's pseudo-liberals and pseudo-conservatives. We usually think of a liberal as someone who advocates personal freedom but who is able to rationalize the restriction of economic freedom. A conservative is generally thought to be someone who favors economic freedom but desires restrictions on personal freedom. Libertarian-centered conservatives reject such contradictory line drawing. They believe in across-the-board freedom, though they recognize that social organization is essential for a civilization to survive and prosper.

As such, the libertarian-centered conservative is incapable of prejudice when it comes to human rights. All people—rich and poor, strong and weak, informed and ignorant—are entitled to sole dominion over their own lives and property. Custom, tradition, and existing law do not influence the libertarian-centered conservative's reasoning when it comes to freedom. People have a right to be free, and their freedom can be taken away only by force.

Human Freedom

Virtually everyone claims to be in favor of freedom, but few people seem to be able to agree on what it actually means. To the laissez-faire business-man, freedom means an end to government regulation. To the communist, freedom can be achieved only when individual incentive has been crushed and "the people" own everything. Homosexuals believe they will be free when gay marriage is legalized in all fifty states. Those who oppose gay rights believe that freedom includes being free from the flaunting of homosexuality. Some people believe that job quotas for certain minority groups promote freedom, but to a person who is anti-discriminatory in the truest sense of the word, quotas and seniority considerations violate freedom.

People's notions concerning freedom are limitless. Hitler believed that only the extermination of all Jews would allow Germans to be free. Obviously, then, just because someone is in favor of freedom does not mean you should assume he is a person of high moral standards.

The reality is that one person's idea of freedom can eradicate another person's freedom. To one individual, liberty means doing what he wants with his own life, while to another individual it means doing what he wants with *other* people's lives. Therefore, each type of person says that the other person's concept of freedom is tyranny.

Based on the evidence, I think we can safely conclude that throughout history men have miscommunicated on the subject of freedom. Because conservatives, liberals, bigots, fascists, communists, environmentalists, and every other kind of group imaginable all claim to want freedom, they obviously cannot be talking about the same thing. The problem stems from the ability of people to stretch the meaning of a word just enough to suit their particular objectives.

The dictionary defines *freedom* as "being free." In turn, *free* is defined as "not under the control or power of another." How can there be such confusion over a definition so clearly stated?

First, people have a tendency, in reference to freedom, to think in terms of freedom for themselves. In other words, freedom is a license to do as they please.

Second, throughout history utopian thinkers have insisted on confusing freedom with equality. But nothing could be more incorrect. No matter what one's moral desires, nature has made freedom and equality totally incom-patible. Will and Ariel Durant pictured nature "[smiling] at the union of freedom and equality in our utopias. For freedom and equality are sworn and everlasting enemies, and when one prevails the other dies."

As the U.S. government steps up its attempts to defy nature and bring about equality, it finds it necessary to employ force. And when force enters the picture, some people will come under the control or power of others. Exit freedom.

Thus, you may be surprised, after a little probing, to find that when people espouse freedom, often they are referring to their freedom, not yours. Worse, you may conclude that the gaining of their freedom necessitates the violation of your freedom.

What happens when one person's freedom interferes with the freedom of others? If freedom is to be subjectively defined by each individual, it is reduced to a meaningless abstract. As we shall see, the only way freedom can be viewed rationally is in its pure, no-compromise form: human freedom.

If we think in terms of human freedom, we must think in terms of freedom for all. Again, freedom is an across-the-board matter. It means freedom for the poor, the rich, the handicapped, the oppressed, the weak, and the strong. It means freedom for everyone.

The idea of absolute freedom raises a number of questions because the concept of man in a state of pure freedom is foreign to us and therefore difficult to grasp. Doesn't civilization need rules? What would happen if everyone did as he pleased?

These are valid questions, and they point up the cruelest paradox of nature: that in order to preserve freedom, freedom must, to some extent, be restricted. Allow freedom to be absolute, and you can be sure it soon would be replaced by chaos. So, it becomes a question of whose freedom needs to be restricted, and to what extent, in order to protect freedom. What I am referring to here is the concept of *social organization*—a generally accepted code of conduct that makes it possible for civilization to exist.

It took a long time, but Rousseau's relativism finally led to the hippie revolution of the 1960s, free love, and rampant drug use. All well and good from a purist libertarian point of view, but what happens when those who simply revile a civilized society are insistent on pushing the relativist envelope to ever greater extremes? Should people be allowed to fornicate on street corners? Should your neighbor be allowed to keep a nuclear weapon in his basement?

The libertarian-centered conservative recognizes that there are no perfect answers in life, so he is always willing to discuss, in a rational, common-sense manner, issues of concern to others. But he lives by the creed: When in doubt, always give the nod to liberty.

Another thought that inevitably surfaces when one talks about freedom is that the concept of freedom is an antiquated idea. Progressives insist that the world is now far more complex and overpopulated than it was at some unspecified time in the past. Men, they believe, need to be restrained by governments for their own good and for the good of their fellow man.

But people who use the complex-society argument usually are among those who do not really want a free society. Many people are unhappy and/or unable to achieve success on their own merits; thus, they yearn for an external power (government) that has the muscle to force other people to conform to *their* standards of right and wrong.

Clearly, most so-called freedom fighters and political terrorists use the word *freedom* only for convenience, because, as history has clearly documented, in most instances in which freedom fighters have succeeded, freedom has become a much less abundant commodity after their success.

Nature of Man

Because governments are not living entities, but consist of groups of men and women who govern other people, the deepest roots of government are embedded in the nature of man. Following are some human traits that are especially important in understanding the birth of government.

- **Survival instinct.** First and foremost, man, as he has demonstrated so well during his long stay on our planet, is a survivor. Survival does not mean merely staying alive. It also means furthering his well-being in every possible way. This trait is sometimes translated into the often-misunderstood term *self-interest.*

    Self-interest does not coincide with the progressive's vision of an avaricious monster trampling over bodies to grasp the last ounce of whatever it is that avaricious monsters are supposed to be grasping. It simply means that all people have needs and desires, and that it is quite natural—and civilized—to try to fulfill those needs and desires to the best of their abilities. And one of man's greatest desires is to be free. It is also his greatest need if he is to function as a human being.

    Self-interest—the survival instinct in man—is not, in itself, a moral or immoral quality. It is the behavior in which this instinct manifests itself in each individual that is either moral or immoral.

- **Expediency factor.** As you will see throughout this book, the expediency factor in man is one of the major forces—perhaps *the* major force—behind the destruction of the American Dream. By *expediency factor*, I am referring to the instinct to seek quick, short-term solutions to problems. This approach to problem solving almost always entails irrational action because any behavior that does not take into consideration the long-term effects on one's own well-being is irrational.

- **Individuality versus conformity.** A human being is inherently individualistic and, as such, unique. At the same time, everyone, to one extent or another, has a desire to conform. This desire to conform tends to be dominant in the majority of individuals. They fear standing out from the crowd, especially if it means standing alone.

- **Power lust versus subservience**. Finally, we get to the heart of the matter, the addictive drive in some people for power and the submissive tendency in most people to serve their leaders. Fortunately for those who aspire to power, most people are of an idolatrous nature and yearn to revere someone they believe to be superior to themselves. Those who longed for power and those who by nature were subservient probably were destined from earliest times to form an institutionalized system whereby one could dominate the other. It was the inevitable union of these two types that has made it possible for governments to enslave people since the beginning of recorded history.

There are many kinds of power—physical power, will power, the power to persuade—but the power I am referring to here is raw power. More specifically, it is power over people. The power to control the lives of others is an end in itself. While there are always financial benefits to be gained from such power, they are bonuses to the genuine power seeker, because his main objective is the fulfillment of his insatiable lust for sheer power. Ruling others gives him that which is most important to him: ego gratification.

Ironically, the impetus that brought respectability to the concept of some men having power over others came from a most unlikely source: those who were strong individualists. The rational individualist knew his needs could best be served by dealing with other men as traders, meaning that all men had to be free. He did not believe in interfering in the lives of his neighbors. The individualist was not inclined to make short-term, expedient decisions, but, because he was human, he did at times fall into the expediency-factor trap . . . and, as we shall see, Nature has never forgiven him for his careless mistake.

The Catalyst

Though we know precious little about ancient history, historians seem to agree on the one phenomenon most responsible for the beginning of civilized man—the Agrarian Revolution. When man discovered agriculture, it freed him, for the first time, from the nomadic life of hunting for his food.*

---

*Though *man* here refers to both genders, there is strong evidence that suggests it was actually women who originally developed agriculture.

He was able to settle down and produce his food from the soil. The evolution of the family unit followed as a natural result of his having roots, of having a place to call home.

For the first time, land was not a hunting stage upon which men stalked wild animals. Land, when mixed with human labor and creativity, acquired value. Land was now property. Men had owned other things before—crude axes, knives, the most rudimentary coverings for their bodies—but these things could be replaced with relative ease. Not only had their values been minimal, but they were easily protected because of their relatively small size. But land—especially improved land—was both valuable and difficult to protect. If people combined their energies with the soil and produced plentiful crops successfully, the food machine they created could be neither quickly nor easily replaced.

The type of individual most likely to succeed by cultivating the earth's crust to further his well-being was the rational individualist. He was now free of the day-to-day struggle for survival that had depended upon his catching prey. His needs and desires could now be fulfilled by staying in one place and investing time and energy in the miracle of agriculture. Having freed himself from the uncertainties of the hunter's life, man had no desire to lessen that freedom. The good life having been discovered, it was more than worth fighting to protect.

But the industrious individual, by nature, has neither the time nor the inclination to fight. This presented a problem, as it has throughout history, because there were always envious people who aspired to steal the food machines created by their neighbors. From the very beginning, outlaws, in their struggle to survive, managed to create irrational justifications for plundering the property of others.

Clearly, the new property owners needed a solution. That solution was to be found in the most unlikely alliance in history, an alliance between industrious individualists who sought protection of their property and those whose chief aspirations were to achieve power over others. Thus, government was born. The floodgates had been opened. One great occurrence—the discovery of agriculture—was the catalyst.

The birth of government gave an air of respectability to a system through which some men could rule others. It was a way of making order out of chaos, of giving structure to society. With social order established, civilization had begun.

From the beginning, of course, the alliance was a contradiction in terms—one side desiring to have its freedom protected, the other side offering to protect it in exchange for controls over that same freedom. Freedom-loving people throughout history, who have given the highest of all values to liberty, have paid dearly for the arrangement ever since.

The contradiction—that in order to preserve freedom, freedom must be restricted—is always with us, and the perfect solution has yet to make its appearance.

Because of this enduring contradiction, friction was inevitable. People who desired to have their property protected obviously intended to franchise power only to the extent that it could accomplish that end. The only legitimate function of government, as granted by the people, is to protect the individual from aggression (i.e., to protect his life and property).

Whenever government goes beyond this basic function and acts in violation of people's rights, it becomes the aggressor. At that point, as we see more than ever today, government itself becomes an illegal entity that is in violation of Natural Law.

The trade-off had been simple and straightforward: "We'll give you limited power to rule us in exchange for protection of our lives and property." Government had no right, nor does it now have the right, to violate the rights of people or grant rights to anyone. Protecting rights is far removed from violating or granting rights.

Nor does it seem likely that men ever intended for government to fulfill the desires of all people or to solve their problems. From history as recent as the American Revolution, we know that the Founding Fathers made it eminently clear they did not want government interfering in their lives and property.

To power seekers, however, government became a means to an entirely different end. As Milton Friedman said, "The power to do good is also the power to do harm." Power seekers now had a vehicle through which they could exercise their compulsion to control other people. To them, their newly acquired power was not a means to the end that had been intended by the grantors of that power. Power itself was, and always has been, the real objective of government officials, even when not consciously acknowledged by them.

In *Nineteen Eighty-Four*, George Orwell, through his character O'Brien, explained the true relationship between power and government:

> *Now tell me why we (the Party) cling to power? What is our motive? Why should we want power? . . . The Party seeks power entirely for its own sake. We are not interested in the good of others; we are interested solely in power. . . . The German Nazis and the Russian Communists came very close to us in their methods, but they never had the courage to recognize their own motives. They pretended, perhaps they even believed, that they had seized power unwillingly and for a limited time, and that just round the corner there lay a paradise where human beings would be free and equal. We are not*

like that. We know that no one ever seizes power with the intention of relinquishing it. Power is not a means; it is an end. One does not establish a dictatorship in order to safeguard a revolution; one makes the revolution in order to establish the dictatorship. . . . The object of power is power.

With such conflicting objectives between the ruled and ruling classes, it is understandable why the history of man encompasses one tale after another of revolutions, ingenious ploys for controlling people, and conquests of one government over another.

CHAPTER 2

The System

S ince they formed that first ill-fated partnership with individuals who desired only to have their freedom protected, the major challenge for governments has always been in coming up with the most practical way in which to maintain control over the people for whom they are supposed to be working. Power seekers have experimented with many systems, using such varying ideological guises as communism, fascism, and divine monarchies, to name but a few.

Regardless of the system used, an institutionalized means of controlling people, supported by a monopoly on the use of force, is one of the two characteristics common to all forms of government. The second is that all governments exist off the surpluses created by the people they rule. The ruling classes (i.e., those who refer to themselves as *governments*) do not produce wealth; thus, their existence depends upon the expropriation of assets from others.

One dictionary definition of *government* is: "the exercise of political *authority, direction, and restraint* over the actions of the inhabitants of communities, societies, or states"; "a system of ruling."

Thus, even though governments have varied in form over the centuries, virtually all have been similar in substance. All governments restrain and rule people; therefore, all governments are totalitarian and authoritarian to one extent or another. (*Totalitarianism* refers to a centralized form of government in which those in control grant neither recognition nor tolerance to parties with differing opinions. *Authoritarianism* is a system of governing that calls for unquestioning submission to authority.)

It is never a question of whether a government is totalitarian or authoritarian, but, rather, to what extent. Most governments throughout history have been outright dictatorships, under the rule of either a single dictator or an oligarchy (a small group of people).

Two obvious examples of extreme totalitarianism are the Soviet Union during most of the twentieth century and Nazi Germany in the 1930s and 1940s. Though their ideologies appeared, on the surface, to be different, neither of them tolerated opposition of any kind. Under Hitler, Nazi Germany was a totalitarian dictatorship, while the Soviet Union was a totalitarian oligarchy. In both cases, however, individual freedom was sacrificed to unquestioning submission to authority.

What about democratic republics and democracies? Aren't they "government by the people"? If it is possible for government to be moral, or at least useful, then surely a government with the lofty stated goal of "vesting supreme power in the people" would be the most likely to qualify for that description. The analysis of government throughout this book will therefore focus on democratic forms of government.

Pointing out the drawbacks of a democratic form of government is not to imply that other forms of government are better. Winston Churchill explained the issue perfectly when he described democracy as "the worst form of government, except for all the others that have been tried from time to time."

In other words, there are drawbacks to a democratic form of government, and it is in one's best interest to be aware of them. When people are not aware of the realities of a political system, or, worse, when they refuse to acknowledge such realities, they are giving men and women of power a free rein.

The relevant question is not whether democracy works. The question is how well it works and for whom. We know that it works very well for those in power, as do fascist dictatorships. But whether democracy is the best type of government mankind can devise to protect individual rights is a question worth investigating. As Sy Leon has observed:

> *The question . . . is not whether the system works, but whether we like the* way *it works. Just because something works doesn't mean it is desirable. Concentration camps work, if your purpose is to enslave people. Stealing works, if all you care about is money. Lying works, if you don't give a damn about your personal integrity. Literally anything, no matter how monstrously immoral, will work, depending on your desires and how you define the term "work."*

If people were truly free, no government could force them to do anything they did not want to do. If government truly represented you, you could give orders to the government. The reality, of course, is quite the opposite. Notwithstanding what people have been taught to believe, democracy is not synonymous with freedom.

The only way people can be truly free is through an absence of government. On the other hand, to keep people totally under control, a strong totalitarian government is necessary. The only way to make people equal is through a totalitarian government that takes away freedom. But if a mixture of equality and freedom is the objective, democracy is probably the best form of government. The problem is that as a democracy leans toward equality, it leans away from freedom; as it leans toward freedom, it leans away from equality.

History teaches us that great civilizations experience four definitive stages: They are born; they flourish; they decay; they die. This includes the relatively small number of democracies that have been attempted in past centuries. It is interesting to conjecture why democracies, when they have endeavored to achieve both freedom and equality, have ultimately decayed and died.

Historically, democracies, in their decaying phases, usually have evolved into tightly controlled totalitarian governments. Ironically, what brings about this collapse is an excess of democracy, which causes chaos and leads to totalitarian rule. When a democracy degenerates into a free-for-all stampede of citizens vying both for favors and increasing infringements on the rights of fellow citizens, its collapse is inevitable.

And therein lies the major weakness in a democracy. The very nature of a democracy promotes an irrational, destructive human instinct that I like to refer to as the *expediency factor.* A democratic form of government becomes a vehicle through which each citizen, dominated by thoughts of expedient solutions to his own problems, hopes to live at the expense of his neighbors. He accomplishes this through a mechanism known as majority rule—a concept which, by its very definition, implies that it is justifiable to violate the rights of the minority so long as the majority consents to it.

But majority rule, as people have time and again discovered, can be far more lethal than a bullet. By use of this clever device, some people can take control over other people's lives, expropriate their wealth, and generally do as they please to them without having to resort to physical violence. In short, majority rule is the most ingenious scheme ever contrived by governments to control their subjects.

Majority Rule

Majority rule must be examined from three viewpoints: morality, logic, and reality.

Morality

Assuming one accepts the premise that people need to be governed to one extent or another, the inevitable question regarding all rulers and rules is: Who shall decide?

Shall it be God? This might be a satisfactory solution to many people, but I suspect that God has more important things to do than become involved in secular politics. And in His absence, there seem to be several million differing interpretations of His laws.

Shall it be the minority? Common sense dictates that minority rule would be an unjust concept.

Through process of elimination, majority rule seems to be the method most preferred by those who believe in the need for government, but who seek as much individual freedom as possible. The danger lies in confusing the word *best* with *moral* or *good*. To say that a system is best has nothing whatsoever to do with whether it is moral.

When one says that a certain method is best, he is not assigning any sort of absolute rating to it. He is merely making a comparison. Being the best could mean simply being the least immoral. As Lysander Spooner asked nearly 150 years ago, "Suppose (the U.S.) be 'the best government on earth,' does that prove its own goodness, or only the badness of all other governments?"

It is important to test the moral validity of majority rule, if for no other reason than to decide whether it deserves the aura of sanctity that surrounds it. Most people have never dared to question the basic morality or logic in the assumption that a majority should have power over a minority.

A majority of people in the South once believed in black slavery. Did that make it moral? What laws, divine or natural, gave the majority a right to hold others in bondage? Whether or not one realizes it, if he believes in the moral validity of majority rule, he does, even if it be unconsciously, believe in slavery—because a majority can impose slavery on a minority any time it wishes to do so.

The reality is that the practice of majority rule violates Natural Law because it interferes with an individual's right to pursue his own happiness without interference from others. It also violates his inalienable right to his own property. If a person's rights are inalienable, then people are not morally entitled to violate those rights just because they happen to do so through group action.

One cannot say he believes in human freedom (i.e., Natural Law) but make an arbitrary exception when an act of aggression is taken by some unspecified number of people calling itself "the majority." If this logic were to be accepted, any small group of people would have the moral right to agree on something, then approach a stranger and force him to go along with it. This is how a lynch mob works, and a lynch mob, too, is a majority. A lynch mob is nothing more than majority rule stripped of its fancy trappings and its facade of respectability.

The most important person in this country is you! In *your* life, *you* are the majority. You have a natural right to live your life as you please, without interference from others—no matter how great their numbers. No group of people, regardless of size, has a right to take the fruits of your labor without your consent. No group of people, regardless of size, has the right to tell you what to do with your property. No group of people, regardless of size, has the right to tell you what you can smoke, drink, or eat.

If you are not committing aggression against anyone, no group of people, regardless of size, has the right to interfere with your life. If you do not believe in interfering with your neighbors, but ten of your neighbors vote to interfere with each other's lives and with yours, you are, morally speaking, a majority of one.

One of the great myths of our world is that the majority is inherently vested with some divine power to choose between right and wrong. In truth, the idea that the majority is morally superior to an individual is a baseless assumption. Such an idea forces the conclusion that the minority is morally inferior.

In reality, majority rule has nothing whatsoever to do with morality, justice, or truth. It means only that more people have voted one way or another on a candidate or issue, and, in actual practice, the *expediency-factor* more often than not makes their choice an immoral one. The highest moral principles are contained in Natural Law, not in laws decreed by the majority.

From a very early age, there was something about majority rule that did not ring true to me. I had followed the concept through to what I believed to be its logical conclusion, and the ultimate implication—tyranny of the majority—seemed an atrocity to me.

Consider: 51 percent of the people in a community have black hair and 49 percent have blond hair. If the members of this community believe in, and live by, the absolute sanctity of majority rule, then the slight minority— the 49 percent who have blond hair—find themselves at the mercy of those who outnumber them by only 2 percent. If majority rule is morally valid, then the black-haired people of this hypothetical community possess the moral right to do with the blond-haired people as they see fit. Even a decision to execute them would be moral on the grounds that it is the will of the majority.

Drawing lines on majority rule does not work, either. One cannot say, "Well, the majority should not be allowed to have the minority executed, but it should have the right to decide on matters that do not violate the rights of others." But all majority rule violates the rights of others if it forces them to go along with actions with which they do not agree.

In a community where gays outnumber heterosexuals, should the majority have the right to outlaw sex between married partners of the opposite sex? In a community where atheists outnumber religionists, should the majority have the right to outlaw the practice of religion? In a community where people over the age of sixty-five outnumber all other ages combined, should the majority have the right to force the others to turn over 90 percent of their wages to them?

Where does one draw the line? The only logical place to draw it is at Natural Law. If Natural Law is used for one's moral foundation, majority rule is against the law because majority rule always involves aggression.

You either believe in human rights or you do not, and majority rule always violates human rights. Those who would like to make majority rule apply to some situations but not to others are advocating that arbitrary lines be drawn, thereby giving rise to the same old question: Who shall decide? The majority? If the majority is to decide on which matters the majority should be allowed to rule, then, in reality, the majority is being given absolute rule.

The fantasy of majority rule is that it is morally virtuous. The reality of majority rule is that it is moral cannibalism. The bottom line of majority rule is that one group of people, simply by outnumbering another group, can do what it wishes to that group. Theoretically, in fact, majority rule could validate literal cannibalism!

In today's society, then, a free individual might appropriately be defined as a person who is allowed one voice in millions in deciding what will be done with him and his property, as well as one voice in millions in deciding what will be done to other people and their property. Certainly the term *self-government* is a misnomer because each person does not govern himself. In reality, self-government today means that each person is governed by all the rest of the people.

All that government by consent of the people means is that a certain number of people have consented to be either governed by certain people or bound by certain laws. The problem is that those who do not so consent are forced to go along with it anyway. Jim Davidson describes this dilemma of the victimized minority by defining democracy as "that form of government where everybody gets what the majority deserves."

In other words, whereas a dictatorship allows only a small number of people to interfere in the rights of others, a democracy makes it possible for great numbers of people to impose their wills on others—through the force of government. Is an act of aggression any more moral if it is carried out by the majority rather than by a dictator? Does a person feel better if he is coerced by the majority rather than a monarch?

Logic

The basic premise of majority rule is that *good* is defined as "that which is best for the greatest number of people." Such a premise, however, is so vague as to be meaningless. Every person in a society has a unique set of circumstances, unique needs and desires, unique personality traits, unique fears, and unique ambitions. A certain political action might be a catastrophe for person A, of no consequence to person B, and very good for person C. Another political action, however, might be great for person A but bad for person C.

In this example, how can one determine which actions are best for the greatest number of people? Clearly, he can't. The reality is that each person's uniqueness dictates which actions are best for *him*. This is why progressive terms such as *social justice* and *the common good* are nothing but red herrings.

Reality

Having examined majority rule from the standpoints of logic and morality, let us see how well the concept works in actual practice.

First, the majority, in reality, does not rule. On the contrary, it is the minority that rules the majority. Because approximately half the eligible voters vote in presidential elections (and fewer in other kinds of elections), it is the nonvoters, along with those who vote against the winning candidate, who actually form the majority. This means that approximately 75 percent of the people are ruled by politicians and laws for which the remaining 25 percent have voted.

In truth, then, *mandate of the people* means the mandate of a small minority of people whose candidates are elected and whose propositions are passed. Hardly what a schoolchild envisions when he is taught about the fairness of majority rule.

A similar myth concerning majority rule is the belief that "the people have chosen." What, in fact, takes place in an election is that two handpicked candidates are propped up before the public, each having been selected by a small group of politically active people. A minority of the people, erroneously described as the majority (as previously explained), then elects one of the two handpicked candidates to rule itself and the majority.

A third fallacy of majority rule is that not only does the majority not rule, the real gut-level ruling—where the worst violations of natural rights occur—is carried out by people in regulatory agencies who are not even elected to office. What the system really boils down to, then, is that officials who are elected by a minority of the population in turn dole out power to nonelected bureaucrats who do not have to answer to voters and who are almost impossible to remove from their jobs.

Majority rule, then, is incompatible with Natural Law and therefore incompatible with human freedom. But there is little doubt that it is the best system for those in power. Democracy's main attraction—majority rule—is ideal from government's standpoint because it gives the illusion of consent. People, through patriotic slogans and mind-twisting logic, are led to believe that the government represents them; thus, they feel content.

When a so-called democratic government does an efficient job of maintaining this illusion, the reward can be a power seeker's dream: the actual support of a large percentage of the people who are ruled.

The Vote

The vehicle through which majority rule supposedly asserts itself is *the vote*—the political process known as an election. An election involves the art of *politics*, defined in the dictionary as "the plotting or scheming of those seeking personal power, glory, position, or the like." What a reassuring definition . . . welcome to the wonderful world of the vote.

One might properly describe majority rule as the window dressing of the system, while the vote is the machine used to do the dressing. Notwithstanding the fact that the average person's life is not improved by the outcome of elections, the outcome matters a great deal to politicians. The politician who wins the largest percentage of the votes cast wins power. The loser must sit on the sidelines and wait until the next time around to try to capture (or recapture) the reins of power. The vote is therefore of utmost importance to the players of the power game in a democracy.

The Four Great Political Realities

So long as a democracy proves to be the most practical method of controlling people, the vote will remain a critical aspect of the political system from the standpoint of politicians. And so long as the vote is a critical aspect of the system, certain realities are unavoidable. Four of the most important of these realities are as follows:

REALITY NO. 1: No person can become a serious candidate for office without having substantial financial backing and/or important political connections. It takes a great naiveté to believe that IOUs, payable in favors, are not issued at the time of the disbursement of campaign contributions, whether such contributions are in the form of money or connections.

REALITY NO. 2: It takes votes to get elected to office.

REALITY NO. 3: To get enough votes to be elected, a candidate must, to put it politely, make unrealistic and contradictory promises to a wide variety of special interests. To put it not so politely, it is virtually impossible to get elected to public office without promising to commit aggression against certain members of society. You might say it's a mandatory condition built into the system. It's the only way the politician can appeal to the expediency factor in most voters.

REALITY NO. 4: Once elected, a politician must violate Natural Law (i.e., he must commit aggression against both voters and nonvoters in an effort to make good on at least some of his campaign promises). Virtually all political action involves violating the rights of various members of society, whether such action entails redistribution-of-wealth programs, government intervention to help certain businesses or industries, favors for special-interest groups, or enactment of victimless-crime laws to satisfy the moral judgments of certain individuals.

The result of The Four Great Political Realities is a relentless appeal to the expediency factor in every eligible voter. It stimulates people to think in terms of expedient, short-term solutions to their problems. The politician's expediency is political (attainment of power), while the voter's expediency is material and moral. Thus, a candidate's chances of winning are dependent upon his ability to convince voters that he will, if elected, commit more aggression than his opponent.

What this boils down to is a description offered by Jim Davidson:

> *You pool your life and property with those of other citizens and cast them into the electoral pot to be put at the disposal of politicians. Those who win the election promise to manipulate you to achieve the "common good." More often than not . . . the politicians are really promising to steal from you to reward special interests.*

The vote borders on being a sport. Indeed, Thoreau saw voting as "a sort of gaming, like checkers or backgammon, with a slight moral tinge to it, a playing with right and wrong, with moral questions; and betting naturally accompanies it."

This is how democracy destroys itself through "an excess of democracy." The voting game brings out the worst in people, its very nature being such that it encourages everyone to claw zealously for his share of the plunder. Politicians recognize this weakness and know how to exploit it to win election and reelection.

Will Durant wrote that Plato observed of ancient Greece, "the crowd so loves flattery . . . that at last the wiliest and most unscrupulous flatterer, calling himself the 'protector of the people,' rises to supreme power."

Can 70 Million Americans Be Wrong?

Citizens are continually urged to vote. Media and celebrity pawns flood us with admonishing slogans such as, "If you don't vote, don't gripe." Even friends and acquaintances make perplexing statements to us like, "It doesn't matter whom you vote for, just so you vote." (Huh? Why doesn't it matter?)

And yet, notwithstanding this constant barrage of intimidating rhetoric, nonvoters continue to be the true majority in every election. In 1960, 37 percent of the voting-age population did not vote. In the 1976 presidential election, the figure had increased to 46 percent. In 2008, due almost certainly to the fact that an African-American was running for the presidency for the first time in U.S. history, the number of nonvoters dropped to a mere 43.2 percent.

But, even so, the result was that Barack Obama was, at best, the choice of only about one-fourth of the eligible voters (approximately 52 percent of the 133 million people who voted, but slightly less than 30 percent of the 231 million eligible voters).

As usual, nonvoters piled up a huge majority—70 percent to 30 percent—over those who voted for Obama. Thus, notwithstanding all the hoopla about change, the reality is that Barack Obama was no different than all other recent winners of U.S. presidential elections. The fact is that no president in modern history has ever received a true majority (i.e., 51 percent of the votes of eligible voters). It is therefore absurd for an elected official to claim that he has a mandate of the people.

Just why people do not vote has been the topic of many interesting discussions, articles, and books. In a survey conducted by Peter D. Hart Research Associates, when asked what might inspire them to vote, 62 percent checked "having a candidate worth voting for." Other polls have shown that people do not vote because they do not believe politicians can do anything about their problems.

And they're right. Each person's problems are unique, and so are those of his neighbors. Remember, majority rule is the abstract concept that good is that which is best for the greatest number of people. The fact is that *you* can best solve your own problems because you understand them better than anyone else and because you care about them more than anyone else.

Most important, polls show that people believe there is no distinction between the two major parties. Doesn't every candidate urge you to vote? Doesn't every candidate urge you to pay your taxes? Doesn't every candidate talk about helping the poor? Doesn't every candidate endorse obeying laws, regardless of whether those laws are moral? It is rarely a matter of differing principles. It is virtually always a case of debating over the degree to which each candidate exhorts you to adhere to traditional government doctrine.

If roughly half the people in this country do not vote, it's obvious they are trying to send a message to the power holders in Washington. But the government, instead of being responsive to the people it supposedly represents, retaliates with an endless barrage of slogans, the essence of which is, "It's your duty to vote."

To say the least, the politician has a closed mind when it comes to the nonvoting phenomenon. He refuses to consider the possibility that people do not vote because they are not satisfied with *any* of the candidates or because they do not wish to be governed by *anyone*. That kind of thinking simply does not fit in with the politician's objective of perpetuating and increasing his power.

In reality, what the United States has is a one-party system—the *Demopublican Party*—masquerading as a two-party system (Democrats and Republicans). No matter whom you vote for, you are voting for the Demopublican Party. Again, if one were inclined to be impolite, he might go so far as to say that the so-called two-party system in this country is a sham.

As history has taught us, when the Demopublican Party feels threatened, it does not hesitate to reveal its totalitarian instincts. And it definitely feels threatened when a new party tries to get in on the action. Remember, the dictionary defines a totalitarian government in part as one in which "those in control grant neither recognition nor tolerance to parties differing in opinion." Other than Ross Perot, who spent part of his own fortune on his presidential campaigns in 1992 and 1996, when was the last time you saw a Demopublican presidential candidate debate a third-party candidate on television?

Many new parties have tried hard to maneuver their way into the power game, usually without making a ripple. And the few that have managed to slip one foot in the door have ended up limping away with a badly swollen foot. The system itself is controlled by the power structure of the Demopublican Party, and so long as it can continue to perpetuate false beliefs about majority rule, it can likely avoid the ugliness, expense, and uncertainty that come with having to resort to violence to keep people in line.

How do the power holders control the voting process? Primarily through two methods: first, through the hard reality of legislation. Because the Demopublicans are in control, they can pass any law that suits them—including laws that make it difficult, if not impossible, for a third party to compete. There is one law that, in effect, gives only Demopublican candidates access to taxpayer money to finance election campaigns. Another law refuses Secret Service protection to "outsider" candidates, with but a handful of past exceptions.

The most potent of all laws, however, are state laws that deny voters the opportunity to vote for anyone other than the Demopublican candidates.

The laws in most states make it so expensive, time consuming, and difficult to qualify as a legitimate party that very few outsiders have managed even to get on the ballot.

The second method for controlling the vote is far cleverer because of its subtlety. The totalitarian concept of not granting recognition to parties of differing opinion is not lost on the Demopublicans. Thus, its major weapon against competition is simply to ignore it. "Great is truth," said Aldous Huxley, "but still greater, from a practical point of view, is silence about truth. By simply not mentioning certain subjects . . . totalitarian propagandists have influenced opinion much more effectively than they could have done by the most eloquent denunciations."

A good example of this was the silent treatment the Demopublicans gave to Ron Paul in the 2008 primaries, even though he was technically a member of the Republican wing of the party. His libertarian-centered conservative message was based on across-the-board freedom for everyone, with clearly stated intentions to dramatically reduce regulations, taxes, and, in general, the size of government. He also advocated a return to the gold standard (which will be explained in a later chapter) and the elimination of victimless-crime laws.

Needless to say, the media cooperated by giving Ron Paul, whom polls showed was wildly popular with millions of voters, little or no coverage. Even before he was mathematically eliminated from the primaries, the major networks and cable stations dropped his name (and the number of primary voters who had voted for him) off their screens. The system does, indeed, work very well for those in power.

You might be wondering, "If the vote is nothing more than a meaningless ritual, why even bother with elections? Why don't the Demopublican power holders just vote among themselves?" Answer: because the vote is a process of legitimization. In reality, the mechanics of representative government amount to nothing more than a validation of the system by the citizenry.

In his book *The Third Wave*, Alvin Toffler explained:

> *Yet from the very beginning it [representative government] fell far short of its promise. By no stretch of the imagination was it ever controlled by the people, however defined. Nowhere did it actually change the underlying structure of power in industrial nations— the structure of sub-elites, elites, and super-elites. Indeed, far from weakening control by the managerial elites, the formal machinery of representation became one of the key means by which they maintained themselves in power.*
>
> *Thus elections, quite apart from who won them, performed a powerful cultural function for the elites. To the degree that everyone had*

a right to vote, elections fostered the illusion of equality. . . . Elections symbolically assured citizens that they were still in command—that they could, in theory at least, dis-elect as well as elect leaders. In both capitalist and socialist countries, these ritual assurances often proved more important than the actual outcomes of many elections.

In other words, representative government is pretty much an illusion. Letting people vote every few years is the equivalent of throwing them a piece of raw meat. Once the election circus is over, they learn once again that they have virtually no power.

Candidates make a point of telling us, "It doesn't matter whom you vote for, just so you vote." Why is it so important to a politician that you vote, even if you may not vote for him? Because by casting your ballot, you cast a vote for the system—the system that can satisfy his urge for power and provide him a way to live in luxury without having to produce anything of value. Thus, by casting your ballot, you help perpetuate the illusion that the people have chosen. If politicians were honest, they would encourage a person to vote only if he sincerely believed in one of the candidates.

Politicians like to create the impression that a large voter turnout is a sign of a healthy political system, but this idea disintegrates rather rapidly when one is reminded that in the old Soviet Union, nearly 100 percent of the people voted in every election. (*Hmm* . . . I wonder why.)

In many countries, including Australia, voting is compulsory even today. At present, nonvoting brings only a fine in Australia, but it does not take great powers of prophecy to envision nonvoters, not only in Australia but also the United States and other Western countries, being jailed for refusing to vote. Interesting logic: If you don't vote to preserve your freedom, we'll take your freedom away from you by force.

When people say you have to participate to change the system, it sounds great until you try it, only to find that the fundamental and routine violations of the Constitution never change regardless of who is elected. Today, of course, Americans are reeling from the fact that things have changed as a result of the last presidential election, but it's not the kind of change they naively believed they would get.

Nicholas von Hoffman quotes Sy Leon as saying that "voting is like going through one of two doors. Whichever one you take you wind up in the same room." Von Hoffman goes on to say that "such talk [about having to participate to change things] has a convincing ring until one has participated, elected his man, and then found out he might just as well have supported the loser for all the difference it made."

In short, the players change, but the game does not. The power holders give us a choice of two candidates, each of whom is acceptable to the general aims of the Demopublican Party. When given the opportunity to vote on issues, there are likewise only two alternatives, each of which falls within the framework defined by the government.

The alternatives are whether to increase restrictions on the freedom of some people (or, in some cases, all people) or whether to decrease restrictions on freedom. The choice is never between restriction of freedom and complete freedom. Political debates, when stripped of their politicalese, always boil down to discussions of whose freedom should be increased or decreased and to what extent.

The fact is that our political system offers choice, but not free choice, and there is a substantial difference between the two. A prisoner who is told by his captors that he has the right to die either by shooting or hanging is given a choice. If he were given a free choice, however, he obviously would choose a third alternative not presently available to him.

One might justifiably describe our democracy as a system through which everyone has the freedom to elect officials to restrict his freedom. "A man is none the less a slave," said Lysander Spooner, "because he is allowed to choose a new master once in a term of years."

Government by the people, then, really means government by approximately one-fourth of the eligible voters who vote for the winning candidates and issues from among those made available to them by the government. Or, to cut through all the hocus-pocus, government by the people really means government by those in power.

The Nightmare of the System: Expediency

The overall result of the system—culminating in the vote—is a nation of expediency factors run rampant. And the trait seems to feed on itself. As more and more people base their decisions on the expediency of the moment, more and worse problems are created and more chaos results.

As each person sees his neighbor getting a bigger slice of the government pie, he feels he must take quick action to assure that he does not get shortchanged. Working and minding one's own business have become outdated virtues. The name of the game is *grouping*—aligning oneself with others whose situations vaguely resemble one's own and then letting the candidates know they either must meet your collective demands or lose your votes. H. L. Mencken summed it up succinctly when he described an election as "an advanced auction of stolen goods."

Grouping is one of the banes of man's existence. It is irrational and degrading. It robs a person of his individuality. It encourages a moral person to rationalize the taking of immoral action in the name of the cause. The cruel irony is that it links, under common banners, dishonest people with hardworking, honest people. It calls upon honorable men and women to do the expedient thing to defend the group against the injustices of society.

Politicians, who rarely base their decisions on anything other than the expediency of the moment (meaning, whatever will translate into the most votes at election time), are acutely aware that the vote revs up people's expediency mechanisms, and they play this weakness to the hilt. Through the vote, politicians pit union members against businesspeople, blacks against whites, law-and-order advocates against civil-liberties supporters, rich against poor, young against elderly. Government represents power, the power to protect ourselves from our greedy neighbors—to help us get our slice of the pie before they gobble it all up.

This is a delightful state of affairs for power holders because it motivates virtually everyone to vie for the government's attention. Want a lollipop? There is only one place to get it: government. Only government has the power to tax. Only government has virtually unlimited borrowing power. Only government is allowed to print fiat paper dollars. Only government has the legal right to use force. The bureaucratic process is completely controlled by politicians through the marvelous invention known as the vote, an invention that preys upon the ever-destructive human weakness known as the expediency factor.

Because the end of the largest rainbow is in Washington, it is not surprising that there are now 35,000 registered lobbyists—up from "just" 10,000 in 1980—maneuvering to get the attention of those who hold the reins of power. Also headquartered in Washington are thousands of national groups, all of whom fight to satisfy the expediency factors of those they represent.

The Private Club

Today's government is really just a private club whose members we refer to as "politicians." One of the reasons government acts in such confusing and contradictory ways is that each member, at any given time, says and does what he believes will gain him the broadest possible voter support—and thus the most power.

Government malfunctions as a problem solver for individuals because it consists of thousands of elected officials, each of whom tries to please a wide variety of groups whose aims are conflicting. That is why you hear the same politician espousing the merits of capitalism one day while preaching socialism the next. Political expediency means not only that the decisions of politicians must be based on immediate results for the greatest number of people, but also that such results must be easily identifiable. Long-term consequences are of little concern to the politician because they are almost always too difficult for the average voter to identify.

Thoreau certainly was right when he likened the vote to a sort of gaming. Each politician has to take his best guess as to which combination of expedient demands by the public will bring him the greatest number of votes. A demographic study of the population eliminates much of the guesswork, but even so it can sometimes be a tricky business. Further, each politician's opponents have access to the same statistics. A politician's job, then—like the participant in any game—is to win.

But the fact remains that no human being has the God-given right—let alone the competence—to direct the lives of other people. That is the danger inherent in the system—that it gives ordinary men and women the power to commit aggression. "The ordinary man with extraordinary power is the chief danger for mankind—not the fiend or the sadist," warned Erich Fromm.

As previously noted, the one qualification all office holders have in common is an excessive drive for power over the lives of others, and their expedient actions are based on this drive. Their code of ethics is a simple one: That which increases or cements one's power base is good; that which lessens or threatens one's power base is bad.

Does this make all politicians evil? Evil may be a harsh word, but in the context of Natural Law, I consider them evil to the extent they desire to rule other people (i.e., commit aggression against others). Some politicians may be upstanding human beings in many respects. A politician may be a good family man, kind and considerate toward his neighbors and friends, and, outside of the political arena, practice sound ethics.

As previously mentioned, most politicians probably do not consciously acknowledge to themselves that their chief aim is power. They may realize that the facts are contrary to their desire for political power, yet they choose to ignore those facts and cling to their magnanimous belief that they are acting in the best interests of others. In other words, they simply block out all information that contradicts their artificially established belief structure, which can result in a stressful state of mind that psychologists refer to as *cognitive dissonance*.

Most politicians, I believe, have a mental disorder that causes them to believe they are missionaries of God, put on this earth to protect others and, though strangely contradictory, keep them in line. It is the politician who deludes himself into believing that his violations of Natural Law are for the good of society who poses the greatest threat to freedom. An individual who rationalizes aggression as the means to a self-proclaimed virtuous end has mentally positioned himself to justify the commission of virtually any kind of atrocity.

The entire election process, then, boils down to form rather than substance. A politician's success depends a great deal on his physical appearance, personality, and speaking ability. The person who does the best job of convincing the greatest number of people that he will give them more of everything stands the best chance of grabbing the brass ring of power. All candidates run on virtually the same platform, so what they say is not a factor. What is important is how good they are at saying it.

These are rather odd criteria for picking an individual to rule a country, as Plato, paraphrased here by Will Durant, pointed out: "In politics we presume that everyone who knows how to get votes knows how to administer a city or a state. When we are ill . . . we do not ask for the handsomest physician, or the most eloquent one."

Sadly, many Republicans, when campaigning, try to convince voters that, if given a chance, they can be just as liberal as their Democratic counterparts in the Demopublican Party. And Democrats, even while running up record deficits, try to convince voters that they are fiscally responsible and that they are simply trying to clean up the financial mess left to them by the Republicans.

With Democrats trying to act like Republicans and Republicans trying to act like Democrats, it's no wonder that the Demopublican Party resembles a barnyard full of chickens scurrying about in every direction, frantically searching for worms. Over the long haul, however, the Demopublican Party has patterned itself more and more after the preachings of its Democratic socialist wing. This has led to the Republicans having virtually no identity of their own, and, as a result, they are on the verge of extinction.

The reason for leaning toward Democratic socialist rhetoric is to be found in the numbers. The Democratic sales pitch has a much more expedient ring to it: "Vote for us and we will give you more of everything, no matter what it costs or from whom we have to take it."

Politicians promise billions of dollars in services and direct payments in exchange for votes, yet they have no means of producing wealth on their own. No one ever got elected by promising less. Remember, one of the two conditions common to all governments is that they exist off the surpluses of others. If a politician fails to deliver the goods to voters, he risks being thrown out of office the next time around.

To add to the problem, when a new president ascends the throne, more often than not he develops delusions of being loved by all of his subjects. Power breeds in him the absurd notion that he is the protector of the people. Each new president longs to go down in history as the benevolent leader who solved everyone's problems. This delusion only increases a president's already dangerous kleptomaniacal habits. Once he starts believing that he not only has to deliver, but deliver to *everyone*, his only way out is to borrow, tax, and print on a massive scale.

Sy Leon has suggested that what all politicians really are afflicted with is Politicoholism, and he offers this solution to their problem:

There seems to be but one remedy for acute Politicoholics. They should be placed in a comfortable institution, beyond the reach of dangerous weapons, where they can act out their fantasies with each other, unencumbered by the real world. They can make speeches, solicit the votes of other inmates, plan the lives of one another, levy taxes in play money, issue decrees, and start imaginary wars for the good of their institution. Clearly, this is the only humanitarian solution to the problem of acute Politicoholism.

CHAPTER 3

How People Get the Things They Want

W hile most of today's government functions can be invalidated on moral grounds, it nevertheless is important to understand the economic consequences of government's actions. If one understands why policies are economically disastrous in addition to being immoral, it is easier to see why a political system based on the expedient actions of more than 300 million people is a prescription for national suicide.

I believe a majority of Americans find it difficult to make the connection between human rights and property rights, which is unfortunate. They relate economics to property matters only, viewing property as something inanimate, totally separate and apart from a person's life. Economics, therefore, is of little concern to them. But the fact is that economics is at the very heart of the human-freedom issue.

Why? Because money for people programs comes from *people*. There is no such thing as a government function that does not have an economic reality attached to it because every so-called function makes those who work for a living worse off.

Having said this, my discussion of economics will be restricted to certain basics that I feel are crucial to analyzing the functions of modern-day government. I will say at the outset that fundamental economics is relatively simple and can therefore be explained in simple language. Adding technical jargon does nothing whatsoever to change basic economic principles. Beware the economist who cannot explain matters in simple terms. Unclear expression is a sign of unclear thought.

People often wonder why professional economists so often disagree on economic issues. First, they are human beings, and like all human beings, they have biases, political beliefs, economic motives, and a wide variety of values and social interests. All these may be subconscious, but they do exist. The wide disparity of opinion among economists once prompted a pundit to say that if all the nation's economists were laid end to end, they would point in all directions.

One dictionary definition of *economics* is "the science that deals with the production, distribution, and consumption of wealth (i.e., goods and services)." Simple translation: Economics is the study of how people get the things they want.

By "the things they want," I am referring to the material goods people desire. Economics does not deal with love, religion, ethics, philosophy, or emotional issues. These and many other subjects may be of interest to people, but they have nothing to do with the science of economics. It is critical to keep this in mind when thinking in economic terms.

More specifically, "things" refers to what the economist calls *wealth*. Wealth is food, clothing, television sets, automobiles, and other products desired by individuals. To a business owner, wealth also may consist of factories and equipment, things that can be used to produce products and services desired by consumers. But money itself is not wealth. Money is a medium of exchange, used for the purpose of acquiring products and services that individuals desire.

What stimulates economic growth—the production of wealth—is voluntary action on the part of individuals trying to improve their well-being. It is unfortunate that the idea of individuals' becoming wealthy bothers some people. Whatever their moral or ideological reasons, many of these people seek to interfere with the natural process of individuals striving to obtain what they desire through consenting-adult transactions. What is more unfortunate, many of these people are economists who advocate the strong arm of government as the most effective way to interfere with the right of people to improve their well-being.

When such interference occurs, the first fundamental law of economics—*the law of supply and demand*—is violated. It is the workings of this law that create a relationship among prices, wages, and costs. For example, if prices go up, demand drops, which causes employees to be laid off, which causes wages to go down, which causes fewer goods to be produced.

Using another example, if natural conditions create an excess supply of goods in the marketplace, these goods will be offered at a lower price, which increases demand, which pushes up prices, which attracts more entrepreneurs to that particular industry, which attracts higher wages and more employees . . . and on and on the cycle goes. Unless, of course, government intervenes to stop the natural flow of the market.

What is good about the creation of surplus wealth is that it leads to an increase in plants and equipment, which leads to the creation of both new jobs and new products. The sale of these products leads, hopefully, to profits, a large part of which are then reinvested in still more plants and equipment or in research and development. Thus, economic growth continues and everyone's well-being is improved.

But what if all profits are not reinvested? The fact is that surplus wealth must lead to growth in virtually all cases, even if it is not reinvested in the business from which it was derived. Suppose, for example, a man builds a successful business and then sells the business for millions of dollars. He has no desire to produce anymore. He just wants to enjoy the good life. What, then, is the economic result of his leading a retired life of luxury?

If he buys a car, he helps employ auto workers and automobile salespeople. (Obviously, I'm referring to "foreign" automobiles made in the United States, since, for all practical purposes, the original U.S. auto industry no longer exists.) If he takes a vacation, he helps employ travel agency employees, airline employees, luggage factory workers, and hotel personnel, to name but a few. If he builds a mansion, that, too, stimulates the economy, because it requires a wide variety of laborers and craftsmen.

Even if he puts his money into stocks, bonds, or savings accounts, he stimulates the economy by making money available to other businesses. About the only way he can escape contributing to the economy is to hide all his money in his home, a highly unlikely scenario, to say the least. But even then he would require certain products and services just to live.

One can see why Ayn Rand proclaimed that money is the root of all good. Surplus wealth stimulates the economy, which is critical to the poorest people in any society. The greater the surplus wealth, the greater the chances that those at the lower end of the economic scale will begin to reap benefits. Sorry, progressives, but trickle-down economics really *does* work.

Here is the second fundamental law of economics, one that few politicians seem to understand: *There is no such thing as something for nothing.* Wealth cannot be created out of thin air. Only productive effort can create television sets, refrigerators, automobiles, and houses. By contrast, today's money *can* be created out of thin air (actually, out of paper), because, as previously mentioned, money is not wealth.

The reality is that you cannot have more without creating more. There are no magic formulas by which to create wealth, even though the public has been cruelly led to believe otherwise. Income to the people of a nation must not exceed their output (i.e., what they produce). If it does, the nation experiences what is known as *false prosperity.* When output increases, real income (i.e., income derived from productive effort) increases. When output decreases, real income decreases—no matter how much more money people receive.

When a person finds that his higher income of today buys less than his income of five years ago did, he is living in a country that is being deluded—and destroyed—by false prosperity. He is living in a nation where the combined income of the population exceeds the total production of goods and services. He is living in a nation that is courting economic collapse.

Some economists, in what seems like a desperate attempt to justify government interference in the marketplace, argue that false prosperity is better than risking a depression. (The polite phrase is *severe recession.*) They could not be more wrong. A depression is an adjustment period in the supply-and-demand cycle that forces people and businesses to become more efficient. Like children, people are reprimanded for being naughty. This happens when they treat themselves to the fantasy that prosperity can be created without work. The more irresponsible their actions, the worse the reprimand—in the form of a recession or depression—hence, like children, the better they learn their lesson.

Not everything that is good for us feels good, and so it is with a depression. Long term, a depression is a healthy process—a financial catharsis of sorts. Prices fall to levels where merchandise can be sold, overvalued investments drop to realistic plateaus, and, when everything reaches its natural level once more, the market is once again healthy. Just as it is in the long-term best interest of children to experience an occasional spanking, so it is with adults who have misbehaved.

Which brings us to the big question: What politician has the courage to spank more than 300 million people? Certainly not one who is tied to the vote.

And now for the shocker: That is the end of your lesson in economics. I can hear the screams of economists from New York to Tokyo: "What about macroeconomics and microeconomics? What about the Gross National Product? What about elasticity of demand? What about the consumer price index?"

Answer: All of these things are related to supply and demand and/or the principle that there is no such thing as something for nothing. One can sermonize patronizingly about oversimplification, about the world of today being much too complex to be explained away in such an elementary fashion, and about a thousand-and-one other factors that must be considered, but the reality is that each of these leads us right back to the two basic laws of economics.

Attitudes toward Economic Laws

While the basic laws of economics never change, there are, theoretically, two different attitudes governments may take toward these laws. They may either obey them or choose to violate them, depending upon their economic systems.

At one idealistic extreme, any government that allowed laissez-faire capitalism would thereby show a healthy respect for the law of supply and demand. It would demonstrate, through its actions, that it understood that wealth cannot be created without effort. At the other extreme is communism (in its theoretical form, as opposed to communism as it is practiced in the real world). Theoretically, communism refuses to acknowledge the unrelenting law of supply and demand and implies that wealth can be produced without labor.

It should be pointed out that neither of these systems challenges the concept of division of labor, which might properly be referred to as *industrialization*. It is this division-of-labor concept that has allowed man to advance technologically in quantum leaps. Man's vastly superior brain gave him the capacity to make tools, which was the beginning of his technological climb. A tool is an object that allows people to produce more with the expenditure of less time and energy.

The next great advance in man's technological evolution was the discovery that he could produce far more through the division of labor (i.e., through each person's specializing in one craft rather than meeting his daily needs by producing every item himself).

The division-of-labor concept was further refined during the Industrial Revolution in England when it was discovered that the multiplication of output was even greater if large groups of people were organized to produce just one product, with smaller groups within the same factory specializing in just one aspect of a given product.

Division of labor in industry is practiced by all modern nations, though it is interesting, as we shall see, why some succeed at it far better than others. No one, other than green-is-good nutcases, advocates the vague concept of "returning to nature," to pre-technological times when disease, poverty, suffering, and early death were horrors that awaited each newborn child. Only fools and romantic dreamers talk of returning to a preindustrial period when people were clean, well-fed, healthy, and happy—indeed, a period that never existed!

Industrialization, fortunately, is not the issue. The only issue is, who will *control* the means of industry? If industry operates in a free environment, people can be organized by mutual consent to increase production. If industrialization takes place through coercion, people are forced to produce against their will.

Respecting Economic Law

Capitalism is technically defined as "an economic system characterized by private . . . ownership of capital goods, by investments that are determined by private decision rather than by state control, and by prices, production, and the distribution of goods that are determined mainly in a free market."

In other words, capitalism is an economic system that works through the absence of controls, a system that works through individuals. The term *free enterprise* is generally synonymous with capitalism, and for the purposes of this book, the two will be used interchangeably. So that there will be no confusion over what I mean by the terms *capitalism* and *free enterprise*, let me make it clear that whenever I use these terms, I am referring to laissez-faire capitalism and laissez-faire free enterprise (unless specifically stating otherwise).

Laissez-faire is a French term meaning "a doctrine opposing government interference in economic affairs beyond the minimum necessary for the maintenance of peace and property rights." Note that this definition specifically spells out the original intentions that led to the birth of government—protecting people's lives and property.

The truth be known, capitalism of the laissez-faire variety has never been tried on this planet. When one realizes what capitalism has accomplished *despite* government interference, he cannot help but wonder what the well-being of mankind might be *without* government intervention. Capitalism is not an idea whose time has passed. The sad reality is that capitalism, in its pure form, has yet to be discovered.

The very thing that makes the free-enterprise system work is the absence of interference. Free-market competition assures the public of the widest variety of goods at the lowest possible prices. To the degree the market is not regulated, it responds naturally to the law of supply and demand, and both producers and consumers are better off. To the degree the market is regulated, the law of supply and demand is negated, causing the market to be less efficient and more costly, and causing both producers and consumers to be worse off.

Many people have been taught that capital is the only thing rewarded in a capitalistic society and that labor is cheated. Let us examine how capitalism works and see if there is any merit to this charge. The capitalistic cycle requires four elements: ideas, capital, labor, and management.

Obviously, the idea must come first, but an idea has no value until someone is willing to invest capital (i.e., surplus wealth) in it. So the backbone of capitalism is creativity and risk taking—the entrepreneur who has the ability to come up with an idea and the investor who is willing to risk money on his idea. The entrepreneur and the investor also must have the creativity to organize the idea and the money into a plan. Clearly, then, the entrepreneur is the "first cause" in the capitalistic cycle.

But without workers and managers, ideas and capital are useless—unless the entrepreneur is willing to build his product, piece by piece, through his own efforts. Which is exactly what people did, for the most part, before the Industrial Revolution brought on a refinement of the division-of-labor concept.

Summarizing, then, the capitalistic cycle works like this: An entrepreneur comes up with an idea, risks his capital (or the capital of investors), and organizes a venture. To operate the tools in which he has invested, he must hire employees, which means job opportunities are created. The more he modernizes his facilities (i.e., invests in new equipment), the more the productivity of his operation increases (i.e., there is an increase in the output of each worker). This greater output increases the production of goods and makes them available to consumers at lower prices.

Though everyone benefits from the cycle, it may justifiably be argued that the person at the lowest end of the income spectrum benefits most from capitalism, for several reasons.

First, he is free to take a job at any wage, and, in fact, both employment and wages usually increase in a free market.

Second, he is free to start a small business of his own, without the necessity of obtaining a license or having to comply with costly regulations that only large companies can afford.

Third, free-market capitalism keeps prices down, which allows him to buy things he would not be able to afford in a government-controlled economy.

And if all goes well, the entrepreneur makes a profit—hopefully, a very large profit. Big profits generate surplus capital that can be invested in more and better plants and equipment, which means more employment, more products, lower prices—and so the cycle continues, unless and until it is interrupted by government intervention.

The thing that enables capitalism to work so smoothly and to be of benefit to all producers is each person's desire to improve his own well-being. Adam Smith pointed this out more than 230 years ago in his book *The Wealth of Nations*. Contrary to what the public has been led to believe, Smith was not particularly sympathetic to the businessman. Rather, his emphasis was on the "invisible hand" of the marketplace that would assure the masses of gaining more than through any other system. He pointed out that even if a man were not interested in the welfare of other human beings, when he based his actions on the profit motive (in a free market, without committing aggression), those actions would automatically benefit others.

How much easier it is to sleep at night knowing that your well-being will be improved because of the desire of other people to pursue their own well-being, rather than to depend on the highly suspect altruism of politicians and professional do-gooders.

The reason capitalism works so smoothly is because it is in harmony with nature—with man's natural instincts. If people have the freedom to engage in economic activities to improve their well-being, innovations will come about and economic growth will occur. The result is that civilization advances, meaning that more people are healthier, wealthier, and happier. On the other hand, when such freedom is restricted, growth is slowed or, in extreme cases, halted, and a civilization retrogresses.

In simple terms, a free market is a freedom-of-choice voting system. In a free market, a person does not have to go along with the desires of the majority. That is, he can "vote" to buy any product he desires, without regard to whether others want it. In addition to giving the individual free choice, a free market offers him a wide diversity of products and services. But when government intervenes and imposes regulations, price restrictions, and other controls, businesses and people are forced to conform and the individual's choices are restricted.

Common Fears about Capitalism

Capitalism, of course, has its faults, as does any system, but these are offset many times over by its merits. It is the myths about capitalism I wish to address here, myths that have been perpetuated through ignorance, envy, and/or the desire to control people's lives.

Myth: *Didn't the Industrial Revolution prove that businessmen, when unregulated, will subject workers to inhumane working conditions, long hours, and low wages?*

The Industrial Revolution, which occurred in England from roughly 1760 to 1840, brought about the greatest improvement in the well-being of man since the Agrarian Revolution. Prior to the Industrial Revolution, the Black Death, scurvy, rickets, and other diseases regularly wiped out large segments of the populations of Europe. For the average person, life was day-to-day misery. Before the Industrial Revolution, most people knew no other life but work, and their work was almost always under inhumane conditions. Those who were lucky earned enough to keep their families alive.

The truth is, the Industrial Revolution changed all this. Industrialists did not roam the countryside with shotguns, rounding up workers for their factories. On the contrary, as word of the new opportunities spread, people invaded the cities by the thousands, aggressively competing for the "inhumane" jobs. There's no question that wages were low—but only by today's standards. There's no question that hours were long—but only by today's standards. There's no question that conditions were bad—but only by today's standards.

The point that enemies of capitalism miss is that it was not today's standards that the eighteenth-century laborer used as a measuring stick.

What caused him to migrate to the cities to seek employment in the so-called sweatshops were the filth, sickness, and inhumane conditions he left behind.

By comparison, conditions in the factories were like the Promised Land to him. Never before had he lived so well. One time, loud and clear: People do not voluntarily leave one job for another if the new job offers lower pay, longer hours, and inferior working conditions. People gladly left their terrible lives behind for the vastly improved living conditions made possible by the Industrial Revolution.

The fact the rich may have grown richer is only one aspect of the Industrial Revolution. Just as important is the fact that industrialization lifted the living standards of the masses to a level never before imagined. One may properly say that it lifted them to a level that, for the first time, made the average worker conscious enough of better living conditions to complain about long hours, low wages, and bad working conditions. Eric Hoffer referred to such people as "the newly poor." When people are struggling just to stay alive from one day to the next, such thoughts do not occur to them.

Today, the nationwide illegal-alien problem in the United States is a modern-day example of what happened during the Industrial Revolution. Stories of the deplorable living conditions of victimized aliens abound, yet they flood our borders by the thousands. Why? To live under deplorable conditions? Yes—because those deplorable conditions are so much better than those they left behind in Mexico that they are willing to take great risks to attain the lifestyle of an illegal alien. Having lived in Mexico, I speak from firsthand observation.

Myth: *Didn't the Robber Barons prove that if big business is not regulated, men will amass fortunes through unethical means?*

The so-called Age of the Robber Barons occurred in the United States roughly between 1875 and 1910. In America, as in England, not only did the rich get richer, but never before had so many people lived so well. The Rockefellers, Carnegies, and Fords did not accumulate wealth by printing money. They produced oil, steel, and automobiles, all of which necessitated the employment of thousands of workers. And in order for workers to be able to afford to purchase their products, they had to be paid decent wages.

I do not mean to imply that all businessmen of that era were honest. There are honest and dishonest entrepreneurs, just as there are honest and dishonest laborers. But the only person I would consider to have amassed his fortune through unethical means would be one who used coercion (i.e., force or the threat of force) to achieve his ends. Unfortunately, then, as today, all too many businessmen colluded with the government to gain special favors, protection from competitors, and legislation that gave them a dishonest advantage in the marketplace.

In other words, it was the availability of government power—government intervention itself—that gave men the opportunity to acquire wealth unethically. To the extent businessmen of that era used government aid to accumulate wealth, I would consider them to have been dishonest. But to the extent they amassed great fortunes by providing better products and services at prices the public voluntarily paid, I admire them and believe that the people of this country owe them a debt of gratitude.

Myth: Didn't the Great Depression prove that capitalism does not work without government controls?

As is so often the case, people have been led to view the cause as the solution. The Great Depression in this country occurred roughly between 1929 and 1940. By 1929, government intervention in the economy had become pronounced (relative to earlier standards) and had begun to disrupt the workings of the free market.

One of the worst contributions the government made to bringing about the Great Depression was the passage of the Federal Reserve Act in 1913. The Federal Reserve Act will be discussed in a later chapter, but for now let it suffice to say that it put government in a position to, among other things, arbitrarily inflate the currency and provide easy credit for unknowledgeable amateurs who thought they could get rich quick in the falsely inflated stock market.

Also in 1913, government passed the Sixteenth Amendment, which created the present-day income-tax structure. Then, in the 1920s, government's meddling in the economy reached into the areas of collective bargaining, national old-age insurance, and many other aspects of the economy. Public works were increased, employers were persuaded to divide time among their employees to spread the work, and industries were encouraged to expand for the sake of keeping the economy from collapsing.

To make matters worse, government officials continued to assure the public that the economy was healthy and that the future of the country looked great, just as government officials do today. When the Federal Reserve Board did try to slow credit and inflation, people complained to their congressmen that the big operators on Wall Street were trying to cut the little man out. Political expediency being the disease that it is, congressmen, of course, responded to these complaints by seeing to it that easy credit continued.

Once things started crumbling, government added to the deterioration of the economy by delaying necessary liquidations, lending money to shaky businesses, further inflating the currency, and artificially propping up prices and wages. In general, government, as always, made matters worse by increasing its intervention rather than getting out of the way and allowing the free market to adjust itself as normally and rapidly as possible.

The point is that capitalism did not fail. As always, it was government controls that caused the economy to fail.

One other significant feature of the Great Depression era worth noting is the way in which the expediency factors of the general populace contributed to the conditions leading up to it. Like today, a something-for-nothing attitude prevailed, which is in violation of one of the two cardinal rules of economics. In those days, however, the something-for-nothing urge was satisfied through unrealistic investment in the stock market. People were appallingly irresponsible in their investments, pushing stock prices to totally unrealistic levels.

As was discussed earlier, the free market reprimands financially imprudent people with a blunt instrument known as a depression. The more the laws of economics are violated, the worse the reprimand. The indiscretions of the late 1920s were very bad, hence the very bad depression that followed.

Myth: If greedy businessmen are not controlled, wouldn't they make unreasonable profits through price gouging?

Here we have a rather impressive array of anti-capitalistic terms. Let us examine them one at a time.

Greed is a subjective term used to describe what someone believes to be excessive desire (usually for material gain) on the part of someone else (i.e., it is one person's opinion as to whether another person tries too hard to improve his well-being). But the desire to further one's well-being is a trait common to all people and is not dependent upon anyone's opinion.

The difference in people fulfilling their desires is not so much one of extent, but of the different ways in which they go about it. Clergymen may fulfill their desires by helping others. Dedicated medical researchers may fulfill their desires by discovering cures for diseases. Successful businesspeople may fulfill their desires by creating better products and services at a profit. Single-issue crusaders may fulfill their desires by imposing their moral standards on others. Rapists and murderers may fulfill their desires by committing aggression against their victims.

Each of us, knowingly or unknowingly, attempts to further his well-being (i.e., act in his own self-interest), but the actions of some do not involve aggression, while the actions of others are clearly in violation of Natural Law.

What are *unreasonable profits?* An opinion, to be sure. How does one determine if a profit is unreasonable when every risk is different, every person's efforts are different, and every situation is different? How can there be an absolute standard for determining how much profit is too much? When a person invests in a venture, he has no guarantee that there will be any profit at all. If it turns out to be a losing proposition, is there such a thing as an unreasonable loss?

In truth, a reasonable profit is whatever profit a person can make by selling his product or service at whatever price the public is willing to pay—without the use of coercion. The fact is that profits are never too high. The higher the profits, the better for the economy in general, for all the reasons previously discussed.

Henry Hazlitt put the necessity for profits in another light: "The function of profits . . . is to put constant and unremitting pressure on the head of every competitive business to introduce further economies and efficiencies. . . . In good times he does this to increase his profits further; in normal times he does it to keep ahead of his competitors; in bad times he may have to do it to survive at all."

Disregarding the fact that high profits allow for higher shareholder dividends and greater investment in production facilities, profits should be welcomed if for no other reason than because they give workers the security of knowing that the company they work for is solvent. It certainly does not give workers peace of mind to know that their company is barely profitable.

Finally, we come to *price gouging.* Again, a subjective term. One could just as easily argue that an unskilled worker making $7.25 an hour as a result of government-enforced minimum-wage laws is guilty of price gouging. The same line of reasoning can be used here as was used to discuss unreasonable profits. In the absence of coercion, there is no such thing as price gouging. A seller of anything is entitled to the highest price that the market is willing to pay him.

But that does not mean he will get any price he wants. There is a limiting factor. Competition determines whether someone's prices are too high. And, as we shall later see, everyone has competition in a free market—though, once again, the public has been misled into believing otherwise. Only government force can protect a business from the necessity to compete.

All this brings us back to the law of supply and demand. People will buy a product according to how badly they want it and how high it is priced. Its price also will be determined by the existing supply of the product. That's why some professional athletes make millions of dollars a year, while the annual salary of a great scientist may not exceed $100,000. The fact that some people believe this to be unjust is irrelevant. That is merely their opinion. The reality is that enough people apparently believe it is right; otherwise, they would not be willing to pay big money to see an athlete hit a home run or dunk a basketball.

The law of supply and demand can never be wrong because it allows people to vote freely for what they want. What others think they should want is of no concern to them. Every good marketer knows this and has probably learned it the hard way.

Price gouging is not possible in a free market because, contrary to what the collectivist believes, both sides profit in a voluntary transaction. They profit in the sense that each person receives what he is willing to accept. Capitalism rejects the notion that one person's gain is another person's loss. When dealing on a voluntary, non-coercive basis, that is not possible. It's a virtual axiom that all parties to a voluntary transaction automatically gain.

Myth: If there were no government controls, wouldn't small operators be put out of business?

I am particularly sensitive to this charge because I've had so much firsthand experience with it. I've always been able to trace my failures to my own imprudent actions or government intervention. In not one instance was competition from big businesses a factor.

In fact, I found quite the opposite to be true. I've always felt that big companies could not compete with me because I was on top of my situation at all times. I could move swiftly, without having to consult cumbersome committees, and I could afford to give my personal touch to every transaction.

This is why ambitious entrepreneurs, even in the face of ever-increasing government meddling, have been able to start from scratch and build companies such as Microsoft, Amazon.com, and Google in industries already dominated by corporate giants such as IBM, Barnes & Noble, and Yahoo. The fact is that the giants are too busy trying to keep pace with other competitive giants to watch the young entrepreneurs who are creeping up behind them. And by the time they are aware of an industrious, enterprising upstart, it's usually too late.

It is true that laissez-faire capitalism helps put some people out of business, but that's a good feature of capitalism because it automatically weeds out inefficient producers who are not competitive—a process commonly referred to as *creative destruction*, which is necessary to a healthy economy. It is efficient businesses that produce the best products at the lowest prices, employ the greatest number of people at the highest wages, and reinvest surplus profits to increase efficiency and continue the process onward and upward.

One of the effects of this process is that workers from unsuccessful companies are absorbed by successful companies. Owners of businesses who cannot keep pace have no divine right to remain in business if they cannot compete. They have a natural right to pursue a business venture, but not a government-guaranteed right to be successful.

Many people simply do not understand that it is in everyone's long-term best interest for inefficient, antiquated businesses to fold as new, efficient businesses take over. That is what keeps the economy healthy and helps keep unemployment low. Only government intervention in propping up dead companies—such as General Motors and Chrysler—can interfere with this natural, healthy process.

Capitalism is not the dog-eat-dog system that many have decried it to be. In a free society, men do not put others out of business by being ruthless, but by providing better products and services at lower prices. A capitalistic society is one in which individuals are free to trade with other individuals, at their sole discretion, without interference from anyone.

Is Wealth Really Evil?

Many other myths about capitalism have become trademarks of free-enterprise antagonists over the years. All of them, however, can be answered with indisputable facts and logic. At the root of these myths about capitalism is that too many egalitarian minds are, quite simply, envious of the success of others. As a result, they try to believe that the wealth of one person impoverishes his neighbor—as though there were a fixed amount of wealth on our planet.

This, of course, is nonsense. A nation as civilized as the United States can afford rich people. As a matter of fact, it cannot afford not to have rich people, because it is the opportunity to become rich—the ultimate material symbol of the American Dream—that provides the best hope for the impoverished.

The billion-dollar empires built by men like John D. Rockefeller, J. Paul Getty, Andrew Carnegie, Cornelius Vanderbilt, and Henry Ford symbolized hope. Every man who started from humble beginnings and built a financial empire represented living proof that everyone had the opportunity (not the guarantee) to go as far as his talent and ambition would take him. Financial empires gave every impoverished young man hope that he, too, could achieve great success.

Just as important, the great financial empires of yesteryear provided a value system for the people of this country. There was no confusion about the moral way to achieve financial success. People clearly understood that the marketplace was the arena for financial gain and that winning in the marketplace led to material well-being.

As the system slowly changed the rules of the game to include needs and desires—as defined by anyone politically active enough to bring about government intervention in the marketplace—expediency factors went into high gear, people began to resent those who accumulated great wealth, and, eventually, the envy-based, anything-goes attitude that prevails today came to replace the concept of getting ahead by producing value for others.

Again, free enterprise offers the greatest opportunities for those at the lowest end of the economic scale. I believe that the best insurance for having a "chicken in every pot and a car in every garage"—on a permanent basis—is for ambitious, risk-taking entrepreneurs to know that they have the opportunity to have ten chickens in their pots and ten cars in their garages if they are able to earn them. This means, in simple terms, that the poor are only as secure as the rich.

If the progressives now in power are successful in shifting an ever-greater percentage of the tax burden to the wealthiest among us, the building of super fortunes will become an anachronism of our country's past. When there's no pot of gold at the end of the rainbow, it destroys incentive. Government sends the message to its subjects, "Forget about the evils of wealth. 'Tis better to have security from the cradle to the grave." And as incentive drops, it will bring the economy down with it.

Envying successful people is a self-destructive mistake, but one that power-hungry politicians prey upon unmercifully. Equating wealth with evil is an offshoot of such envy. As William Simon put it, "The crude linkage between wealth and evil, poverty and virtue, is false, stupid, and of value only to demagogues, parasites, and criminals—indeed, the three groups that alone have profited from the linkage." It is the production of wealth, in spite of government intervention, that has brought man to his present living standard, a living standard impossible to conceive of just a few centuries ago.

But perhaps an even greater mistake is the refusal of those who know the truth to speak out. As Eric Hoffer said, one of the tragic curiosities of our day is the loss of courage on the part of talented and successful people, particularly those in positions of leadership. Again William Simon put it succinctly in *A Time for Truth*:

> *As is so often the case in our society, when the liberals orchestrate a nationwide uproar over good versus evil, all those defined as evil suffer an acute loss of nerve. Businessmen and bankers, who seem to value respectability more than their lives, are incapable of tolerating this moral abuse. Invariably they collapse psychologically. And whatever they may think and say in private, in public they either go mute or stumble frantically over their own feet as they rush to join the moral bandwagon.*

Progressives generally believe that to seek one's own happiness without concern for the rest of society is uncivilized. On the contrary, I believe that to thwart man's basic instinct to improve his well-being is uncivilized and tyrannical. What it boils down to is that some people wish to take it upon themselves to restrict the freedom of others. Nobel-Prize winner Dr. Milton Friedman pinpointed this presumptuousness by noting that "a major source of objection to a free economy is precisely that . . . it gives people what they want instead of what a particular group thinks they ought to want. Underlying most arguments against the free market is a lack of belief in freedom itself."

Those who hammer away at the injustices of capitalism would do well to recognize that never have so many people lived so comfortably as in modern-day America, even though its capitalistic system is stifled more each year by government. And as the last vestiges of laissez faire are dissolved by omnipotent politicians, the threat of losing that comfortable way of life is becoming more ominous each day.

I would argue that the robber barons were not the great industrialists who amassed mega-fortunes by giving Americans the highest living standard in the history of mankind. The real robber barons are those power-hungry and envious collectivists in our government who want to control you and all that you produce and own. What these robber barons desire is for you to relinquish your individuality and deliver control of your life into their hands. They want you to have faith that their superior judgment and morality will protect you from the temptation to pursue your own well-being.

Disrespecting Economic Law

Communism is technically defined as "a theory advocating elimination of private property; a system in which goods are owned in common and are available to all as needed; a totalitarian system in which a single authoritarian party controls state-owned means of production with the professed aim of establishing a stateless society; a final stage of society in Marxist theory in which the state has withered away and economic goods are distributed equally."

Regardless of how this definition may strike you, the one overriding fact about communism is that it does not work, neither in theory nor in practice. When I refer to *theory* and *practice*, I mean that theoretical communism, as described by Marx, Engels, Lenin, and other historically prominent communists, bears virtually no resemblance to real communism (i.e., communism as it has been practiced in so-called communist countries).

Theoretical Communism

Can we make any sense of the dictionary definition of communism? How are goods owned in common? Does this refer to some sort of utopian partnership among individuals? And what is meant by "available to all as needed"? Who determines who is in need? Who determines what it is that they need? Who determines how much they need? The same, age-old question relentlessly stalks us: Who shall decide?

Several years ago, I had an occasion to ponder this muddled concept of the way communists believe people should live. It happened during a dinner party at a friend's beach home. While standing on his balcony, I became engaged in a discussion with a woman and her husband. During our conversation, the woman offered her opinion that it was not right for people to build private homes on the beach. When I asked why, she answered that "all the ocean frontage should belong to 'the people.'"

Her statement interested me because I felt she sincerely believed her viewpoint to be morally valid. Pursuing my curiosity, I began asking her questions. "Who is it you are referring to when you use the term 'the people'?"

"Everyone," she answered.

"Do you mean that you and I should be joint owners, along with millions of other people, of every square inch of this beach?"

"Of course," she replied with certainty.

It seemed to me that such an involuntary partnership held the potential for a whole bunch of practical problems.

"What happens if both you and I want to sit on the same four square feet of beach at the same time?"

"You're getting overly technical," she protested. "That would be highly unlikely to occur."

I silently translated the real meaning of her response to be "I can't answer that."

In reality, common sense told me that it was precisely this sort of problem that would, in fact, continually occur in a common-ownership society. Worse, it would occur on a much larger scale.

For example, in a utopian communist society, what would stop a gang of people from getting up early each morning and staking out fifty yards of the most desirable beachfront in a given area? After all, because they would own every square inch of the beach in common with everyone else, they would have a perfect right to do so. Is this what the original communist theoreticians had in mind—a chaotic society that would operate on a first-come, first-served basis?

But wait a minute. Why should the gang have to get up early each morning to lay claim to its preferred area of the beach? Does communism provide for a time limit on the use of commonly owned property? Why not just have a couple of gang members guard the property at night? Technically, they would merely be exercising their right to use common property. It's just that in this particular case, their use would be continuous.

To carry this line of reasoning to its ultimate conclusion, why not just live on that particular area of the beach on a permanent basis? You guessed it: That would be the precise point at which "the people" would be engaged in something called *private ownership of property.*

It seemed clear to me that, in real life, the vague concepts of "elimination of private property" and "goods owned in common" could mean only that land and other wealth should be taken from their rightful owners and made available to the strongest person or group to come along and claim them. In which case, it is theoretical communism, not capitalism, that is a dog-eat-dog system.

The only meaningful way in which to think of property is that someone either owns it or does not. As discussed in Chapter 1, the true tests of ownership are whether you may do anything you desire with your own property and whether anyone else may take all or any part of it from you. You might also recall the listing of only three possible ways in which property can be viewed. Theoretical communism seems to favor the first of those three views—that anyone may take anyone else's property whenever he pleases.

Another aspect of theoretical communism is the notion that the individual is unimportant and that it is therefore moral to sacrifice him for the good of society. But because *society* is nothing more than a term for a group of individuals, this means that every person is subject to sacrifice, at any time, and that such sacrifice is subject to the whims of any subgroup of individuals strong enough to enforce its will.

This is precisely the kind of society that existed in pre-civilized times. Men lived communal lives to protect themselves from beasts and the hazards of nature. Cannibalism was considered moral, because only one individual needed to be sacrificed to feed the group. This is especially interesting because one of the standard arguments of free-enterprise antagonists is that capitalism is outdated. Advocates of freedom are labeled as "old-fashioned thinkers." But, in truth, it is communism that has been outdated since man first discovered the miracle of agriculture and began his climb toward civilization.

A final aspect of theoretical communism that should be mentioned is the so-called labor theory. This is the rather vague concept that calls for a laborer to receive all the fruits of his labor or insists upon the right of a laborer to the products of his labor. But in a division-of-labor society (which, as previously noted, exists in all civilized countries today), how does one determine how much labor (in terms of money) each laborer has put into a particular product?

Theoretically, the Marxist believes that if a man puts $100 worth of labor into the making of a product (and assuming he makes every aspect of the product himself, which is almost never the case), he is being exploited if someone buys it from him for $100 and resells it for $125. The Marxist would argue that the additional $25 belongs to the laborer who made the product.

Of course, the Marxist does not explain what happens if the next person sells the product for only $75. Should the laborer then refund him the $25 loss he incurred? And how does one keep track of each laborer from whom he has bought a product, so that, say, ten years down the road, he can send him the profit realized from reselling the product at a higher price?

And how do you define physical labor? Is writing a book physical labor? Or should an author's profits go to the workers who do the typesetting, printing, shipping, and other physical tasks related to the manufacture and distribution of his book?

It is obvious that the labor theory, aside from relying on the immoral concept of forcible interference, is unrealistic to the point of having no practical meaning. It is an unintelligible notion that has no way of being explained in the real world—or any other world. And yet these kinds of abstract notions, such as "the laborer should not be exploited for profit," persist, particularly on college campuses. It is sad—and dangerous—that young people are being taught to believe in such nonsense.

Unfortunately, few college professors are intellectually honest enough to explain the connection between freedom and free enterprise. Before there can be physical labor to perform, someone must come up with an idea, someone must invest capital, and someone must organize people together for productive purposes.

Even if it were possible to define the labor theory in an intelligible way, it still would overlook the fact that cost, price, and value are three distinctly different considerations. Cost relates to how much capital (including that invested in labor) it takes to produce a product. Price is what is being asked for the product. Value is what any particular person at any given time believes the product is worth. You and I may buy the same item at the same time for the same price, but you may value it more than I do. Thus, you may have been willing to pay a higher price for the item, had it been asked, while I may not have been willing to do so.

The labor theory is just another example of the anti-capitalist mentality that in every transaction one person must win and another must lose.

This, of course, is totally untrue, for the same reason that every person in a voluntary transaction theoretically profits because he exercises free choice. The only way the labor theory can make any sense (although it would be impossible, as well as undesirable, to apply) is if every person were an individual entrepreneur producing each item in its entirety. And a society of entrepreneurs is hardly compatible with the goals of hard-line communists.

Like laissez-faire capitalism, theoretical communism has never existed on this planet. The difference, however, is that capitalism is a very simple concept and is in harmony with Natural Law and man's natural instincts. Theoretical communism, on the other hand, is not only unintelligible, it violates every canon of ethics concerned with human freedom.

Real Communism

Real communism is quite different from theoretical communism and quite easy to understand. Whereas communist leaders would like to have the gullible masses believe that the people own everything, the reality is that real communism turns out to be a dictatorship in which the dictators own everything. *Everything* includes not only all land and material wealth, but also people's lives. Every citizen of a communist country is a literal slave— unless, of course, he is part of the power structure.

In truth, communism (as it is theoretically proposed) is a myth. While it purports to have as one of its main objectives "common ownership of all property," in reality no one (except the dictators) owns anything. An owner, as we have discussed, has absolute say-so over what will be done with his property.

People in countries such as Cuba and North Korea have no say-so whatsoever about what will be done with any property, including their own lives. They are told what jobs they will perform. They are told where they will perform them. They are told what hours they will work. They are told how much they will be paid for the work they do (which is hardly in accordance with the vague notion of the labor theory). And not only may they not quit their jobs like workers in capitalist countries, they can be imprisoned for even daring to challenge any of these commands.

In light of the facts, the notion that people in communist countries own everything in common is absurd on its face. For 70 years, the Soviet Union's iron-fisted totalitarian government exploited its workers unmercifully. The tools of industry, like everything else in communist countries, were owned by a small group of men who controlled the government. These men were the actual owners, because an owner is someone who can say what will be done with his property, without interference from others. And you can be sure that when the Soviet Union's dictators wished to do something with any property held within its borders, no citizen dared to challenge them.

Earlier I said that freedom and equality are incompatible goals and that this incompatibility is one of the things at the heart of democracy's problems. Democracy strives for balance, but has difficulty keeping the scales tipped away from equality and toward freedom. Under communism, however, there is *no* freedom and glaring *inequality*. It is true that there is some degree of equal misery among the masses (in whose name revolutions are always carried out), but you can be certain that government leaders do not live like the rest of the population.

There is one aspect of theoretical communism that is also a grim reality of real communism—the belief that the individual is nothing and that the state is supreme. Which is precisely why communism does not work. Remember, the state consists of nothing more than millions of individuals. How can the individual be nothing and the state be everything when the state *is* individuals? Rose Wilder Lane, in her evolution from communism to libertarianism, described the precise moment when this incongruity first struck her: "When the capitalist is gone," she asked, "who will manage production? The State. And what is the State? The State will be the mass of toiling workers. It was at this point that the first doubt pierced my Communist faith."

If you recall our earlier discussion of the capitalist cycle, the impetus for the productive process is the investment of surplus wealth. How, then, does a communist country carry out an industrial venture? First, it invests whatever wealth has been accumulated by the government through the efforts of its subjects. Second, it utilizes the country's huge pool of slave labor, which represents a vast reservoir of surplus wealth for the dictatorship.

In other words, the government merely invests slave labor in its projects, along with whatever surplus wealth it has amassed through the efforts of those same slaves. This is precisely how Lenin, Stalin, and subsequent Soviet leaders built subways, factories, dams, railroads, and virtually all other large-scale projects in their country.

If Karl Marx were alive today, he would undoubtedly be disappointed by the realities of communism. Marx naively predicted that the dictatorship established by the communists would be temporary, that it would eventually be dissolved because there would be no need for it. He believed that people, after seeing how wonderfully communism worked, would be happy to work for the good of society.

Needless to say, the hundreds of millions of people who have been enslaved in communist countries around the globe have not been happy to work for "the good of society." That is why brutal security forces have always been maintained to keep people from escaping. Which raises the question: If communism is such a wonderful way of life, why aren't people, particularly those in Western nations who praise the cultures of communist countries, not storming their borders trying to get into those countries? The flight has always been most decidedly in the other direction.

And, needless to say, no communist dictatorship has ever intentionally dissolved itself. Recalling George Orwell's words once again: "One does not establish a dictatorship in order to safeguard a revolution; one makes the revolution in order to establish the dictatorship." The excuse for a revolution is always to free the people or to give all power to the people. But revolutionary heroes almost always turn out to be as bad as, and usually worse than, the oppressive governments they overthrow.

After Lenin overthrew the existing Russian government in 1917, one of his first moves was to set up a bloody and efficient network of secret police to stalk enemies of the people. But long after Lenin died, the secret police force (which became known as the KGB) remained—much larger, much stronger, and much more oppressive with each passing year. Long after the all-power-to-the-people ether of revolutionary heroes wears off, people find themselves still enslaved. The people to whom all power goes always turns out to be the small group of people (and their successors) who led the revolution. Napoleon admitted bluntly, "Vanity made the revolution; liberty was only a pretext."

The sad truth is that those leaders who have cried the loudest for collectivist equality have been the bloodiest and most inhumane of all dictators. It is estimated that Lenin and Stalin combined murdered some 60 million of their own countrymen in an effort to accomplish their aims. Were the 60 million lives worth it? From the standpoint of the dictators, yes. Perhaps never before in history has the enslavement of a people been carried out so efficiently. Its brutal methods, which included its incredibly effective secret police force, prevented serious threats of uprisings against it until Mikhail Gorbachev came on the scene and *glasnost* and *perestroika* were implemented.

Thus, communism works very well for those in power. Because of the realities of communism, however, its leaders must direct more of their energies toward crushing dissent, whereas politicians in so-called democratic societies are obliged to direct their energies toward winning the vote.

But from the standpoint of the masses, communism has been a colossal failure. The cruel irony is that the greatest technological advances made by the Soviet Union came from Western capitalist nations. Within a matter of a few years after Lenin took power, conditions were so bad in Russia that he was on the verge of being confronted with another revolution. As a result, he threw open the doors to "despicable" Western capitalists, inviting them to help industrialize the Soviet Union. Major U.S. corporations scurried off to Russia to help save the country from its own system.

Meanwhile, the Soviet Union was able to use its slave-labor force to concentrate on the production of armaments, while American farmers and manufacturers eased its domestic difficulties. Interestingly, Eric Hoffer noted that, though "communism is a failure as an economic system [it] may triumph as a military instrument."

The famous dissident Alexander Solzhenitsyn, author of *The Gulag Archipelago*, explained that without the help of the United States, Russia's communism would almost certainly have collapsed much sooner:

> *It is American trade that allows the Soviet economy to concentrate its resources on armaments and preparations for war. Remove that trade, and the Soviet economy would be obliged to feed and clothe and house the Russian people, something it has never been able to do. Let the socialists among you allow this socialist economy to prove the superiority that its ideology claims. Stop sending them goods. Let them stand on their own feet, and then see what happens.*

The reality is that the communist all too often has been allowed the luxury of keeping his collectivist cake while eating off the fruits of capitalism. When college students suddenly see the light (i.e., read about communism for the first time) and run about preaching the goodness of collectivism and the evils of capitalism, they should be reminded that after decades of misery in countries like China and the Soviet Union, communists in those countries came running to evil Western capitalists to show them how to become capitalistic. This one fact tells more about the merits of capitalism and the failure of communism than any book could ever do.

Nor is this naiveté limited to the young. So-called liberal adults in this country love to talk about the purity in the cultures of places like Vietnam and China, failing to note that it is communist countries such as these that are so obsessed with industrial growth that it has resulted in their evolving into hybrid-communist countries (i.e., communist dictatorships that allow some capitalist activity). In China, industrialization has long been placed head and shoulders above communist ideology, and for good reason: Real communism resulted in poverty and misery for the masses.

Amid all the hubbub of China's whirlwind initiation into the world of capitalism in the 1970s, the most important point about China's overtures to the West was missed by most of the media. When China opened its doors to Western capitalists, the message was clear: "We admit it; the revolution failed. Communism does not work." With a per-capita annual income of $350, China's leaders decided, after thirty years of experimentation with a system wherein "goods are owned in common and are available to all as needed," it was time to throw in the towel.

Communism does not work because it defies human nature. There's nothing in it for the individual. This same kind of restraint of human nature was a key factor in keeping the slave-oriented economy of the Old South perpetually depressed. If people know that everyone will receive the same regardless of how much they produce, they have a tendency to become more needy and less productive. When motivation is eliminated, producers tend to disappear. That is why, as Rose Wilder Lane noted, a communist economy is a static economy. No ideology can change the nature of man.

As a result, both China and the Soviet Union ultimately resorted to "creeping capitalism." Out of desperation, they began to give peasants small incentives for increased production. The communism of China and the Soviet Union soon lost its so-called purity.

One of the most glaring examples of capitalism versus communism could be found in the late 1970s by comparing Taiwan, a tiny nation of 17 million inhabitants at the time, with China, whose population was then only a billion people. Taiwan, notwithstanding its size, was one of the top twenty trading nations in the world. Its foreign trade in 1977 was $17.9 billion compared to Communist China's $16.4 billion.

It is no coincidence that a country more than fifty times the size of Taiwan could not equal it in production. Nor was it a coincidence that in countries like China, where free enterprise was outlawed, human freedom was most restricted. The connection between freedom and free enterprise is always there: Without property rights, no other rights are possible.

Before leaving the subject of communism, I feel it is my duty, as a libertarian-centered conservative, to point out that if people wish to enter into a communal existence voluntarily or form communistic societies without forcing others to join, that is certainly their right. The key word, as always, is *voluntarily*.

Few people, however, choose such a life voluntarily—including those in Western nations who are the most vociferous in singing its praises. I believe communism will always fail (when it comes to making life better for the masses) because of the reality that people naturally seek to improve their own well-being. That is why any communist society can be held together only by a firm dictatorship. Communism, as an ideology, is not a threat to freedom-loving people. The threat of communism stems from the fact that its dictators have been remarkably effective in assembling powerful armies and mighty arsenals of weapons.

The Economics of Nothingism

I like to refer to socialism as *nothingism* for two reasons. First, theoretical socialism, by dictionary definition, is virtually the same as communism.

Therefore, if one were to be concerned only with the theoretical aspects of socialism, there would be little reason to use the term at all; *communism* fits the bill quite well. The only significant difference between the definitions of socialism and communism is that socialism is referred to as a transitional stage of society between capitalism and communism.

In view of the rapidly accelerating trend toward collectivism in all Western nations, especially in the United States, this is a rather discomforting thought. Marx, in other words, foresaw the current trend toward collectivism. He viewed socialism only as a temporary, intermediate step, with communism ultimately becoming firmly established. The only catch is that Marx did not live to see what communism would be like in real life. In real communism, the state does not "wither away" (as in the definition of communism). The state stays on to terrorize its people, and no one but the state has any rights.

The second reason I view socialism as a nonsystem is that real socialism is neither fish nor fowl. It is, in fact, a contradiction. In all Western nations, both capitalism and communism exist, with the mixture referred to as socialism (though the governments of most countries, such as the United States, conspicuously avoid using that term). In some countries, the tilt is toward capitalism, while in others, the balance is shifted closer to real communism. But socialism, in the real world, is nothing more than a mixture of impure capitalism and impure communism.

The reason so many countries cling to the contradictory system of socialism, as opposed to communism, is that it provides the opportunity for politicians to meet the expedient demands of citizens by exploiting what works—capitalism. Ironically, it is capitalism that fuels the socialist economy, with much of the fruits of capitalism being confiscated to help vote-hungry politicians meet the expediency-minded demands of their constituents.

While the expediency factors of both citizens and politicians put constant pressure on governments to lean more and more toward socialism, there are two other factors that help flame socialist fires. The first is fear. Governments make clever use of fear, urging citizens to conform or run the risk of being left out in the cold, particularly in old age. It is this drive for conformity that leads frightened people down the collectivist path like sheep, a path at the end of which the god of socialism is presumed to be waiting, ready to wave his magic wand and instantly dissolve one of nature's strictest laws—the inequality of human beings.

The second factor that inspires socialism is envy, which is at the heart of the true socialist's anger. The hardcore socialist is bothered by the fact that, in a free society, people can rise to the level of their ambitions, abilities, and willingness to work. Through socialism, the envious socialist hopes not to make everyone well off, but to make everyone equally miserable. It is no wonder that the socialist admires societies like Cuba, where most of the population lives barely above the poverty level.

Socialism leads us to where government has evolved today, with its distorted concepts of what the functions of government should be. With the gradual, 100-year ascent of the progressive movement in the United States, which was one of the last bastions of substantial capitalistic activity, our country is now rapidly accelerating down the path to socialism—and perhaps beyond.

In vying for the vote, one of the excuses politicians use for injecting ever-greater dosages of socialism into society is the *mysterious-multiplier* concept. This is the curious notion that the laws of mathematics, economics, and common sense somehow change when one goes from small to large transactions. While government successfully perpetrates the myth that as society becomes larger and more complex, problems are too difficult for individuals to solve, quite the opposite is true. In reality, the more complex problems become, the better they can be solved by individuals—or at least at the local level.

This is because an individual has his own well-being at stake. An individual knows himself better than some bureaucrat in Washington who has never met him. An individual understands his own needs and desires, his own personality, his own special circumstances—none of which are exactly like those of his neighbors. The larger a society grows, the *less* capable government is of solving the problems of individuals.

In addition to the mysterious-multiplier concept, government works hard to try to make voters believe that economic law can be ignored and that something can, in fact, be created out of nothing. People are led to believe that when money is taken from one group and handed to another, something greater results. Again, the exact opposite is true, for two reasons.

First, on the way from one group to another, a substantial portion of the booty ends up in the hands of the government employees who administer such transfer-of-wealth programs. Second, there is a loss, not a gain, when wealth is confiscated. What are lost are the new technology, products, services, and jobs that could have been created with that wealth.

What allows government to violate economic law so blatantly is its adeptness at using the magician's ploy of getting the audience to look at one hand while performing the trick with the other. As we've seen with the beyond-the-pale stimulus packages and overall spending of the current administration, the silver-tongued politician distracts his audience by emphasizing the hand that holds the short-term benefits of his actions. This, he hopes, will translate into votes. But the hand he hides behind his back holds the long-term ramifications of his expedient, vote-getting plans. And the long-term effects are almost always disastrous—even to the people who receive the short-term benefits of such actions.

It is the continual use of this short-term-patching approach that, when combined with the normal bungling, inefficiency, and corruption of government, is most responsible for our national insolvency. Plain and simple, it does not work. The use of short-term, politically expedient solutions to cure the perceived problems of individuals is akin to trying to bail water out of a sinking ship by using a bucket riddled with holes. Government effectively succeeds in keeping the public's attention focused on all the water it throws out of the boat (the short-term benefits), but it succeeds even better at hiding the fact that the ship is sinking a little more each day.

This is precisely how our economy got to where it is today. Barack Obama didn't create this mess all by himself. He was merely a facilitator for the progressives' long-term agenda of universal everything—and a darn good one at that.

This short-term-patching approach was also facilitated by the works of the late John Maynard Keynes, the British economist. Keynes believed in injecting varying dosages of socialism into a capitalistic economy, which means he believed in a contradiction. So-called Keynesian economics is the belief that increased government spending stimulates the economy during periods of recession, thereby decreasing unemployment, while decreased government spending slows the economy during inflationary periods.

The 1970s, however, shattered Keynes' theories, because the United States experienced both unemployment and inflation (*stagflation*), the worst of all possible worlds for the average worker. What Keynes did not understand were the realities of the system and its dependency on expediency factors. He was politically naive in that he believed that power-hungry politicians actually would cut back on government spending during inflationary times.

But the realities of the vote have made the politician's spending habits like the proverbial snowball accelerating downhill. He can't stop spending because voters are hooked on benefits. People always want more, not less. Either you give it to them or you don't get reelected. That's why even so-called conservatives act like socialists once they achieve power. It's officially referred to as "lack of courage and conviction."

When people blame capitalism for the mess in which the United States today finds itself, they are looking in the wrong direction. Unfortunately, we have never had the opportunity to try laissez-faire capitalism in this country. And though capitalism has done well even with one hand tied behind its back, ever-increasing government intervention has rendered it less and less effective. In truth, what has failed is our mixed economy (i.e., a contradictory economy comprised of some free enterprise and ever-increasing government intervention).

Socialism must fail in the long run because it is an irreconcilable contradiction. Freedom and restraint cannot coexist—especially when the emphasis is on restraint. The failure of our economy would make Karl Marx look like a prophet but for the fact that it is Marx's own socialism that has failed, not capitalism. Also, it is not Marx's theoretical utopian communism toward which we are rushing. On the contrary, we are moving rapidly toward the same kind of totalitarian societies that exist, and have existed, in other communist countries throughout the world.

Socialism tends to evolve into extreme totalitarianism because it destroys incentive. As we have been witnessing through decades of welfare-state growth, lack of incentive in turn helps cause a nation's economic collapse. Ultimately, this collapse can trigger anarchy and chaos, which forces government to resort to strong-armed totalitarian measures to restore order.

Progressives make the presumptuous mistake of believing they are the only people who would like to see everyone in the world well off. But among freedom lovers and people of goodwill, such a desire is assumed without a second thought. The disagreement lies in the most appropriate method for improving the welfare of the greatest number of people.

The Nightmare Results of Political Promises

At this point, we are in a better position to appreciate the ramifications of the functions modern government performs. These functions are a direct result of the lethal combination of expediency factors and the vote. The equation is straightforward:

$$\text{Expediency Factors} + \text{The Vote} = \text{Government Functions}$$

Because the realities of the vote bring out the expedient worst in people, when a politician attempts to make good on his campaign promises, the resulting government functions require violations of human freedom. It is precisely because of politicians' promises to deliver more of everything to everyone that the once-limited function of government has been transformed into the fulfillment of as many of those promises as possible, no matter how immoral in concept or how economically unfeasible they may be.

Obviously, these functions have little to do with the Constitutional function of government. We already know that government's only legitimate function, assuming it is to be conceded any function at all, is to protect the individual from aggression. For true libertarian-centered conservatives, this means, at most:

1. Providing physical protection for the lives and property of citizens.

2. Providing a system of arbitration for contractual disputes.

3. Providing for a national defense.

Protecting a person from aggression, with his explicit consent, certainly is within the framework of Natural Law. But whenever government goes beyond this basic function and acts in violation of people's natural rights, *it* becomes the aggressor. Consequently, for some people to take it upon themselves to try to solve the problems of millions of others, either against their will or at the expense of their fellow citizens, necessitates a violation of Natural Law. The American Revolutionists were well aware of this, which is why there were no provisions in the original Constitution providing for government to fulfill the needs and desires of individual citizens.

Nevertheless, the reality of the system is that it takes votes to get elected; it takes expedient promises to get votes; and it takes expedient actions to stay in office. And what the politician's expedient actions translate into are a new set of functions for government, functions far removed from those originally outlined in the Constitution.

Throwing out the Constitution

Though the erosion of the American Dream began more than 200 years ago and evolved into out-and-out progressivism beginning with Theodore Roosevelt and Woodrow Wilson in the early part of the twentieth century, a tremendous acceleration in the rate of that erosion occurred in the 1930s under Franklin Delano Roosevelt. Said FDR: "Government has the definite duty to use all its power and resources to meet new social problems with new social controls." (Really? Definite duty? You could have fooled me.)

With those words, FDR took it upon himself to, in effect, throw out the Constitution of the United States and redefine the function of government. At best, his statement was unintelligible; at worst, immoral.

First, government has no power (i.e., legitimate power) except that granted to it by the individuals who explicitly consent to be represented by it.

Second, government has no resources except those that it arbitrarily expropriates from its citizens.

Third, there are no such things as "social problems"; only individuals have problems. And since each individual's circumstances are unique, so, too, are his problems.

Fourth, the government has no duty, either moral, divine, or legal, to "meet" anyone's problems.

Finally, there are no such things as "social controls." Society is an abstract entity, and controls can be imposed only on individuals. (Even businesses are composed of individuals.) From a Natural Law point of view, government has no right to control the lives of individuals in any way except to prevent them from forcibly interfering with others. All other government control is aggression and is therefore immoral and illegal.

Logic and morality notwithstanding, FDR was determined to be a generous man—with other people's money. Among a seemingly endless list of short-term, expedient actions, he established the Social Security Act, introduced farm subsidies, brought us minimum-wage laws, and created a multitude of government jobs programs. (He also tried, illegally, to pack the Supreme Court with progressive justices, but, fortunately, Congress stopped him in his effort.)

Worst of all, FDR initiated the soak-the-rich policy of taxation that subjected persons with high incomes to unequal tax treatment, thereby initiating the economy-crippling trend toward lack of incentive—a forerunner of Barack Obama's war on prosperity nearly 80 years later. While the New Deal may have put a chicken in every pot, the long-term consequence, as is always the case with socialist reforms, was a gradual erosion of personal freedom. The New Deal was a classic example of political expediency—emphasizing immediate benefits to certain voters while ignoring the inevitable long-term damage caused by such actions.

Roosevelt was, indeed, a generous man. And today, all these decades later, we are still paying for his generosity. Even FDR could not create wealth from nothing—although, to his credit as a politician, he was able to defer the payment for his actions far longer than were any of his successors. As a result, he did not live to have to face the long-term consequences of his actions.

It was the Great Depression of the 1930s that allowed Roosevelt to change the rules of the game dramatically. Long before Rahm Emanuel infamously explained that "You never want a serious crisis to go to waste," the Great Depression gave progressive politicians a far greater range of issues to use in vying for the vote. It allowed them to hold out more carrots to more people, because virtually everyone was in need. As a result, politicians offered redistribution-of-wealth programs to the poor, business subsidies to favored businesses, and, eventually, special legislation to special-interest groups to "promote the general welfare."

Now, in our rapidly crumbling democracy, government's function has been tragically altered. Today, government's main business is "helping people fulfill their desires." What this means is that government attempts to fulfill the needs and desires of people who cannot do so on their own in a free society, a society that gives them the opportunity to deal with their fellow man on a voluntary basis. And when men no longer fulfill their needs and desires on a voluntary basis, the code of ethics necessarily becomes every man for himself and anything goes.

In the next three chapters, I will analyze some of the most notable functions of modern government—functions fathered by the expediency factor and mothered by the vote. Again, we should carefully consider both the moral validity and economic realities of these functions.

Morally, there isn't much to debate. An action either complies with Natural Law or it does not. If a government function violates the natural rights of any individual, it is immoral. As I stated earlier, liberty must be given a higher priority than all other objectives. Personal integrity demands that one's belief in Natural Law not be betrayed on an emotional whim. The good that a particular government function may purport to accomplish for some people is not a justifiable reason for committing aggression against others. No end justifies the violation of any individual's right to his own life and property.

I again emphasize that people do not have the right to force others to be concerned, sympathetic, helpful, or charitable toward others. No one has the right to dispose of other people's lives or property, no matter what his personal rationalizations may be. If needs and desires were relevant, then any group of people would be justified in taking forcible control over other people's lives merely by claiming that such action is necessary in order to fulfill their needs and desires.

It should also be mentioned that when people speak of problems or injustices that need to be corrected, they are merely voicing their opinions. When one bandies about an abstract term such as *social justice*, he is doing nothing more than stating his opinion that an injustice does, in fact, exist. In addition, he is advocating the use of government force to fulfill his desire to change a circumstance that he chooses to define as an injustice.

As a result, when government intervenes to correct what certain voters deem to be an injustice, it virtually assures that a greater injustice will be committed. More often than not, the injustice originally alleged is merely a reflection of someone's moral beliefs—usually relating to his personal needs and desires. And because government itself does not produce wealth, such needs and desires can be satisfied only by instituting real injustices against those who do produce wealth.

CHAPTER 4

The Gourmet Banquet

Conservative economists used to refer to it as the *free lunch*, while trying in vain to explain to the public that there was no such thing. But we've come a long way since FDR. What started out as a ham sandwich and a glass of milk has evolved into a gourmet banquet, with more than 300 million people pushing and shoving one another in an effort to stuff themselves with as many free delicacies as possible.

This mania is a result of Government Function Number One: *redistribution of wealth.*

Though U.S. currency isn't worth much anymore, money still talks. So the expediency-minded politician, through the vote, strikes up a bargain with the expediency-minded voter. After all, a candidate cannot just come right out and tell people he wants power over them. He must promise them something. Sy Leon, in *None of the Above*, describes the understanding this way:

> If [the politician] simply laid his cards on the table and said, "I want to give you orders," he would be ignored or despised. So he comes bearing gifts. "I will give you education, or food, or housing," he says, "and all you have to do is give me some control over your life. Let me make the important decisions for you, and I will reward you."

In the final analysis, the main plank of every candidate's political platform promises redistribution of wealth. The only differences lie in the degree and method each one advocates.

The late Senator S.I. Hayakawa once described how congressional decisions are made with regard to doling out government largesse as follows:

> A member of the committee will say, for instance, "Here's an appropriation for such-and-such. It was 1.7 for 1977. So for the 1978 budget we ought to make it 2.9." So all we do is add 1.2; that's not

hard. The next item is 2.5. The members discuss it back and forth, and someone says, "Let's raise it to 3.7." They look around at each other. "Everybody in favor?" "Yes, sir. Okay." So in five minutes we have disposed of 2 billion bucks—2 billion, not 2 million. I never realized it could be so easy. It's all simple addition. You don't even have to know subtraction.

Hayakawa went on to point out the obvious fact that the people of the United States never amended the Constitution to change the government's main function to redistributing wealth. Franz Oppenheimer described this unapproved redirection of government purpose as "the institutionalization of the 'political means' of acquiring wealth."

As every mature, rational individual knows, wealth can be produced only through effort. Redistribution of wealth as government's chief function poses many uncomfortable questions—for example, how much of whose wealth shall be given to which people? Which again raises the inevitable question: Who shall decide?

If one believes in Natural Law, he knows there can be only one moral answer to the last question: Each individual must decide for himself. The reality, however, is that politicians take it upon themselves to decide. And their decisions, of course, are tied directly to the vote. What does this mean in numbers? Obviously, that politicians must take from the smallest number of people possible and give to the largest number possible if they hope to stay in office.

And who constitutes the small and large numbers? This is an interesting question because the original majority (the poor) has now become a minority and the new majority (the middle class) has fuzzy demarcation lines.

Rich versus Poor?

Even though the original majority has become a minority, I believe it's important, before analyzing today's majority, to understand some realities concerning the original voting groups. George Orwell viewed them in three categories:

Throughout recorded time, and probably since the end of the Neolithic Age, there have been three kinds of people in the world, the High, the Middle, and the Low. . . . The aims of these three groups are entirely irreconcilable. The aim of the High is to remain where they are. The aim of the Middle is to change places with the High.

The aim of the Low . . . is to abolish all distinctions and create a society in which all men shall be equal.

These three groups are created by nature, and the circumstances of each individual within each group are unique. Thus, to change the groups through artificial means is to ignore the instincts, abilities, and circumstances of individuals. This artificial change may be instituted by majority rule or through violent revolution, but in either case, nature, in the end, will have its way. Will and Ariel Durant described this inevitability as follows:

. . . violent revolutions do not so much redistribute wealth as destroy it. There may be a redivision of the land, but the natural inequality of men soon re-creates an inequality of possessions and privileges, and raises to power a new minority with essentially the same instincts as in the old.

The Promise of Equality

Over the centuries, many have attempted to eradicate inequality. Virtually everything has been tried, but, in the end, nature always reasserts itself. Marx's ideological dreams were grandiose, indeed, but inequality has never been erased in any communist country. In Cuba, for example, shoemakers, carpenters, and truck drivers still live like shoemakers, carpenters, and truck drivers, while baseball, basketball, and track stars live like privileged elite. And, of course, members of the ruling class drink champagne and eat caviar.

Why is the reality of inequality so difficult for many people to accept? Speaking for myself, I am grateful for the fact that there are so many men and women whose unequal abilities make it possible for them to create the products I want, entertain me with their music, and cure diseases. All of these talents make the world a better place for you and me.

I believe one of the factors that has caused inequality to become an obscene word in today's world is confusion over the phrase "all men are created equal" in the Declaration of Independence. The document itself makes it clear that the founders of our country had no illusions about transforming nature. There can be little question that the phrase "all men are created equal" was intended to mean that all men have equal *rights*.

This is so self-evident that no serious person of goodwill would deny it. Everyone has an equal right to sole dominion over his own life—meaning that he has the right to do anything he wishes with his life, so long as he does not forcibly interfere with that same right in others. Every individual has the natural right to pursue his life, his liberty, and his happiness without fear of aggression from his neighbors. These rights are inalienable. But other than their natural rights, people most certainly are not born equal.

In our increasingly socialistic society, however, equal rights has come to mean unequal rights for some. It has come to mean that those who produce the most wealth do not have the same rights as those who produce the least. It is interesting to note that in the phrase "life, liberty, and property," there is no mention of equality. This is because life is *not* equal. Liberty and equality are conflicting objectives, and property rights and equality have no relationship to one another.

If one believes in equal rights, he cannot simultaneously believe that some people should be allowed to force others to share the fruits of their labor. This means facing up to the reality that if one person has $1 million and another person has only $1, no one has the right to force the person with the $1 million to give any part of his wealth to the person who has only $1. On the contrary, it means that the person with the $1 million has just as much right to keep everything he owns as the person with only $1. Why? Because it's *his*!

Unfortunately, many economists are influenced by the question of inequality—both among individuals and nations. They simply cannot accept the fact that freedom and free enterprise only give people a better opportunity to improve their well-being but do not make everyone equal. Egalitarianism is a philosophical issue, and philosophy has nothing to do with economics.

As we have discussed, one of the chief causes of the eventual collapse of all democratic experiments throughout history has been the clash between equality and freedom. In their zealous efforts to achieve equality, utopian proponents have had a tendency to violate the rights of those whom they deem to be the rich. And when the rights of any person are violated, cracks begin to appear in the structure of a democratic civilization.

No matter how hard they try, progressive do-gooders can never escape the inevitable questions: Who has the omniscience and moral authority to decide who is poor? Who has the omniscience and moral authority to decide who is in need? Who has the omniscience and moral authority to decide how much of whose assets should be confiscated to help the poor? Who has the omniscience and moral authority to decide at what point a person should no longer be considered poor?

Let us first consider need. How do we define it? Is a person in need if he earns only $15,000 a year? Or should the figure be $20,000? Or $30,000? What about the individual who earns $40,000 but has five children and elderly parents to support, a wife who is dying of cancer, and a house that is badly in need of repair? Or the person who has an income of $100,000 a year, but owes $300,000 in bills and is on the verge of bankruptcy?

Now let's take a look at the term *desire*. How about the desire for a decent living? What, exactly, is a decent living? Is everyone entitled to one? Is everyone entitled to a home? We've already ridden the Barney Frank Foreclosure Express to that answer.

Is everyone entitled to a car? A Ford? Why not an Infinity, if that is what a person desires? In fact, if desire is relevant, what about the poverty-stricken individual who desires a Roll-Royce? Why should his desire be any less relevant than that of the person who is willing to settle for a compact car? This is not an attempt to be humorous. It is an attempt to demonstrate that, compassion aside, everyone's desires are personal and subjective.

The harsh reality is that if one insists that needs and desires are relevant, moral standards are out the window. It would mean that one man's desire to steal would be on an equal moral footing with another man's desire to work. One man's desire to be free would not have greater moral validity than another man's desire to violate his freedom.

A person who places needs and desires above liberty does not believe in human freedom. What he believes in is freedom for *some* humans. He believes it is moral to violate the rights of certain people to help certain other people whom he deems to be in need.

The relevant question is not whether someone desires something or believes that he needs it. If human rights are to be respected, the relevant question is whether he has the ability to pay for it and/or the willingness to work for it. In a just world, every person would get exactly what he deserves. And what he deserves is precisely what the highest bidder will pay him in a free market, regardless of what he believes he should get or what his desires might be.

That some people are poorer than others is a reality. That these people desire a better way of life is perfectly natural and understandable. And for them to pursue a better way of life is their natural right. But that is where Natural Law draws the line. For anyone to force you to hand over to others an arbitrary percentage of the fruits of your labor is a violation of your natural rights.

Because you have a natural right to your life, liberty, and property, someone else's desire for your life, liberty, or property is morally inconsequential. Needs are subjective opinions, and desires are personal wishes. One cannot sacrifice his standard of ethics to opinions or wishes. Your human rights are superior to any desire I might have to take your property.

Each of us has many personal needs (as defined by us on an individual basis) and desires. These needs and desires are not only of a financial nature, but also an emotional nature. Are emotional desires also to be considered relevant? For example, should others be forced to give love to every person who needs or desires love?

Government likes to cloud the issue of needs and desires versus morality with a strange adaptation of the same mysterious-multiplier concept it applies to economics. The idea is that needs and desires acquire moral validity if one thinks in terms of large numbers of people. It is this illogical notion that forms the shaky foundation for majority rule. If 3 million people vote to steal from 1 million people, proclaiming that the theft is justified because they arbitrarily decide that they need the money for a worthy cause, that does not morally validate the theft.

To demonstrate the absurdity of such a position, eliminate six zeroes from each figure: If three people proclaim themselves to be a society and decide to rob a targeted individual, insisting that their decision is in society's best interest, virtually everyone would agree that their claim is ludicrous.

Which begs the question: How can the same action be declared morally right simply by multiplying by millions? On the contrary, it would be that much more immoral because the number of people whose rights would be violated would be substantially increased.

People of goodwill, who respect the rights of others, must reject the notion that an act of aggression can be justified by arbitrarily claiming it is for a worthy cause. It says something about the moral decay of our society when a fictional character—Robin Hood—is seen as a good guy because he steals from those he deems to be rich and gives the stolen loot to those he deems to be poor. As pointed out in *Fundamentals of Liberty*, the drift toward justifiable aggression in our society makes it easier to understand the corresponding drift toward increased criminal activity in our society.

> *If a man grows up believing that trespass is all right whenever he deems himself as having a "just cause"; if a man is continually reminded that "property rights are not absolute"; and if a man witnesses governments interfering with the property rights of other men, all with the approval of business, professional, civic, religious, and labor organizations; if such is the background in which persons are raised, it is not too difficult to understand why criminal behavior is on the increase. If men who are respected in the community can sanction property trespass and violence, then why not the criminal?*

Economic Realities of Redistribution of Wealth

Assuming that there was an omniscient source capable of deciding who is rich and who is poor, and ignoring the moral aspects of redistribution of wealth for purposes of this discussion, the question of economics still remains.

Nearly forty years ago, Henry Hazlitt calculated that if the government had confiscated 100 percent of the income of every person in the country who earned over $50,000 in 1968, it would have netted an additional $24 billion in tax revenues. Had those soak-the-rich dollars been distributed equally among the approximately 200 million people then living in the United States (assuming no administrative costs whatsoever), each person would have received the grand sum of $120!

That, of course, did not take into account an even more important economic reality: If the government did implement a 100 percent tax rate on the highest income earners, they would simply shrug their shoulders and fulfill Ayn Rand's prophecy laid out in *Atlas Shrugged*. Why in the world would anyone continue to produce if he knew that all of his earnings would be confiscated? This is precisely what the Laffer Curve is all about: Higher tax rates mean *lower* tax revenues.

For much of the past eighty years, excessive tax rates have played a major role in helping to destroy the American Dream. Potentially productive individuals have curtailed their efforts whenever tax rates have risen to a point where their incentives have been reduced by the economically destructive class-warfare philosophy of unequal taxation. The progressives now in power, who still cling to this suicidal policy, would do well to think about the cliché of killing the goose that lays the golden eggs.

The truth is that the welfare state, which politicians would have you believe was designed to aid the poor, is, in reality, devastating to those at the low end of the income spectrum. Among other things, it kills incentive, which decreases productivity, which increases unemployment. In addition, it is a major contributor to inflation, as we shall see in a later chapter, which is one of the worst enemies of those with the lowest incomes.

One of the aspects of redistribution of wealth that I most deplore is the politician's ploy of making it a black-versus-white issue. But, in truth, it has nothing to do with black versus white. The real issue is freedom versus tyranny. Human freedom relates to all people, whether black, white, or yellow. The road to security and economic success is paved with hard work, ambition, determination, and, above all, a respect for human rights. It has nothing whatsoever to do with color.

The New Majority

But the politician does not like to be bothered with mundane issues such as morality and ethics. His focus is on one issue: What group or groups of voters form the majority?

When the lines were more sharply defined by nature alone, the politician's task was much simpler. He could easily see that the vote could be won by offering government benefits to those in the lower income brackets. Had nature made more people capable of becoming rich, you can be sure that the politician would have pandered to wealthiest people instead. It's all in the numbers.

Now, however, government has a dilemma. The wealth has been so thoroughly redistributed that the poor are in the minority. The majority of voters have long been ensconced in the so-called middle class, a group that certainly is not immune to thinking in expedient terms.

Try as government does to pit one member of the middle class against another—through occupation, race, sex, nationality, and even religion— the fact remains that its members are aligned by a common bond: They have been weaned on the milk of false prosperity. When economic reality finally began to set in near the end of George W. Bush's second term, they were looking for change they could believe in.

Which brought to power the Duplicitous Despot from Chicago and a radical progressive majority in both houses of Congress. People were so mad (and panicked) that they didn't even bother to listen to the kind of change that was being promised to them. They were totally focused on propping up the good life that was quickly slipping away from them.

How can people maintain such an attitude of entitlement? By embracing the fantasy that economic law can be violated and that Natural Law *should* be violated. To refuse to believe that such violations are not only possible but moral, one would have to be prepared to give up the false prosperity he has come to cherish over the years. How many people do you know who are willing to do that?

Government now has virtually everyone hooked on getting more and more pie while doing less and less of the baking. Yet the same people who form the middle-class majority have become—through government's redistribution-of-wealth policies—government's major source of funds.

Virtually everyone in the new majority wants "tax reform." Everyone wants government spending to decrease. Everyone wants to see inflation brought under control. Everyone believes that the other guy's benefits are an unnecessary government expense—but no one is willing to accept a reduction in *his* share of the plunder pie.

People, now hooked on the benefits of the gourmet banquet, no longer are capable of being objective. As a result, they give up a little more of their freedom each time they need a quick fix. And that is why the power holders, notwithstanding the dilemma they have created, still hold the trump card. They know that we all want more, so they continue to offer us more in exchange for ever-increasing power over our lives.

The sad reality is that so long as most voters believe they are getting their fair share of a mythical fixed pie, they are willing to submit to serfdom. The secret to maintaining such voluntary control, which is the backbone of the system, is contentment. "Without economic security," said Aldous Huxley, "the love of servitude cannot possibly come into existence."

The Death of Productivity

Of course, as every sober-minded, straight-thinking adult realizes, there is only one way to create wealth—through productive effort. But there are two ways to *obtain* wealth. One is through productive effort; the other is through plunder. Both employers and employees obtain wealth by providing goods and services on a voluntary-exchange basis. Those who receive government checks obtain wealth by taking from those who produce it.

More than three decades ago, Eric Hoffer referred to the new American era as the Age of the Labor Faker. While it is difficult to argue with this moniker, it implies a blanket indictment, so I believe it deserves closer examination.

There are varying degrees of labor faking. At one end of the scale are those who still retain pride in their work, insist on being individualistic, and want nothing from the government. Such people can be found in all occupations and at all income levels. Whether a man is a janitor or a business executive, he is an economic plus to the national economy if he earns his income and steadfastly adheres to the principle of nonaggression.

At the other extreme are those who produce virtually nothing and live off the efforts of producers. This group consists primarily of those who are capable of earning their own way and who would do so if they had no other means of obtaining food, clothing, and shelter.

A smaller percentage of the nonproducing group is made up of those who are physically or mentally disabled to such an extent that they are not able to care for themselves. The circumstances of such people are a concern to every humane individual, and I will address their plight toward the end of this chapter.

In between the maximum producers and the nonproducers are the millions of people who labor fake to one extent or another. Each, of course, rationalizes that his form of government dole is justified, that he is honest and hardworking, and that it is he who is getting the short end of the stick. Few people are able to be objective about the part they've played in helping to fan the flames of false prosperity.

While there is no question that every person must accept responsibility for his own actions, government is the true serpent in the False-Prosperity Garden—offering handouts in exchange for votes. The result is that we have become a society that rewards people for doing less. And in such an environment, human nature assures that people will do exactly that—less. Yet, Barack Obama, at the time of the writing of this book, was proposing still higher cash payments to families below a certain income level. The polite name given to this transfer-of-wealth practice is *negative income tax.*

It doesn't take a great deal of insight to predict the effect of such handouts. So-called guaranteed incomes are death to productivity. The higher the guaranteed income, the greater the number of people at or even slightly above that line who will stop working and take the guaranteed income. And as more and more people take the route of the nonproducer, those left to produce will have to give up an ever greater percentage of their earnings to support the nonproducers.

It's human nature not to appreciate anything that can be obtained with little effort. And things that are handed to us free, with no effort at all on our part, are the least appreciated of all. In fact, human nature is such that rather than being appreciative, we tend to become resentful. The more we get for free, the more we want. Indeed, we become belligerent; we demand more. After all, it's our right.

The inevitable catastrophic climax toward which we are rushing as we jockey for positions at the welfare-buffet table is that the middle class is at the breaking point. It is on the verge of no longer being able to support both itself and the rest of the population. As William Simon stated three decades ago in an interview with *Reason* magazine, ". . . half the people in America work for a living and the other half vote for it." And he didn't even live to see the Obama Welfare Express arrive in Washington.

Today's tea parties are the beginnings of former Secretary of the Interior Walter Hickel's predication in the late 1970s that "the next revolution in this country will be when those who work refuse to support those who don't."

In *The Discovery of Freedom,* Rose Wilder Lane reflected on our evolution into a society in which more and more people demand security without paying for it through their own risk and effort:

> . . . *human beings are fighters by nature. Living is a tough job; only good fighters can do it. Like it or lump it, this planet is no safe place for any living creature. Living is fighting for life, and when anyone does not know this fact, someone else is doing his fighting for him.*
>
> *Anyone who says that economic security is a human right, has been too much babied. While he babbles, other men are risking and losing their lives to protect him. They are fighting the sea, fighting the land, fighting diseases and insects and weather and space and time, for him, while he chatters that all men have a right to security and that some pagan god—Society, The State, The Government, The*

*Commune—must give it to them. Let the fighting men stop fighting
this inhuman earth for one hour, and he will learn how much security there is.*

Living in an age when Stoic virtues are thought to be passé, we cling
to the belief that the world owes us the good things in life. But the accelerating decay of our democratic republic is a warning that neither nature
nor the laws of economics have any intention of bending their ways to go
along with our preposterous notion. In the end, it is they, not we, who
will have their way.

The Nature of the Redistribution Process

When one gets to the heart of most government programs, he discov-
ers that they are nothing more than a potpourri of schemes to redistribute income. Few people, however, recognize the more subtle means of
accomplishing the redistribution process. The schemes they do understand
are those that involve taking money out of their pockets and handing it to
others. This forcible transfer of people's assets has come to be known, in
political jargon, as *transfer payments.*

From Your Pocket to Your Neighbor's Pocket

It would be impossible to discuss here, in detail, even a small percentage
of the transfer-payment programs that exist today. All of them, however,
have one thing in common: They encourage voters to pursue the destructive illusion of something for nothing.

Government would have us believe that it is a boost to the economy
when government puts unearned money into the pockets of arbitrarily
selected groups of people. But, in fact, the opposite is true. When money
changes hands involuntarily, with no product or service being given in
return, no additional purchasing power is created. In this type of transaction, one person's gain is another person's loss. The productive person
who relinquishes the money in taxes has lost the exact amount of purchasing power that the recipient has gained.

But it is not a zero-sum game, because the economy is worse off. That's
because the more workers and businesses have to cough up for transfer
payments, the less incentive there is for them to produce. And because
they produce less and are taxed more, companies have to raise their prices.

The result? Everyone is worse off than before the transfer took place.
The people whose money is taken now have fewer dollars and are faced
with higher prices to boot. And the people on the receiving end can never

seem to get enough unearned dollars to keep up with the steady increase in prices.

The Unemployment Myth

Unemployment compensation is an old wealth-transfer-payment favorite. Government causes unemployment (in myriad ways, including minimum-wage laws, taxation, and draconian regulations) and then uses it as an excuse to increase taxes. After all, transfer payments must be made to the unemployed to keep them from starving to death, which sounds very humanitarian until one examines some inconvenient truths.

There is no question that it's been tough for many people to find jobs during the Obamapression. But even during years of seeming prosperity, when the classified-ad sections of virtually every newspaper in the country were jammed with employment opportunities, millions of folks claimed that they couldn't find work and thus received unemployment benefits from the government. The law of supply and demand obviously was telling us that millions of jobs were going begging because the supply of jobs was greater than the demand for jobs.

And this was because people knew—and still know—that the government will pay them for not working. Thus, unemployed people represent a lot of votes for office holders who support the idea of pay without work—an idea that would have been unthinkable to our Founding Fathers.

The truth be known, when a person says he cannot find a job, you can be sure he is almost always misstating his problem. Most likely, what he really means is that he cannot find the exact kind of job he wants, under the exact working conditions he wants, at the exact wages he wants. There is no such thing as unemployment for the person who is willing to work for wages that the market is willing to pay. Outsourcing has proven this. To put it in Gore-like terms: The debate is over.

One of the things for which I most respected my father was that throughout the Great Depression he never failed to earn enough money to provide food, clothing, and shelter for his family. Even though he had virtually no education, he was always employed, working sixteen- to eighteen-hour days. Whatever it took, he made sure that he brought home the bacon—his bacon, not his neighbor's.

Fundamentals of Liberty states that "no involuntary unemployment can exist . . . in a market where the price of labor is free to fluctuate in response to demand for labor. The only men who would remain unemployed in a free market would be those who voluntarily chose not to work at a given wage."

I remember back in the 1970s when Senator Hayakawa made the point that involuntary unemployment is theoretically impossible. His view was that unemployment statistics were so high because "there has been an enormous increase in voluntary unemployment."

Hayakawa also pointed out that secondary wage-earners (i.e., wage-earners in addition to the primary wage-earners of households) and people who collect unemployment benefits are able to be choosy about the jobs they take. Thus, official government unemployment figures are greatly misleading. Unemployment in the face of eviction or starvation is one thing; unemployment in a case where the head of a household earns a decent living or a person collects unemployment compensation instead of working is quite another.

Far from being inhumane, the abolition of welfare payments would be a long-term capitalistic boost to the poor. By cutting down on the excessive expropriation of producers' assets, productivity would increase, prices would decrease, and employment and wages would rise.

Finally, an abstract that is of utmost importance, those now relying on handouts would regain their self-esteem. The worst part about being poor (and I speak from personal experience) is the degradation that goes with it. In many cases, charity is unavoidable. Forced charity, however, is another matter. Because the recipients of such largesse know that the money has not been given willingly, there is a backlash of bitterness and resentment.

Government, aside from the direct handouts already discussed, also claims to help the unemployed by creating jobs. How is government's creation of jobs for the unemployed a form of redistribution of the wealth? Because the money used to pay for these jobs comes from producers. Worse, the jobs created are ones for which there is no demand in the free market. As a result of the taxes that fund these jobs, businesses have less money to employ people in private industry. Therefore, unemployment is not reduced. Instead, government intervention causes one person to gain at the expense of someone else.

Once again, perhaps this sounds like a zero-sum exchange, but it is not. The job that is lost in the private sector is in a business that creates a product or service that people want. The government-created job provides a service that many or most taxpayers do not want—in some cases, a service that virtually *no one* wants. In addition, because of the bureaucratic waste common to all government programs, it takes more dollars to pay the same employee to do an equivalent amount of work as in private industry.

Finally, the taxpayers who no longer have the money used to create the unneeded government job have less to spend on products and services that they want; thus, production is slowed and unemployment in private industry is actually increased. A typical government solution.

Dr. Milton Friedman, in exposing the age-old political trick of holding out the short-term benefits for all to see while hiding the long-term results behind one's back, described "the visible versus the invisible effects of government measures" as follows:

People hired by government know who is their benefactor. People who lose their jobs or fail to get them because of the government program do not know that that is the source of their problem. The good effects are visible. The bad effects are invisible. The good effects generate votes. The bad effects generate discontent, which is as likely to be directed at private business as at the government.

Government's whole approach to unemployment is upside down. To improve the well-being of people, the emphasis should be on full production, not full employment. You move toward full production as you produce more goods and services people want. If full employment was the horse instead of the cart, government could just put unemployed people to work building pyramids in the Mojave Desert. After a few years, it could have them tear down the pyramids and then start all over again. Obviously, nothing would be accomplished, but you would have full employment.

The point is that merely creating jobs does not produce wealth. An economy will fail if people are employed in jobs that do not produce goods and services that the public wants to buy on a voluntary basis. Stalin's Soviet Union and Mao's China had full employment, but its people had no wealth. Worse, they had no freedom.

Is full employment in a free market possible? Theoretically, yes. But only if government stays completely out of the marketplace, which it never has done at any time in history. While full employment may not be possible other than in theory, one thing is certain: The closer you get to full production, the closer you get to full employment.

In the end, however, I always feel most comfortable falling back on basic civil-libertarian principles. The fact remains that even if the economic realities of government's meddling in the unemployment issue were not harmful to the economy, no one has a right to a job. No one has a right to a decent living. No one has a right to health care. No one has a right to a home, an automobile, or a television set. But everyone does have a right to pursue all of these things by dealing with others on a noncoercive basis.

Those who proclaim that someone has a right to a job really are saying that certain other people do not have human rights—that an unemployed person has a right to force others to satisfy his desires. While it is true that government can, through the use of force, guarantee a person a job—and even a minimum wage—such a person is being led to the dangerous belief that his needs and desires are superior to the liberty of others. But there's a price for everything in life. When government removes the burden of a person's having to sell his services for what they are worth in the free market, the very least he can expect to pay in return is an equivalent loss of freedom.

Life on the Dole

The sad reality is that welfare long ago became a way of life in this country. Few people take seriously the notion that welfare is primarily for those who cannot help themselves. Stories about clever ways to game the welfare system make for entertaining chatter at cocktail parties. It's chic to joke about one's successes in siphoning off ever-increasing portions of the government's redistribution dollars.

Years ago, I was dismayed to hear one such story from an acquaintance of mine. He was a reasonably successful businessman who had just dissolved his partnership. His intention was to go into the same type of business as before, with a new partner, but he was marking time until the conclusion of a court dispute involving his ex-wife. He casually informed me that while waiting for his divorce situation to be resolved, he was drawing unemployment compensation!

At first, I thought he was joking. And he was (i.e., the story was true, but he thought of his accomplishment as something of a joke). If I had a strange expression on my face, it was because I was picturing him taking his transfer payment directly from me—at gunpoint. Because, in reality, that is exactly what he was doing. It was just that the government was furnishing the gun power for him. If taking money from those who earn it has become something to laugh at, Americans have slipped a long way down the moral ladder.

The Social Security pyramid scheme has become the biggest transfer-payment scandal of all, and most Americans now realize that there is no such thing as a Social Security fund. Social Security has long been exposed for what it is: a glorified Ponzi scheme. Ponzi was a famous swindler, who, in 1920, raised enormous amounts of capital from unwary investors, promising to pay them huge returns. Which he did—for a while.

The problem was that his ability to repay both principal and profit to old investors depended solely on his ability to raise money from new investors. After one investor became suspicious, panic spread, new investors were hard to come by, and it was only a matter of time until the whole Ponzi scheme collapsed. This practice, tried many times by both big- and small-time con artists over the years—most recently by the infamous Bernie Madoff—is also commonly referred to as *pyramiding*.

The only way you or anyone else who has been paying Social Security taxes over the years can ever hope to get anything back is totally dependent upon the government's ability to milk ever greater amounts from future generations. There is no fund! Dr. Milton Friedman candidly disrobed Social Security thusly:

> *Social Security is not a system under which "nine out of ten working people in the United States are now building protection for themselves and their families" (as HEW misleadingly describes it). Social Security is a system under which nine out of ten working people pay taxes to finance payments to persons not working.*

The problems inherent in any pyramid scheme are now growing out of control with the Social Security program. Increasing Social Security taxes, coupled with Medicare and astronomical increases in pension benefits for government employees, make a showdown between working people and retired people inevitable. The ominous question is, how much longer will a smaller and smaller segment of the population be willing to support an ever-increasing percentage of the population that is retired?

This is a particularly appropriate question when one considers that, contrary to popularly accepted myths, older people, on average, are better off financially than most other age groups. The highest per capita income is enjoyed by those between the ages of fifty-five and sixty-four, with those over sixty-five not much worse off. In addition, people over fifty normally do not have the financial burdens that face younger people, such as home mortgages and the many expenses connected with raising children.

The Subtle Approach to Redistribution

Redistribution of wealth goes far beyond the blatant transfer of cash from one citizen's pocket to his neighbor's. Government provides thousands of services, on a federal, state, and local level, that accomplish essentially the same thing. For every government service that you either do not want or do not use, your dollars are being taken to supply other people with those services.

The gourmet banquet now includes just about anything you can think of, from welfare items like housing assistance, day care, Medicare, Medicaid, and family planning to seemingly essential public services such as garbage collection, public utilities, fire protection, and mail delivery. Local, state, and federal governments provide legal services, student loans, lotteries, and subsidies for art, publishing, opera, theater, and museums, to name but a few. Whether you want or need any of these services is of no interest to the government. Indeed, you may not even qualify for many of them. But, whether you like it or not, you are required to pay for all of them.

This situation is not quite as galling to taxpayers as are transfer payments because the redistribution of income is camouflaged by the providing of services. The economic problem, however, is that these services do not produce wealth. Therefore, the economy suffers to the extent that money is taken from taxpayers to support such services because the money otherwise would be used to purchase goods and services in the marketplace or for investment in new plants and equipment.

The progressive, of course, argues that the services government provides are necessary and valuable. But he conveniently overlooks three important realities.

First, any service provided by government could be provided better, less expensively, and more efficiently by private industry.

Second, only a small percentage of the population would be willing to purchase most government services if they were offered on a voluntary basis.

Third, many people who receive these services could not afford to pay for them in a free market. Therefore, other people are forced to pay the cost of these services for them. We have already covered the issue of needs and desires versus morality, so I shall not embellish the latter point any further.

Then there is the last-ditch argument that some projects are simply too large to be undertaken without the aid of government. This is, of course, an absurdity on its face, because all projects already are provided with private capital (i.e., "too large" projects are paid for by funds taken from individuals and businesses).

It is preposterous to conclude that the term *general welfare*, as used in the Constitution, was intended to mean that government should have the right to take billions of dollars from citizens and use the money to provide services for others. And it is even more preposterous that government forces millions of people to accept services they do not want.

It should be noted, once again, that those who argue that government, overall, provides valuable and essential services are missing an important libertarian-centered-conservative point: Many other people may not believe that such services are valuable or essential and may prefer to do without them. Again, however, they are forced to pay for them. It always gets back to the presumptuous belief that bureaucrats can, and have a moral right to, determine what is best for individuals. And that belief already has been rejected on both moral and practical grounds.

I am not going to attempt to dissect every government service to make my point. All of them, of course, are invalid from a moral perspective if one believes in Natural Law. I will, however, touch on a small number of these services in order to expose, in addition, their false economic foundations. Also, I hope to bring to light the fact that many services people assume can be provided only by government can, in fact, be provided better, less expensively, and more efficiently by private industry.

Essential Services

People have become so accustomed to government monopolies or near-monopolies in such areas as police and fire protection, garbage collection, education, and operation of streets and highways that it is hard for them to imagine these services being provided by the free market. Often, when one suggests that such services could be provided more efficiently by private industry, on a voluntary basis, the response is one of disbelief. People want to know in detail how such government services could possibly be handled by private companies. The answer is quite simple: They would be handled the same way as everything else is handled in the free market: ingenuity inspired by profit motive.

Consider what would happen if government had for years been providing the public with computers. Some people might get the impression that you were against computers if you suggested that government turn the computer business over to private enterprise. After all, how could people be certain that private companies could handle such a large project? How could they be certain that enough computers would be produced? Who would see to it that the quality would be satisfactory? What if the selling prices were too high?

The answer to all these questions, of course, is the very reason that private enterprise does turn out more than enough high-quality, low-priced computers: profit motive—profit motive that is guided by trial and error, competition, and the law of supply and demand. Entrepreneurs always find ways to create the most desired products and services at the most competitive prices because they know that's the way to make the greatest amount of money.

The exact opposite is true of government services, where low quality, high prices, and inefficiency are trademarks. The U.S. Postal Service is a prime example of this. Everyone has had the experience of standing interminably in line to buy postage stamps or waiting a week or more for a letter to arrive from a few hundred miles away. Yet, while service continues to deteriorate, the cost of postage continues to skyrocket.

Let it suffice to say that what United Parcel Service and Federal Express have accomplished in the package-delivery business—putting the U.S. Postal Service to shame in the process—other companies could accomplish in the delivery of mail. If mail service were a competitive industry, you and I would get the benefit of better service at lower prices. If not, we would take our business to a competitor, just as we do when contracting for pest control, a plumbing job, or a haircut.

For example, for more than fifty years, Rural/Metro Corporation has been a leading provider of emergency and non-emergency medical transportation services, fire protection, and other safety-related services to municipal, residential, commercial, and industrial customers in approximately 400 communities throughout the United States. Local governments simply cannot compete with them.

Not only do taxpayers normally pay for government services used by others, they also pay much more than necessary because of government's insistence on trying to be an entrepreneur. This is not blind stubbornness on the part of politicians. It is based on the reality that the people on the payrolls of those government-provided services represent a lot of votes. By keeping their pay exorbitantly high and their production pitifully low—enough so that the cost to the public is as much as four times what it should be—expediency-minded politicians hope to keep government employees voting for them.

Then there's public education. The idea of the government's not providing everyone with a free education is shocking to some people, but that usually is because they have never considered the moral implications. Like most other government-provided services, the reality is that public education is just another method of redistributing wealth.

Why should a childless couple be compelled to pay for the education of their neighbors' children? As with garbage collection and fire protection, the issue is clouded by the fact that government provides the service. But if all schools were privately owned, the only way government could force some people to pay for the education of other people's children would be through direct transfer payments, the type of redistribution discussed earlier in this chapter. Then the issue of public education could be more clearly seen for what it is—just another redistribution-of-wealth program.

And, as everyone, including those on the far left, knows, the quality of government service in this area is atrocious. In fact, the public-education system long ago became a source of national embarrassment. Students are being whisked through our public-school factories barely able to read and write.

The result of the public-education disaster is that people are rebelling. They are transferring their children to private schools, voting against bond issues for public schools, demanding vouchers that would give them free choice when it comes to picking schools for their children, or making a commitment to home schooling. When people finally begin realizing that redistribution of wealth is not in their best interest, they start to fight back.

There are many books available that deal exclusively with each presently provided government service, but the facts they present are always the same:

1. Government services are always of lower quality and higher cost than could be provided privately.
2. People who do not want the services are forced to pay for them anyway.
3. Some people are forced to pay for the cost of these services for other people.

As Murray Rothbard stated in *For a New Liberty*, the true libertarian does not just want the separation of Church and State. He wants to separate *everything* from the State! This would be a big step toward reducing the size of government and thus cutting back on its politically expedient, but economically disastrous, habit of trying to redistribute wealth.

The Great Revelation

In the old days, the numbers were easy to figure. It was simply rich against poor, and politicians had no trouble calculating that the poor were in the majority. Hence, to win over this majority, vote seekers simply proclaimed their number-one function to be redistribution of wealth.

Thus, government itself created today's voting-class dinosaur (the middle class) and continued to promise these millions of comfortable Americans still more of its magically created wealth. Everything seemed to be going along fine, until a large number of this huge voting bloc came to the realization that no matter how much they received from the government, they still ended up with less.

How can that be? Because with so many of the poor becoming part of the middle class, government had no choice but to start taking from the middle class in order to give to the middle class! Suddenly, redistribution of wealth no longer looked so attractive to the non-rich.

Most members of the middle class had been in favor of redistribution of wealth only because they believed they were coming out ahead. After their emergence to middle-class status, however, few had any concern about helping those less fortunate than themselves.

In conducting your personal financial affairs, you don't buy everything you want. In fact, you realize that would be impossible. Therefore, you consider how badly you want a product or service and how much money you have available, and then make your purchasing decisions accordingly. You are selective—or you are soon broke. Many stubborn politicians, blinded by political expediency, seem unable to comprehend this simple logic.

All this poses an interesting question: If what government has to offer is so good for people—if they really want government services—why does government have to force them to accept such services? Because government services are unconscionably overpriced, low in quality, unwanted or unneeded by millions of people, and a violation of the natural rights of every individual who would not want to pay for them if he were given a free choice.

The Bureaucrat Corps

One would think that government could easily solve its self-created dilemma by recognizing that the vote is now in the hands of the tax-rebelling middle class. After all, helping the poor never was a serious moral objective of most politicians; it was simply a matter of numbers—the most politically expedient method of garnering votes.

But the new majority presents a more complicated problem. Along the way to creating the middle-class majority, politicians also created a mini-monster—millions of government employees who were needed to carry out redistribution-of-wealth programs. Some are officially called *civil servants*; others are unofficially referred to as *bureaucrats*; and today, the highest-ranking unelected big shots are ordained *czars*.

There are now more people employed by government than by manufacturing and construction combined. These millions of government employees now comprise a sizable percentage of the middle-class majority. And, unlike the approximately 100 million eligible voters who did not vote in the 2008 presidential election, you can be sure that government employees do vote—and they never let politicians forget it. They have a good thing going, and they have no intention of moving backward.

I'm sure that the vast majority of these government employees do not understand that they are a major factor in the destruction of the U.S. economy. They do not realize that their false prosperity could result in their loss of freedom in the not-too-distant future. As I said at the outset of this book, most people do not understand the situation. Which is why Barack Obama and his minions have been able to press forward relentlessly with their socialist agenda. They know that government employees have no interest in hearing about the desires of other voters to curtail government spending.

The creation of full-time government jobs is just another method of redistributing wealth. We have already discussed the economic effects of all government-created employment (e.g., job programs), but full-time government employees present uniquely disastrous problems. As we shall see, government employees breed more government employees, which gives the government itself increased voting power, which in turn results in an increase in public-employee salaries and benefits and a corresponding decrease in work.

The growth of government has resulted in its becoming a gigantic, but incredibly inefficient, middleman. A staggering amount of the money that originally was supposed to go from producers to the poor gets lost in the shuffle—and it's shuffled right into the pockets of the roughly 20 million federal, state, and local government employees.

The whole system breeds increases—in numbers of employees, salaries, and dollars spent. Agencies feel compelled to spend whatever monies are allocated to them each year, knowing that their budgets will be cut if they don't. In other words, government agencies work exactly the opposite of private business in that employees are rewarded for being inefficient—for spending more money than necessary.

For example, those who work for welfare agencies have no reason to hope for a solution to poverty. On the contrary, it is in their best interest to see the welfare system grow, rather than decrease, because it means their jobs are safe. This is one of the reasons why poverty statistics do not reflect the billions of dollars received through transfer payments. It is imperative to the administrators of welfare programs that poverty remains a problem.

In reality, all programs designed to help the poor are programs to improve the well-being of those who administer them. The welfare state is most beneficial to those who run it. While Uncle Sam displays the welfare sign in the hand he holds before the public, the hand behind his back contains the real trick—the fact that millions of middle-class-elite government employees make off with most of the funds being redistributed. The bulk of the dollars goes to government administrators, planners, and counselors of the poor.

It's one thing for producers to be forced to support people who are legitimately sick, elderly, and disabled. But to have healthy, financially secure people retiring at fifty years of age puts an intolerable strain on the ever smaller percentage of people still working for a living.

Let me make it clear that I do not believe all government employees have bad intentions, nor do I believe that all government employees are lazy. What I do believe is that government employees, like all of us, have been taken in by the politician's vote-oriented, free-lunch philosophy. Since the days of FDR, millions of Americans have fallen into the trap of believing that wealth can be created without work, and, as a result, a spirit of "let the good times roll" has pervaded the United States for decades.

And it's a spirit that has had a snowballing effect. Government employees, like everyone else, quite naturally have justified their actions with the attitude, "Why shouldn't we get everything we can from the redistribution process?" Most of these employees are innocent to the extent that they have little knowledge of the economic realities involved and certainly have never taken the trouble to think through the moral implications of living off money taken by force from others. How many government employees think about the fact that their income is derived through a violation of the rights of others? Or that government jobs eliminate private jobs?

John Hospers chillingly describes the inevitable consequences of our redistribution-of-wealth policies this way:

> . . . *when it is no longer worth the producers' while to produce, when they are taxed so highly to keep the politicians and their friends on the public payroll that they themselves no longer have a reasonable chance of success in any economic enterprise, then of course production grinds to a halt. . . . When this happens, when the producers can no longer sustain on their backs the increasing load of the parasites, then the activities of the parasites must stop also, but usually not before they have brought down the entire social structure which the producers' activities have created. When the organism dies, the parasite necessarily dies too, but not until the organism has paid for the presence of the parasite with its life. It is in just this way that the major civilizations of the world have collapsed.*

The Fate of the Poor in a Free Society

What would happen to the poor and disabled in a truly free society, a society in which government did not use force to redistribute wealth? This question can best be answered by asking another question: What happens to the poor and disabled in societies that are totally controlled by their governments, governments whose purported purpose is to achieve equality for their people? In all such countries throughout the world, everyone is poor—and remains poor—if they are lucky enough not to be imprisoned or killed.

The question of the fate of the poor and disabled in a free society raises a number of other questions and points. First, we are faced with the same old problem of defining who the poor and disabled are, which in turn gives rise to the same old question of who has the omniscience, let alone the moral authority, to make such arbitrary decisions?

Then there is the assumption that, in our redistribution-of-wealth society, government does, in fact, do a good job of aiding the poor.

Unfortunately, this is a false assumption. As we have already discussed, most of the money earmarked for those in need ends up in the hands of government employees who administer a mind-numbing number of aid programs.

But even if we ignore the problem of defining who the poor and disabled are, and even if we disregard government's waste in administering welfare programs, we still end up with a confrontation between needs and morality (i.e., while it may be true that many people are unable to care for themselves, that does not justify a violation of the rights of those who *are* able to care for themselves).

No matter what the circumstances, trying to solve the problems of some people by using force against others is always immoral. The moral objectives of any individual or group can never transform confiscation into a moral action. The unpleasant result of applying force to a problem is resentment, backlash, and, ultimately, chaos.

Helping the needy is a matter of personal morality, not force. As Lysander Spooner pointed out, even though a man may feel that other men have a moral duty to feed the hungry, shelter the homeless, care for the sick, and enlighten the ignorant, these are personal moral beliefs. If people are to be free, then each person must make his own moral judgment as to how far, if at all, he wishes to go in providing these things.

Many people erroneously believe that to be in favor of personal freedom (i.e., sovereignty over one's own life and property) means that a person is heartless and is against helping those who are disabled. In fact, freedom is one subject, charity another. I believe voluntary charity is admirable so long as the giver is fully aware of the final destination of his contribution.

I am sympathetic toward people who are far less fortunate than I (though I do not presume to be in a position to arbitrarily label some individuals poor and others not), but I also believe in freedom. And because I place a higher priority on liberty than all other objectives, I do not believe that I or any other person has the right to force others to be charitable. Simply put, I am not against charity, but I am against the use of force.

What individual would not like to see every hungry child fed, every disease cured, every disabled person made comfortable? I assume that anyone who had the power to do so would make all misery in this world disappear overnight. But, unfortunately, no one possesses such power— certainly not politicians. The question is not whether people are for or against human suffering; all humane individuals are concerned about human suffering. The question is whether some people should be forced to give money to programs that certain other people feel are helpful to those they deem to be in need.

Charity that involves the use of force is not really charity. In truth, it is the sacrifice of one human being to another. And sacrifice is not the mark of a civilized society. Voluntary charity is not sacrifice, because a person who gives willingly bases his actions on his own moral standards. Voluntary charity does not involve the resentment and bitterness associated with forced redistribution of wealth.

Charity

What would happen to the poor if there were no redistribution-of-wealth programs? In a truly free society, each person would be free to give as much as he wished to charity. Therefore, if as many millions of people are as sincere as they claim to be about helping the poor, they could do two things, in particular, that would go a long way toward easing the misery of those whom they believe to be in need.

First, they could give self-determined percentages of their own incomes to whomever they pleased. Second, they could spend as much time as they wanted working for, and/or forming, voluntary charitable groups to raise money for their favorite causes. And because they undoubtedly would work without compensation, the recipients of their charity would be far better off than they are now because the middleman (i.e., government) would be eliminated.

In response to this proposal, people often ask, "But what if people did not give enough of their money voluntarily?" The answer is that it would mean they did not want to give amounts that others may deem to be enough. In the final analysis, all questions of this nature must be measured against the belief that human freedom is a higher moral objective than the arbitrary fulfillment of certain people's needs and desires.

Fortunately, the history of America is replete with hard evidence that the more free and prosperous a society is, the greater its citizens' desires to give. And, although the creation and possession of great wealth does not need to be defended on the basis of charitable contributions, a comforting bonus to all this is that the wealthiest people in our society have traditionally been the ones to give most to the poor and disabled.

There are thousands of private foundations in the United States that donate billions of dollars annually to causes they deem to be worthy. Among some of the more prominent ones are the Ford Foundation, Rockefeller Foundation, Carnegie Corp. of New York, and the Alfred P. Sloan Foundation.

Andrew Carnegie alone contributed some $350 million (billions in today's dollars) to various philanthropic causes, including more than 2,800 libraries in the United States and Canada. John D. Rockefeller, founder of the Rockefeller family fortune, gave away more than $530 million. His projects included the Rockefeller Institute for Medical Research, the General Education Board (which helped establish schools for Negro teachers and children), and the Rockefeller Foundation ("to promote the well-being of mankind throughout the world"). All told, the Rockefeller family has donated billions of dollars to various charities and charitable programs through the years.

Notwithstanding their charitable acts, however, the greatest contributions the great industrialists have made to the welfare of mankind have been through their use of the free-enterprise system.

My personal belief is that most people are humane and compassionate, and that, given the opportunity to act freely, will respond charitably to those whom they deemed to be in need. But I also believe that people place an even higher value on liberty, and that the less free they are to improve their own well-being, the less charitable they will be. As government has increased its attempts to redistribute wealth, it simultaneously has decreased the desire of taxpayers to be charitable.

And with the massive debt that the progressives now in power are determined to continue increasing, the situation will only worsen. And they are well aware that this will make the poor and disabled ever more dependent on the government.

Charity is just another of the endless array of services in which government should not be involved. People should be left alone to act voluntarily in a spirit of goodwill. A good example of private charity can be seen in the Mormon church. Virtually no Mormons are on public welfare, because the church has its own welfare system. Mormons provide millions of dollars in aid each year to needy members, and they even provide financial aid to non–church members.

The Present Fate of the Poor

The cruel irony is that all the "compassionate" acts of politicians aimed at helping the poor are actually destructive to those who are unable to care for themselves. That's because such acts are based on the vote and consequently are structured to show immediate results—which means short-term solutions.

Long term, however, progressive politicians are setting up a disaster for those whom they purport to be helping. Bureaucratic waste is one of the major factors bankrupting our nation, which can only lead to less for everybody in the long run, including less freedom. If you consider yourself to be a humanitarian and really care about the poor and disabled, ask yourself this question: How will the poor and disabled be better off if our economy experiences a total collapse?

The best way to help the poor is for the government to stop interfering with producers. The results of a laissez-faire economy have already been detailed in Chapter 3. It is unfortunate that so many people who purport to be concerned about the poor do not understand the simple reality that you can only redistribute wealth if wealth exists. If you kill incentive, and production of wealth slows—or grinds to a halt—there is nothing to redistribute.

It's time to restore the American Dream and allow producers to produce so everyone can be better off.

As Murray Rothbard put it in *For a New Liberty*, "What . . . *can* the government do to help the poor? The only correct answer is also the libertarian answer: Get out of the way."

The Gourmet Banquet in Rome

Santayana warned of those who cannot remember the past, but my concern is more with those who do not *know* the past. I believe it's because so few Americans are aware of history that we are now repeating the errors of the past.

The U.S. government is not the first government to offer the gourmet banquet. More than 2,000 years ago Romans enjoyed a glorious redistribution-of-wealth feast under Caesar Augustus. The government took care of every citizen from the cradle to the grave, providing schools, welfare, social security, hospitals, and much more.

In order to pay for all this, taxation reached the point where producers lost the incentive to work. Society became a free-for-all, with lawyers devising ways to evade taxes and government creating new laws to prevent evasion. Everyone was so wrapped up in enjoying their false prosperity that the great productive ingenuity that had built Rome slowly disappeared.

As Rome decayed, the government took an increasingly firm hold over the lives of its citizens, until the original republic ultimately evolved into an extreme totalitarian state. The decline in productivity led to a decline of freedom, which inevitably led to the extinction of the Roman Empire.

Are we reliving the Roman past? If you were to substitute the United States for Rome and Franklin D. Roosevelt for Caesar Augustus in this little history lesson, you would not have a very difficult time trying to pass it off as a history of America since the 1930s. Only the final two steps remain on the horizon: the evolution into an extreme totalitarian state and extinction. And it is these last two steps that I would like to believe most people—rich and poor, blue-collar workers and executives, men and women, blacks and whites—want to avoid. We will either stand together or fall together.

Under the Democratic progressives now in power (and the Republicans before them), more and more people are coming to the realization that there is no need to be productive. Like the gal at the gas pump during the last presidential campaign (the one who was excited over the prospect of not having to pay for her gas or rent once Barack Obama was elected), under the current Obamastration, people are being led to believe that they can enjoy prosperity without having to work for it.

Senator Hayakawa compared this situation to what was happening in the 1960s and 1970s at American universities, when most students were given good grades regardless of the quality of their work. The result was that good students stopped studying, and many even became dropouts. Hayakawa noted that laziness and ignorance were no longer penalized, and he warned, "When there is no such thing as failure, there is no such thing as success either."

Hayakawa concluded the grades analogy by saying that "if everybody is rewarded just for being alive, you get the same sort of effect as you do when you reward every student just for being enrolled. You destroy not only education, you destroy society by giving A's to everyone. This is a philosophical consideration that bothers me very much as I sit in the United States Senate and see its great budget allocations going through."

The redistribution-of-wealth philosophy has led to a prevalent belief that people are not responsible for their own actions, that the burden for their success or failure belongs to society. Worse, it has led to a decline in morality that encourages an anything-goes attitude among citizens. Redistribution of wealth has degenerated into a game of who can get the most benefits for the least amount of work.

Getting a piece of the pie (that mythical pie that, during the last presidential campaign, voters were told they had a right to) has become a misnomer. In today's atmosphere, it would be more proper to describe it as getting a piece of the plunder.

John Hospers, in an article in *Reason* magazine, noted that Albert Jay Nock foresaw this evolution some fifty years ago when he properly described the exploited as those who trade their goods and services on the free market and who are forced to turn over a portion of their earnings to government, and the exploiters as those who receive government checks or subsidies made possible by the work of the producing class.

Government has played a cruel hoax on everyone by making handouts so freely available. First, it has robbed people of their self-esteem—of the desire to succeed on their own. Autonomy and self-responsibility create an environment that breeds goodwill and allows people to develop themselves to the best of their abilities. But by today's progressive standards, such thinking is considered cruel and calloused.

Second, most of those on the receiving end do not understand that loss of incentive is a dire consequence of government benefits. Not just loss of incentive on the part of those who benefit most from government's generosity, but, worse, on the part of society's most productive individuals. An obvious but too little discussed fact of redistribution of wealth is that people simply become less willing to risk their time, energy, and money if they know that an inordinate amount of what they earn will be confiscated.

Make no mistake about it, the money for people programs does, indeed, come from people. Government is now at a crossroads. As David Walker, former Comptroller General of the United States, has been warning for years, politically expedient promises long ago exceeded all possible resources. And this was *before* Obama and his congressional allies began passing new legislation in the trillions of dollars. The bloated middle class is taxed to the point of revolt, aware that it now pays out much more than it receives in benefits, and the productivity rate of the United States is rapidly declining.

Redistribution of wealth does not work—and has never worked—if the goal is to achieve the greatest amount of financial well-being and freedom for the greatest number of people. Will Durant, who studied every redistribution-of-wealth experiment in recorded history, assured us that, in the end, nature will have its way on the subject of inequality:

> . . . *periodically wealth is redistributed, whether by the violent confiscation of property, or by confiscatory taxation of incomes. . . . Then the race for wealth, goods and power begins again, and the pyramid of ability takes form once more; under whatever laws may be enacted the abler man manages somehow to get the richer soil, the better place, the lion's share; soon he is strong enough to dominate the state and rewrite or interpret the laws; and in time the inequality is as great as before.*

This sounds like an exact description of where the United States is today—especially the part about "dominate the state and rewrite or interpret the laws." What made the American Revolution unique was that the Revolutionists made no pretense of a desire to redistribute wealth. Their only objective was to throw out the government. They wanted to be free. They wanted every inhabitant to have an equal right to life, liberty, and the pursuit of happiness. This was the foundation of the American Dream.

But from the day the Constitution became law, politicians began experimenting with the utopian idea of wealth without work. And ever since this philosophy gained a full head of steam under FDR, the United States more and more has come to resemble Rome under Caesar Augustus.

Should we suffer a total economic collapse, you can be sure that those who are now in power will take firm hold of the political reins and establish a totalitarian state. That has been the plan of American progressivism since at least the early part of the twentieth century. If it should occur, it will represent the overdue bill for our false prosperity. "In nature," said Emerson, "nothing can be given, all things are sold." If every-day Americans do not fight back and force out of office those who violate the Constitution on a daily basis, the ultimate price tag for the gourmet banquet will be a total loss of liberty.

Though the popular question during the Lyndon Johnson years was whether the United States could afford both guns and butter, I never for a moment thought that to be the most relevant issue. I believed then, and believe so even more today, that the most important question is whether we can afford both freedom and equality. And both nature and history have repeatedly given us the answer to this all-important question: no.

I urge every American to heed the advice of my late friend William Simon:

> *Stop asking the government for "free" goods and services, however desirable and necessary they may seem to be. They are not free. They are simply extracted from the hide of your neighbors—and can be extracted only by force. If you would not confront your neigh-bor and demand his money at the point of a gun to solve every new problem that may appear in your life, you should not allow the gov-ernment to do it for you. . . . This one insight understood, this one discipline acted upon and taught by millions of Americans to others could do more to further freedom in American life than any other.*

CHAPTER 5

Taking the *Free* out of Free Enterprise

Technically speaking, all government functions redistribute wealth to the extent they are paid for involuntarily by people who may not want government to perform such functions. The redistribution-of-wealth function discussed in the previous chapter is more easily discernible because it involves actions that take money from some people and give it to others in the form of either money or services.

As a result of the vote, however, modern government performs a multitude of other functions, all of which share the objective of appeasing various voter groups. Government Function Number Two—business regulation—involves a multitude of differing personal opinions. As a result, government intervention is almost always confusing, contradictory, and wasteful. To satisfy thousands of differing expedient demands is, of course, impossible. But that doesn't deter the politician from trying to do it anyway. Heaven forbid he should lose even one prospective voter, no matter how harmful that voter's demands may be.

Business regulation is just another form of personal regulation in that every action government takes to interfere in the marketplace directly affects individuals. As we shall see, government interference in the business world causes increases in, among other things, the cost of living, taxes, and unemployment. It also causes shortages in, if not complete elimination of, goods and services desired by individuals.

If the average person truly understood not only how the free-enterprise system works, but also the extent to which government regulation of business damages his well-being, there would be as great a revolt against business regulation as there is against excessive taxation. Taxes, after all, are just one of the many harmful effects of business regulation in that it takes tax dollars to support the regulatory bureaucracy.

Federal agencies alone that regulate business range from worker safety and environmental protection to antitrust enforcement and consumer protection. The Federal Register, which lists these regulations, contained 2,620 pages of regulations when it was first printed in 1936. Today, the number of pages exceeds 78,000.

The Price Tag

Like money for people programs, money for business-regulation programs also comes from people. The one certainty about all government intervention in the marketplace is that the consumer ultimately bears the cost. Unfortunately, the vast majority of Americans do not realize they are paying for these regulations, not only through higher taxes necessary to support the bureaucratic agencies that implement them, but also through higher prices of goods and services. These higher prices are in great part the result of the billions of dollars industry must spend to comply with government regulations.

Of course, the Marxist argument is that business should be prevented from passing the increased cost of government regulation on to the consumer. Which sounds wonderful, so long as you disregard the fact that a company that cannot raise prices to cover the higher costs of doing business goes *out* of business. The results of such a solution, therefore, would be decreased productivity, greater unemployment, higher prices, and scarcity of product.

It's bad enough that excessive regulation often makes it nearly impossible for a company to do business, but the time and money consumed in either conforming to regulations or trying to fight them is enough to break even giant corporations, let alone small and medium-sized businesses. The use of potentially productive time and energy to fill out tax forms, safety forms, sanitation forms, equal-opportunity forms, and environmental-protection forms, to name but a few, has become a way of life for the businessperson, a curious substitute for the American Dream that government regulation has been helping to destroy.

Milton Friedman brought business regulation down to a personal level by maintaining that it is the greatest example of violation of human freedom one can imagine. Among other things, he mentions having to obtain a government license to engage in an occupation, being prevented from selling a product at a price one wishes to charge, and not being allowed to grow the amount of crops one wants to grow. These are sometimes referred to as *economic restrictions*, which is a nice phrase, but the fact remains that they are restrictions of *freedom*. Try as collectivists may, they can never manage to separate freedom and free enterprise.

Business regulation is an integral part of the wealth-is-evil philosophy. Over the centuries, ignorant, envious zealots have convinced great numbers of people that profit is sinful and that large concentrations of wealth are dangerous. This is the irrational attitude that has prompted excessive taxation and overregulation of business in avalanche proportions. Which in turn has helped destroy the lifeblood of the American Dream—free enterprise— the dream that inspired the technological progress that has given Americans health, comfort, and material well-being unimagined in past centuries.

Those who favor such destruction display the same shortsightedness as people who revere redistribution-of-wealth legislation. When a self-anointed morally superior person believes that a problem exists, too often his solution is to appeal to government to pass a new set of laws and create a new agency to enforce them. This results in violating still more rights of more people in an effort to try to solve what certain individuals believe to be a problem by creating bigger problems.

The Rulers Who Don't Answer to the Vote

An especially ugly aspect of the ever-growing regulatory monster is that it is the most visible sign of creeping totalitarianism. Most regulatory agencies operate outside the law, with non-elected bureaucrats in control, and act as judge, jury, prosecutor, and executioner. The new army of czars put in place by the current Marxist regime in Washington can virtually make or break a company or individual businessperson at will. A company or businessperson is deemed guilty until proven innocent, a concept that is in direct contrast to America's founding principles.

What kinds of experts are these non-elected rulers? Just as Senator Hayakawa was shocked when he was named to the Senate Budget Committee, so, too, was William Simon when Richard Nixon appointed him chairman of the Oil Policy Committee (which made him, said Simon, a virtual dictator over the energy resources of the United States). The problem? Simon himself told Nixon that he knew nothing about oil!

Like civil servants who administer welfare programs, government regulators spend most of their time maneuvering to protect their vested interests— which means trying to increase the size of their agencies. Because they have no way of proving tangible results, government regulators, like their counterparts in people-program agencies, must increase paperwork, which in turn increases staff size. And an increase in staff regulators brings still more regulations, which continues the cycle by bringing still more regulators.

It is imperative that bureaucratic regulators find problems, even if they do not exist. As is true of so-called poverty programs, if problems were solved and new problems could not be found, they would be out of jobs. This destruction of our economy and freedom by non-elected bureaucratic dictators calls to mind an all-too-true statement by Ayn Rand more than fifty years ago: "The man who has no purpose, but has to act, acts to destroy others."

How the Destruction Game Is Played

Business regulation, on the surface, appears to be an enigma. While unelected bureaucrats implement the regulations and have dictatorial powers, the agencies themselves are set up by politicians who pay homage to the vote. Therefore, though business regulation for many people is an extension of their wealth-is-evil philosophy, others want business regulated for different reasons. In fact, virtually everyone wants business regulated, including, sadly, businesspeople.

The enigma arises from the contrasting types of business regulation desired by various groups and individuals. Because virtually all business regulation grows out of subjective opinions and moral desires, and because no two people share the exact same opinions and moral desires, how can government possibly please everyone?

The answer is that it can't. But because of the unremitting pressure of the vote, it tries to do so anyway. Which is why business regulation sometimes takes the form of consumerism; at other times burdens industry with totally unreasonable environmental and safety restrictions; and at still other times doles out special favors, on a selective basis, to companies and businesspeople.

The Persuaders

All this manifests itself in a phenomenon known as *lobbying*. The playing field for the lobbying game on a federal level is Washington, D.C. Politicians realize that lobbying groups represent votes. And in the case of business lobbying, in particular, there also are ancillary benefits to be enjoyed, such as campaign contributions and other forms of help from powerful businesspeople. It is no coincidence that the lobbying game gets bigger and bigger as the American Dream continues to diminish in size.

Moral desires show up in the lobbying game through groups of politically active people. The objective of these groups is to persuade government to force business to abide by their opinions regarding protection of the environment, worker safety, the size of companies—virtually an infinite number of moral positions they believe should be imposed on others.

The people who have wrought such destruction upon millions of individuals and on the economy as a whole tend to have visions limited to single issues that distort their view of the world. Nevertheless, I believe that if these people were the only regulatory problem America had, producers might eventually be able to cope with them.

I am sorry to say, however, that they are not the only problem. A problem that is just as bad, and perhaps worse, is that cry-baby businesspeople run to the government to seek an edge over their competitors. Unfortunately, virtually all businesspeople are guilty of this to one extent or another. The result is the philosophical dilemma many businesspeople have been trying to resolve for years: how to have their free-enterprise cake and eat it, too. In other words, how to bring about government intervention in the marketplace that favors their specific companies or industries, while holding down regulation detrimental to their own interests.

Thus, when I sing the praises of capitalism, do not take it to mean that I am praising businesspeople. There are moral businesspeople and immoral businesspeople. There are businesspeople whose operations are virtually dependent upon obtaining special favors from government; there are businesspeople who reluctantly ask for government help only because "everyone else is doing it"; and there are businesspeople who rarely seek government intervention and who, given a choice, would favor the implementation of the world's first laissez-faire economy.

Both small and big businesses are guilty of inviting government intervention into the marketplace. All are well known for their appeals to government to step in and protect them. Small businesspeople often decry the unfair advantages of big business, but many of them are just as guilty as giant corporations when it comes to government collusion. If you've ever read any literature put out by small-business associations, you realize they are not asking for an end to government regulations. Rather, they are asking for less regulation of small business and more regulation of big business. This short-term, expedient outlook has the same destructive effect on society as the expedient demands of welfare recipients, civil-service workers, and the unemployed.

Tariffs are a favorite type of government protection that has been around for years, always helping inefficient domestic producers by forcing consumers to pay unnecessarily high prices for imported goods. While tariffs foster the impression that the government is protecting workers in a particular industry, the long-term effect is an increase not only in prices, but also unemployment. Because tariffs force people to pay higher prices, people have less to spend on other goods and services, which results in less employment in the industries that produce such goods and services. What is hidden is that the job protected by a government tariff is at the expense of a worker in another industry.

Then there are the companies that appeal to government to keep newcomers out of their industries, claiming such industries are overcrowded. These claims are, of course, nonsense, because if an industry is overcrowded, profits should be inordinately low. If so, why would anyone want to invest capital in such an industry? The truth is that the entrenched businesses do not want the extra competition that would force them to become more efficient and produce better products and services at lower prices.

Government subsidies and bailouts to selected businesses are the same story. What really happens is that money is taken from efficient producers to keep inefficient producers in business—all at the expense of consumers in the form of higher prices.

As Henry Hazlitt emphasized, it is important that antiquated, inefficient companies die out so new, efficient companies can grow faster. As a result, capital and labor find their way into more modern industries. Hazlitt used the automobile industry as an example (long before management and the United Auto Workers destroyed it), pointing out that if government had tried to keep the horse-and-buggy trade alive through subsidies, the automobile industry would have suffered, which would have meant a loss of great wealth and a subsequent loss of improved living standards for all.

It is ironic that businesspeople who encourage government regulation use the very same tactics employed by antibusiness moralists who press for safety and environmental regulations—the same moralists whose actions businesspeople so deplore. Businesspeople who seek government favors are, in effect, admitting they cannot compete on the basis of their ability to produce products and services the public wants, and that they therefore wish to see the free-enterprise system revised to suit their needs.

Antitrust Mythology

Many business regulations imposed by government are instituted under the guise of protecting the public from monopolies that otherwise, so the theory goes, would be able to charge virtually any price they desired for their products. If so, it seems rather strange that it is often big companies that bring so-called antitrust or monopoly suits against competitors. Usually the objective is to either keep another company from entering their field or get government to restrict a successful company in ways that would give the suing company advantages it has not been able to acquire on its own merits.

Antitrust and anti-monopoly legislation comprise yet another fraud perpetrated on the average American. The truth is that companies rarely are able to obtain a monopoly in an industry without the aid of government. It is interesting to note that the term *monopoly* originally meant "an exclusive grant or franchise from the king to operate in a given area, free from competition."

Few people realize that the infamous trusts and cartels of the early American business giants failed, mainly because each company in a cartel was always trying to gain an edge over the very companies with whom it was allied, which any student of human nature would expect.

As a result of these failures, some of the bigger corporations got the bright idea to use the coercive machinery of government to pass antitrust laws to knock out competition they themselves could not eliminate in a free market. Industry's antitrust alliance with government is probably the biggest mistake capitalists have made since prehistoric property owners agreed to allow power seekers protect their lives and property.

Today, government awards strict monopolies in most of the biggest industries in the country and monopolies of one kind or another in literally thousands of other businesses. Service businesses such as gas, electricity, and trucking are some of the more obvious examples. While claiming that its regulation of prices protects the public from unfair high prices, the truth is that government rate-setting protects the companies it is supposed to be regulating from having to charge lower prices. Such companies are virtually guaranteed a fixed profit for their products and services.

This charade is exposed whenever some maverick comes along and tries to break into an established industry by offering better products or services and/or lower prices. In such cases, entrenched industry giants usually run to the government to protect them from the new price competition they claim will cause chaos (i.e., lower prices) in their industry.

In truth, licensing laws of all kinds are monopolistic because they mean, plain and simple, that people are not free to compete with established businesses or individuals without government consent. No matter how much one may be used to thinking to the contrary, the same principles hold true even for such businesses as law, medicine, dentistry, and pharmacy.

As in the area of public education, I appreciate that it is difficult for most people to accept this seemingly extreme point of view, having been accustomed all their lives to believing that government licensing is practically divine and that government possesses omnipotent powers to protect the public from incompetent and unscrupulous operators.

However, even with government-monopoly licensing laws for most professions, incompetent and unscrupulous operators abound. And the fact always remains that elimination of competition through licensing, regardless of the nature of the service, lessens the motivation for efficiency, raises prices, and lowers quality, all at the expense of the consumer.

One of the more interesting results of the lobbying/antitrust game is that confusing and contradictory antitrust legislation has now made it technically against the law just to be in business in the United States. Consider:

- If a company charges higher prices than its competitors, government reasoning is that it must have a monopoly in its field or else it would not be able to charge such high prices.

- If a company charges lower prices than its competition, the government assumes that it must be trying to acquire a monopoly by undercutting other companies in its field.

- If a company charges the same prices as its competitors (without government approval), then, of course, it is guilty of price fixing.

What once was the American Dream has been replaced by the notion that virtually every businessperson is breaking the law simply by being in business!

The truth about monopolies is that they seldom could occur in a free market, and even if they did occasionally exist, such companies could not charge any price they desired. This is so because in a free market, even if a company did hold a monopoly, it still would have competition. As pointed out in *Fundamentals of Liberty*, three kinds of competition always exist:

1. **Parallel competition**. There are always alternatives to any product or service. If the price of anything—including seemingly essential products such as gas and oil—becomes prohibitive, consumers will seek a substitute. They may not like the substitute as well, but at a certain point they become willing to sacrifice some degree of comfort and convenience for price.

2. **Dollar competition**. People have only so many dollars to spend, and, unlike government, they weigh their needs, desires, and income against the cost of various products and services, then make decisions to purchase some and do without others. Again, they may not like doing without certain items, but if the prices of these items are too high, that is precisely the decision they will make.

3. **Invisible competition**. No matter how entrenched a company may be, if it raises prices to levels considered exorbitant by consumers, it is practically inviting new companies to enter its field to compete with it at lower prices. Potential competition is always out there in the form of ambitious entrepreneurs looking for ways to increase their wealth by offering better products and services at lower prices.

The greatest regulator is competition, and there is always competition in the absence of government intervention. Above all, the fact that every consumer is interested in buying the best products and services at the lowest possible prices guarantees competition in a free market. This is precisely what makes black markets flourish. A black market is nothing more than a free market asserting itself in spite of government regulation. Only government intervention in the market—usually through antitrust legislation—can interfere with the natural forces of competition in laissez-faire capitalism.

The example of Alcoa Aluminum is cited in *Fundamentals of Liberty* to reinforce the point that a monopoly earned in the free market does not necessarily translate into higher prices for buyers. Notwithstanding the fact that for years Alcoa had a monopoly on aluminum production in the United States, it lowered its price over the years, so much so that it was only charging 20¢ a pound in the 1930s as compared to $8 a pound in 1888. Why would Alcoa do such a thing? Because it recognized the power of invisible competition.

But, in the end, government made sure that the consumer was forced to pay higher prices by bringing an antitrust suit against Alcoa. Bureaucrats, using their infinite powers of political reasoning, determined that Alcoa's defense—that other companies did not enter its field because it operated too efficiently—was not valid. The government, in effect, decided that it was illegal for a company to be too efficient!

In the case of antitrust laws, consumers pay not only for the millions of man-hours required to comply with federal regulations and fight antitrust suits, but also what is probably the biggest cost of all: the monopolistic rates government sets for virtually all major industries.

Worker- and Consumer-Protection Mythology

All government regulatory agencies play the dual role of being both anti-business and pro-monopoly to one extent or another. Some agencies, however, lean more toward imposing the opinions of various consumer and labor groups on the business world. These agencies make it possible for virtually anyone who is willing to spend his time crusading for an issue to disrupt the free market. Whether the issue is consumer safety, worker safety, or environmental protection, the actions of such agencies always involve forcing business to abide by the opinions of lobbying groups concerning what is unsafe or unfair.

What complicates the problem is that not only do these groups make their demands known to vote-conscious politicians—politicians who create agencies and jobs for the non-elected bureaucrats who carry out the interference—but also, more often than not, the non-elected bureaucrats themselves get carried away and impose their own moral standards on business. Under their guidance, so-called consumerism has evolved into a sort of social fascism.

Some brief comments on just a few of the better-known agencies that forcibly interfere with the free market under the guise of consumer, safety, or environmental protection:

- **Securities and Exchange Commission (SEC).** The SEC is one of the most Gestapo-like of all governmental regulatory agencies, continually expanding its powers into areas far removed from its original purported purpose of protecting investors. It arbitrarily makes the law, then passes judgment on whether a person or company has violated it.

  Like all government agencies, the SEC's efforts not only violate human rights, but also result in the opposite of its stated purpose. For example, over the years it has forced public companies to increase the detail of their annual reports and prospectuses to such an extent that it is now virtually impossible for the average investor to understand them. It takes a very sophisticated investor to be able to make sense out of the endless facts, figures, and footnotes that have long been mandatory in corporate public reports and prospectuses.

  Incredibly, when the SEC accuses a company or individual of wrongdoing, it does not have to prove guilt beyond a reasonable doubt, but is required to show only "a preponderance of evidence." Further, defendants, in effect, are virtually forced to provide SEC investigators with evidence against themselves.

  Customarily, an SEC investigation results in individuals or companies signing a consent decree, a nasty little document that states they consent to an injunction, "without admitting or denying the allegations." The result is that the SEC achieves its desired objective of damaging the reputation of the target company or individuals without having to prove that any violation of the law has actually occurred.

  The damage comes from the bad publicity that accompanies such investigations, which causes investors, company suppliers, potential merger candidates, and others to assume that where there's smoke, there's fire. And that assumption usually leads to a drastic drop in the price of a company's stock, which hurts the very investors the SEC claims to be protecting.

- **Food and Drug Administration (FDA).** This is a virtual life-threatening agency in that, among other things, takes it upon itself to outlaw various drugs and medicines that might improve the health of seriously ill people—or, in some cases, even save lives. Every year in this country people die who conceivably could have been saved by drugs outlawed by the FDA.

The question here is not whether certain drugs in certain cases help or harm individuals. This gets at the very heart of the libertarian foundation of true conservatism. Government simply has no business deciding what medications companies should or should not be allowed to sell, and certainly has no right to make it a criminal offense for people to take whatever medications they desire. In addition, there prevails, once again, the general false assumption that government has some mysterious, omniscient power to make such decisions, decisions that can be better made by individuals—both consumers and businesspeople.

■ **Environmental Protection Agency (EPA).** The EPA probably does more to cripple the U.S. economy and endanger lives than any other agency.

Ironically, it is those who ramble on about the evils of capitalism and the need to curb technology to protect the environment who apparently place very little value on human life. Such people are afflicted with tunnel vision, being totally obsessed with "cleaning up the environment" at any cost. By stifling technology, they also stifle the very thing that has ended so much misery for the masses, prolonged people's lives, and made life more comfortable for virtually everyone.

It is curious that people relate capitalism with environmental problems. As pointed out earlier, even the most socialistic countries use the division-of-labor industrial system—though less successfully due to a lack of incentive on the part of workers. As everyone knows, there is far more pollution in China than in the United States.

As with regulation, the price tag for environmental controls is hidden from taxpayers. Everyone wants clean air and water, but not at any cost—certainly not at the cost of losing our freedom. There is nothing wrong with being concerned about the environment, but it is impractical and tyrannical to allow it to dominate virtually every decision regarding technological advancement and business planning.

Energy is one of the most critical areas being endangered by the fascist environmental attitudes of small numbers of bureaucrats and politically active groups. Our legal system—appropriately referred to by some as *trial by endurance*—makes it possible for small groups to block, for interminable periods of time, what could be life-saving energy projects.

The famous Three Mile Island nuclear incident in 1979 immediately brought to the fore professional environmental agitators who, to this day, use this isolated incident as an argument for preventing the construction of nuclear power plants in the United States.

Such obstructionists are a threat to our comfort, safety, health, and, above all, freedom—not to mention that of future generations. If one gives them the benefit of the doubt and assumes that these crisis crusaders are not consciously trying to cause millions of people unneeded suffering, one must also assume that their actions are based on a lack of knowledge.

In the case of Three Mile Island, for example, these crusader types were protesting for all the wrong seasons. In effect, they were protesting against free enterprise and advocating more government intervention. If they felt an irresistible urge to protest, what they should have been protesting was the fact that it was government intervention that created the Three Mile Island problems in the first place.

A rational, well-informed person might be more inclined to analyze the Three Mile Island incident in the following manner:

- Not one person died in the incident.

- No one, to my knowledge, has ever died as a result of the negligent operation of a nuclear-power plant anywhere in the United States.

- If a fatality should ever occur as a result of a nuclear-power-plant accident—or even if many fatalities should occur—the solution would not be to outlaw nuclear-power plants. The solution would be to allow free individuals to correct the problems that caused such deaths—just as we do after all kinds of accidents. Government does not have unique powers to solve nuclear-plant problems. Again, it does not have unique powers to solve *any* problems. Individuals, motivated by the desire to improve their well-being, solve problems. Government bureaucrats, motivated by the vote, succeed only in impeding progress.

- Again, the automobile-accident analogy: There are more than 40,000 automobile-accident fatalities a year in the U.S., yet rational people do not advocate the outlawing of cars. Because one is in favor of the free use of automobiles does not mean he is indifferent to the 40,000+ deaths a year caused by automobile accidents.

- While progressives love to paint businesspeople as evil capitalists who will do anything for profit, common sense tells one that people who operate nuclear-power plants have no desire to fill the air with nuclear radiation. Remember, these people know that they, too, have to breathe the air on this planet.

- Should someone suffer physical damage as a result of the negligent operation of a nuclear-power plant, he (or his heirs, in the case of his death) certainly should have the right to institute civil and/or criminal proceedings against the nuclear-plant owners, just as a person is able to sue an automobile manufacturer if the manufacturer's negligence results in damage to him. This is precisely what prevents businesspeople in every industry from endangering the lives of other people just for the sake of profit. Existing laws against aggression already cover such incidents.

If government intervenes on behalf of an industry, however, as it did in the late 1950s and 1960s when the Atomic Energy Commission, through the Price-Anderson Act, limited the liability of nuclear-power-plant developers and utilities, it practically invites the companies in that industry to be negligent and thus negates this free-market principle. Government intervention, then, is the real problem in the nuclear-power-plant industry because such intervention is detrimental to both energy companies and consumers.

It seems that some people will never understand that the solution to every problem—particularly environmental problems—is not to outlaw the cause of the problem and set up a policing agency to enforce the law. Isaac Asimov made this point by reflecting on prehistoric times, when men first discovered fire and learned that it provided a source of warmth for cold nights and winters. When these men brought the fire inside, however, they found that it filled their caves with smoke. But because there was no agency around to outlaw the use of fire in caves, man instead resorted to his greatest asset—creative ingenuity, inspired by a desire to improve his well-being. As a result, instead of creating a new regulatory agency, he invented the chimney.

Narrow-minded environmentalists who want to eliminate all risks for mankind are forcing us to take the biggest risk of all: destruction. A risk-free society is a dead society. While the Washington progressives want to eliminate all risk (a preposterously naive objective), what is really needed is for the people of this country to recover the willingness to *take* risks. It was the risk-taking, spirited quest of a better life that made America the healthiest, wealthiest, and strongest country in the history of the world.

The Hopeless Cause

Depending on popular voter notions that may be circulating at any given time, government intervention in business may also take the form of wage-and-price controls. The implication is that the government can use force to negate the law of supply and demand. Short term, interference can appear attractive to voters. Long term, however, it never works. And, more often than not, it does not even work on a short-term basis.

What's amazing about wage-and-price controls is that they have been tried for centuries by governments throughout the world and, though they have never worked, governments still get away with using this ill-fated political scheme. They are able to do so because most people do not understand the real consequences of wage-and-price controls.

Basically, wage-and-price controls do not work because it is impossible, without the iron hand of a totalitarian regime, to put price ceilings on every product and service that exists. The result is that producers will produce fewer of those products on which prices are restricted; thus, people will have more money available for products whose prices are not controlled, which will cause the prices of the nonrestricted products to rise faster than normal.

Following are two examples of wage-and-price controls:

- Rent control is one of the most popular forms of price controls. Wherever rent control is implemented, it virtually assures renters in the area that rents of the future will be beyond the reach of all but a small percentage of the people.

  Renters foolishly believe that the government is doing them a favor by using force to hold down rents, but the result is always the same: Regulation of rents makes apartment construction an unappealing investment, which means there will be fewer apartments built, which results in a shortage of rental units, which, ultimately, results in higher rents. Isn't it amazing how government regulations consistently achieve the exact opposite of their stated objectives?

- Again, the energy industry must be mentioned, particularly the petroleum business. Government intellectuals continue to ignore official data and insist there is an oil shortage. But the only shortage is the one artificially created by government intervention. Environmental regulations make it almost impossible to drill for oil profitably; in addition, by artificially restraining prices, government kills off the incentive to engage in costly oil exploration.

  The economics of oil drilling work just the same as with apartment construction. Higher oil prices mean higher profits, which allows for more exploration and, hopefully, more oil. More oil, in a free market, means lower prices—*naturally* lower prices. The profit motive would find us all the oil we need if government would just get out of the way and let oil companies drill. It is a cruel irony that U.S. government restrictions on domestic oil drilling has the effect of subsidizing oil imports and keeping us dependent on other oil-producing nations.

Promoting Unemployment

Similar to government's wage-and-price-protection schemes are laws that force employers to pay artificially high wages or charge artificially high prices ("fair pricing"). Artificially high wage levels include both minimum-wage laws and laws that force employers to negotiate with unions, no matter how unreasonable their demands. The long-term result, of course, is detrimental to those who are supposed to be protected by such laws.

There is a business axiom that says if force is used to increase wages, business simply hires fewer workers (or lays off employees). In the case of skilled union-shop workers, what good does it do a man to be told by his union that his skills are worth $75 an hour if he's unemployed?

On the surface, it may appear that the United Auto Workers Union got around this economic fact of life by coercing the big three automakers to give laid-off workers absurd unemployment benefits through their Orwellian "jobs banks." But, in the end, the realities of the marketplace won out, and GM and Chrysler are, for all practical purposes, out of business. They have been reduced to nothing more than shell companies that serve as wealth-transfer conduits for buying the votes of all those who benefit from the scam. Only a police state can prevent the entire house of lies from collapsing.

For unskilled people at the lowest end of the wage scale, the problem is much worse. By pricing these people out of the labor market, government all but forces them to accept welfare. Yet the minimum wage— that great creator of unemployment—keeps rising relentlessly, the latest increase (in July 2009) being to $7.25 an hour.

Minimum-wage laws promote unemployment because people who might otherwise be hired at a lower wage are simply not hired. This is especially oppressive to minority groups, on whose behalf progressives always claim to be acting. Every increase in the minimum-wage rate since 1948 has brought an increase in the black teenage unemployment rate relative to whites. The bottom line is that government achieves an amazing feat for workers by substituting unemployment for low wages.

During a more laissez-faire period in our history, Henry Ford did not need government force to raise wages. He voluntarily doubled the wages of his employees because he was smart enough to figure out that such a move would increase production and profits. It was the invisible hand of free enterprise, not government, that raised the wages of his workers. At a very early stage of our industrial development, Henry Ford understood that increased productivity (i.e., increase in output per man-hours worked) makes it possible to increase wages without increasing prices. In a free market, wages should, and will, rise according to increased productivity.

It goes without saying that minimum-wage laws and union-enforced minimum wages are paid for by consumers, in two ways. First, in the form of the welfare and unemployment-benefit payments they bring about. Second, in the form of the higher prices that result from higher wages. The latter also means that the increased wages are really an illusion to the worker who receives them because everything costs him more.

Does Anyone Benefit?

While it is true that many companies benefit from special government licenses, government-granted monopolies, and government subsidies, I believe that anyone who gains anything through government intervention will suffer right along with everyone else in the long term. The professional welfare recipient and the corporate executive who vies for special government favors both are contributing to the destruction of our economy and our freedom.

The regulatory game is one of destruction. Regulatory agencies help cause higher prices and unemployment, stifle technology and production, and grant monopolies and subsidies at the expense of the overall economy. All these actions lead America closer to a financial collapse and a loss of liberty.

As I stated at the outset of this chapter, business regulation is an off-shoot of the wealth-is-evil philosophy, and politicians love to play that game. The regulation of greedy capitalists, we are led to believe, will somehow help the poor. We already have been through all the reasons why that is not true, but government nevertheless clings to the political poetry of defending the poor against the evils wrought by capitalism.

But the fact is that business regulations are most stifling to those who are the most impoverished. A person from such a background rarely has the means to cope with oppressive government regulations; thus, he is restricted from becoming a businessperson himself. It is no wonder that the American Dream, which certainly included the freedom to start a small business on a shoestring, has become nothing more than a myth to such a person. John Hospers clearly spells out this predicament in his book, *Libertarianism.*

> *Though the regulations and taxes are enough to discourage anyone to the point of giving up, the effects have been especially harmful to racial minorities, such as the Negroes. Many blacks have had to leave farms in the South because of government intervention: the government paid large subsidies to the big farmers, but the small ones were put out of business by the thousands. They left home in droves for the large industrial cities, only to find that they had been priced out of the labor market by minimum-wage laws and government-created unemployment. For some of them, there was still another possibility: start your own business. But the taxes and regulations described above were enough to prevent that possibility in most cases, or to bring them to financial ruin if they did start.*
>
> *The liberals pretend to be friends of the Negro; but they have been the advocates of the very restrictions and regulations which stopped the*

Negro at every turn—as farmer, as worker, as businessman. And so there was no way out but the government dole, year after year, and life in a ghetto which would have been no ghetto if enterprising building constructors had not been shackled by government regulations and taxes. The message to the black race should be clear: the government is not your friend! And those who are responsible for all the government regulations which stop you at every turn are not your friends either, though they may wring their hands for you in their newspaper columns; if they know what their "humanitarian" measures are doing to you and support them anyway, they are hypocritical; and if they do not know, they are hopelessly ignorant of the economic facts of life.

As incentive continues to be smothered, Atlas is beginning to shrug. Businesspeople increasingly knuckle under to oppressive demands by government, especially since progressives took full control of the reins of power in Washington. It is now common for companies, particularly small ones, to comply with regulations out of coercion, realizing that to try to fight the regulatory bureaucracy is suicide. The number of businesspeople simply giving up continues to increase, as they come to the conclusion that it is no longer worth the battle to stay in business. When too many producers give up, that infamous pie Marxists love to talk about will stop growing. And when the pie stops growing, there won't be any pieces left for anybody.

These regulatory protectors of the ecology and enemies of "business greed" are, as William Simon put it, "not protectors of life, (but) . . . heralds of slow death." What is humanitarian about destroying the wealth-producing machinery that has brought us technological innovation and scientific discoveries that have made us the most advanced nation on earth?

Anything that is done to discourage business investment is bad for everyone. On that basis, business regulatory agencies would have to be classified as a disaster for people at all income levels. But are vote-conscious politicians aware of this fact? As Simon further stated, "It takes an immense resistance to logic and fact not to know that one cannot simultaneously control prices, inflate costs, ban production, increase taxes, grant counterproductive subsidies—and expect healthy, vigorous production to result."

Many politicians may be economically illiterate, but the truth is that most of them are just hopelessly hooked on the vote. As a result, government refuses to do what is necessary to save the economy: Totally disengage itself from economic matters. Totally! The more government neglects business, the better off the economy will be. It is because professed conservative

Republicans have lacked the courage to say this that the Republican Party is now on the verge of extinction.

Senator Hayakawa, expressing deep concern over our inability to rid ourselves of government intervention in the market, warned that "Washington is full of power-hungry mandarins and bureaucrats who distrust abundance, which gives people freedom, and who love scarcity and 'zero growth,' which give them power to assign, allocate, and control. If they ever win out, heaven help us!" Postmortem note to Senator Hayakawa: The power-hungry mandarins and bureaucrats are now on the verge of winning out! Heaven help us.

Man can survive pollution; environmentalists can relax about that. The question is whether he can survive regulation!

CHAPTER 6

Promoting the General Welfare

Government function number three is a sort of catchall. It attempts to cover most of the other expedient desires of people (i.e., desires not directly related to matters of wealth and business). There is, of course, an overlap among these areas, but, for the most part, the function of promoting the general welfare covers moral desires outside the wealth-is-evil philosophy. Politicians are aware that the votes of many people can be won by promising to fulfill their desires to impose their moral standards on others.

Any such attempts to do so obviously are flagrant violations of Natural Law, and anyone directly or indirectly involved in helping carry out such violations is guilty of committing aggression. Yet, virtually all regulations concerned with promoting the general welfare are, in reality, attempts to impose the moral desires of certain individuals or groups on others. Personal morality is not a good guide for lawmaking, because people's ideas of morality change from place to place and time to time, so much so that, as Will Durant said in paraphrasing Anacharsis, "If one were to bring together all customs considered sacred by some group, and were then to take away all customs considered immoral by some group, nothing would remain."

We have already discussed needs and desires versus morality, so we need not belabor the obvious point that it is immoral to force some people to abide by the desires of others—particularly when it comes to moral desires.

It certainly would be presumptuous, irrational, and dogmatic—as well as immoral—to force the teachings of any religion on millions of others as a moral guide. A rational person realizes that it is unreasonable to attempt to base the law on religious beliefs, if for no other reason than because the tenets of various religions contradict one another. Therefore, for one religion to be completely right, all others would have to be wrong. To complicate matters, different sects within each religion sharply disagree on fundamental issues (e.g., Methodists, Baptists, Catholics, and Mormons are all Christians, but many of their doctrines are quite different).

Unfortunately, the reality is that human beings determine by which moral standards other human beings should live, and some of them go so far as to claim they are acting on the word of God. Aldous Huxley showed his skepticism regarding such claims when he said: "The gods are just. No doubt. But their code of law is dictated, in the last resort, by the people who organize society; Providence takes its cue from men."

There is a grave danger in putting men in a position to decide what is right and wrong for everyone in a society. Yet that is the power we hand to politicians via the vote. Through the workings of the system, the definition of *sin* becomes, as Bertrand Russell put it, "what is disliked by those who control education."

The term *general welfare* is meaningless for the same reasons that the definition of *good* as "that which is best for the greatest number of people" is meaningless. As pointed out in Chapter 2, every individual is unique; therefore, his welfare is enhanced by actions different from those that may be in the best interest of his neighbor.

Promoting the general welfare, then, translates into violating the natural rights of some people to satisfy the desires of others. This is because, in reality, there is no such thing as general welfare; there is only individual welfare. And every individual should, and certainly has the natural right to, accept responsibility for his own welfare.

The fact remains that people's moral beliefs concerning matters of conduct, even when such conduct does not infringe on the rights of others, have been used as political tools by government since time immemorial. While this gives politicians issues to bandy about at election time, it causes deep-seated friction and hostilities among people. Because every individual uses his unique circumstances, his personal standard of ethics, and his own reasoning power to decide what is and is not moral, forcing him to abide by someone else's moral guidelines can lead to some very ugly problems.

The desire to save people from themselves or prevent them from doing things that other people feel are immoral is not sufficient cause to commit aggression against them. John Stuart Mill explained this point eloquently in his essay "On Liberty":

> *The sole end for which mankind are warranted, individually or collectively, in interfering with the liberty of action of any of their number, is self-protection. The only purpose for which power can be rightfully exercised over any member of a civilized community, against his will, is to prevent harm to others. His own good, either physical or moral, is not a sufficient warrant. He cannot rightfully*

be compelled to do or forbear because it will be better for him to do so, because it will make him happier, because, in the opinions of others, to do so would be wise, or even right.

Remember, a free person is one who is "not under the control or power of another." Freedom, in other words, is self-control. To the degree someone is controlled by others, he is enslaved. People living in what appear to be relatively free countries may find it surprising to be told that they are enslaved, but I believe it is just this sort of blindness to reality that has allowed progressives to move us gradually toward a collectivist hell.

All laws, therefore, that do not involve protecting individuals from aggression are laws that give government unwarranted power and control over its citizens. To the degree that a person is restricted by such laws, he is not free. A person in China, for example, is not as free as a person in the United Kingdom, but he is more free than a person in Darfur. Each of the three, however, is enslaved. Only the degree of their enslavement differs. It would therefore be just as correct to say that the people of the United States have been among the least enslaved people on earth as it would be to say that they have been among the freest people on earth.

All laws that criminalize conduct that does not involve aggression (rape, murder, theft, fraud, etc.) may be viewed as victimless-crime laws. If there is no victim, there can be no crime. People who oppose victim-less-crime laws tend to think only of laws prohibiting such things as por-nography, certain types of drugs, and various forms of consensual adult behavior regarding sex. These are legitimate areas of debate, and, once again, common sense must prevail.

But victimless-crime laws (i.e., laws governing actions that do not involve a real victim) must, by definition, include laws that not only pro-hibit certain noncoercive acts by individuals, but also force people to take action against their will. Any control over a person's desire to act or not act, other than to prevent him from committing aggression against others, is unwarranted if such action or inaction does not harm anyone else.

The notion that someone is committing a crime because he does some-thing to himself that others may believe to be immoral, self-endangering, or in some way harmful to him is ignorant, irrational, presumptuous, and arrogant. What actually happens to the person who insists on doing things that the law says are harmful to him is that the government makes him a victim of its own aggression. In other words, though he himself has not committed aggression against anyone, the government may choose to commit aggression against him.

Laws that force an individual to take action against his will are just as bad as those that prevent him from taking action. In fact, they are worse because such laws, in reality, make victims of those whom they force to take such involuntary action.

In either of these cases, external control is exercised, as opposed to self-control. And external control of human beings is slavery, no matter how one tries to dress it up with respectable-sounding words.

Whether laws keep you from exercising your will to do things you desire to do or force you to take action against your will, they have one thing in common: They all imply that the government, rather you, owns your life.

And because legal authorities throughout the country spend billions of dollars stalking, bringing to trial, convicting, imprisoning, and fining persons guilty of so-called crimes against no one, police are too busy to protect taxpayers from real criminals.

Compulsory Victimless-Crime Laws

Compulsory victimless-crime laws are laws that force you to take action against your will. Can a man be defined as free if others can force him to do things involuntarily? Those who believe in Natural Law and respect human rights believe that such a contradiction is impossible. Following are some examples.

The Draft

No matter what name one ascribes to it, when a person is compelled to spend part of his life training for the military or, worse, risking his life in combat, he is a victim of involuntary servitude. The Selective Service System is a travesty on human rights. One may preach endlessly about the duty to defend one's country, but the fact remains that conscription is slavery.

While enslavement can be made to seem respectable by the use of such phrases as *military duty* and *serving in the armed forces*, words do not change Natural Law. No one has the right to take a peaceful citizen away from his family and put him into a kill-or-be-killed situation against his will. The desires of some people to fight wars, or the opinions of some people that the draft is necessary to protect the country, are not sufficient grounds for violating the human rights of free individuals. If one were to adhere to Natural Law, the only way in which the people of a nation could rightfully provide for a so-called national defense would be through the voluntary financial support of an all-volunteer army.

The bodies of millions of innocent men and women that lie in military cemeteries throughout the world serve as a monument to the real-life meaning of promoting the general welfare. If government must make laws, it should pass a law requiring that all congresspeople who are in favor of war lead the charge on the front lines.

It goes without saying that everything I have said here is true for any and all kinds of involuntary public service. A truly free person cannot be forced to do anything against his will. A politician's moral opinions as to what is and is not a worthy cause are irrelevant in the matter. Natural Law negates the use of force against anyone who is not committing aggression against others.

Compulsory Education

Many of us remember the case of John Singer, a Utah man determined to demonstrate that government had no right to force him to relinquish his children to its authorities. After a long legal battle, the government eliminated any doubt about its willingness to use force, when necessary, to make it clear to everyone that the lives of all people belong to the state. On January 18, 1979, Singer was killed by government lawmen on his own property. At the time, he was armed in a last-resort preparation to defend his natural rights.

All Mr. Singer wanted was to educate his children his own way, without interference from the state, contending that he had a "God-given right to bring up his family the way he wanted." He did not feel that his children were getting the kind of religious and practical education he desired for them.

In addition to the immorality of government's claiming to own your child, compulsory education has been a disaster from the standpoint of results. Many children who might be better suited to learning a trade are forced to attend public schools, which explains why such a high percentage of high-school graduates are functionally illiterate. When a person is compelled to learn something, his mind tends to block it out. You can use physical force on people, but, as slave owners in early America discovered, you cannot force them to absorb information.

Finally, there is the false notion that formal schooling is necessary for a person to be educated. Not so. A child learns when he plays, when his parents and others talk to him, and from everything he does in life. As he gets older, he learns through reading, his job, and conversations with others. I personally consider my formal schooling to have amounted to only a small fraction of my education. Karl Hess, legendary libertarian speechwriter for Barry Goldwater, once said that he loved learning, which is precisely why he so disliked public education.

Obviously, one of the reasons government insists on educating your child is so he will grow up learning history, philosophy, and government itself from government's point of view.

Affirmative Action

I have yet to hear anyone categorize violations of so-called affirmative-action laws as victimless crimes, but they most definitely are. These laws are but another case of government's applying force to a situation of personal choice.

Supposedly free individuals are told that if they do not hire people whom the government says they must, they will be punished. Although one tends to think of affirmative action as an anachronism, the sad reality is that the practice is still alive and well in both the business world and academia. Not only does affirmative action infringe on the freedom of employers and college administrators, but it also creates another victim—the person who loses out on a job or college admission as a result. Again, the only victims in this type of victimless crime are those created by government force.

While many people, particularly in government, would like to make the affirmative-action issue one that pertains primarily to blacks, the fact is that it is a people issue. Racism is not discrimination against any specific minority. It is discrimination against anyone. And the quota system—which has come to be known as *reverse discrimination*—is one of the most frustrating forms of discrimination.

Thomas Sowell gave part of the answer to this problem in an article he wrote in *Commentary*:

> *. . . supporters of numerical policies have the powerful drive of self-interest as well as self-righteousness. Bureaucratic empires have grown up to administer these programs. . . . The rulers and agents of this empire can order employers around, make college presidents bow and scrape, assign schoolteachers by race, or otherwise gain power, publicity, and career advancement—regardless of whether minorities are benefited or not.*

In other words, blacks have been used as political pawns in the affirmative-action scam. It is just another appeal to people's expediency factors. Libertarian writer Anne Wortham, an African-American, makes no qualms about it when she says, "It is plainly not in the interest of black leaders and the State that blacks become individualistic, no more than it was in the interest of slaveholders that slaves learn to read and write." In other words, if politicians and other progressive leaders were to lose the black-versus-white issue, it would not be in their best interest.

Affirmative-action laws not only are victimless-crime laws, and therefore immoral, but they also do not achieve their purported objectives.

They do, however, achieve two other results: They create resentment and negative feelings between blacks and whites, and they discourage blacks from self-reliance. Ms. Wortham, who grew up in a segregated social system in Tennessee, also states:

> *During the first 20 years of my life . . . the federal government made five major advances in behalf of the civil rights of blacks. . . . With the possible exception of the right to vote, not one of these policies or the programs derived from them had any effect on my everyday life in segregated Tennessee. . . . Had my personal liberation and individuation depended on the knowledge that the State was in the process of increasing my civil liberty, I would have embarked on the road to adult maturity with no self-identity, self-respect, self-interest, self-sufficiency or self-initiative. . . . I would not be the person I am; I would not be such a passionate defender of human individuality and the philosophy of individualism.*

A Rand Institute study supported the conclusions of black individualists like Ms. Wortham and Professor Sowell, noting, among other things, that "our results suggest that the effect of government on the aggregate black-white wage ratio is quite small and that the popular notion that . . . recent changes are being driven by government pressure has little empirical support."

What, then, is it that has allowed blacks to make important civil-rights advances? Primarily, it has been the positive actions of blacks themselves, particularly black leaders who have encouraged self-reliance. In truth, government force regarding such programs as affirmative action and busing has created resentment and backlash, actually retarding the cause of African-Americans.

One of the most shining examples of what can be accomplished through peaceful means was the movement led by Martin Luther King, Jr., in the 1960s. King not only gave millions of blacks a new feeling of self-esteem, but, just as important, was successful in raising the consciousness of millions of whites to the injustices that blacks had endured over the years. While King's movement, in some instances, may indirectly have led to unwarranted forcible interference on the part of government, the real gains for blacks, as pointed out by Ms. Wortham and Professor Sowell, came as a result of their new feeling of pride and the emotional commitment on the part of millions of whites.

What is particularly insulting to blacks is that the quota system implies that most African-Americans lack talent. Minority-group members, like everyone else, want respect—particularly self-respect—which is not achieved by being given special treatment for jobs and college admissions through government force. Says Professor Sowell:

> *The message that comes through loud and clear is that minorities are losers who will never have anything unless someone gives it to them. The destructiveness of this message—on society in general and minority youth in particular—outweighs any trivial gains that may occur here and there. . . . By and large, the numerical approach has achieved nothing, and has achieved it at great cost.*

Many black leaders make a grave mistake by calling for laws to force people to act against their wills. Some of them thoughtlessly accuse people of being racists if they are not in favor of affirmative action. But, in reality, it is they who advocate racism by calling for a clear distinction among blacks, whites, Mexican-Americans, and other racial and ethnic groups, and by favoring special treatment for some people at the expense of the human rights of others. The fact that their ancestors were victims of slavery makes it ironic that they should wish to see others forced to act against their will.

Affirmative action is morally wrong on at least three counts:

1. No employer should be forced to hire anyone who is either not qualified for a job or not as qualified as another applicant, because such force is to the detriment of the employer's business.

2. Innocent people should not be made to pay for the wrongs of others. The mainstay argument behind affirmative action is that because blacks were treated unfairly in the past, society now must compensate new generations of blacks for that treatment. But how can people living today arbitrarily be held liable for the wrongdoings of people in the past? By the same token, why should members of a minority group receive special treatment today because other people were victims of discrimination in the past? Notes Professor Sowell:

   > *The past is a great unchangeable fact. Nothing is going to undo its sufferings and injustices, whatever their magnitude. . . . Neither the sins nor the sufferings of those now dead are within our power to change. Being honest and honorable with the people living in our own time is more than enough moral challenge, without indulging in illusions about rewriting moral history with numbers and categories.*

3. But the most important reason that affirmative action is immoral is that it defies Natural Law. The owner of a business, whether black

or white, has the right to hire and fire whomever he pleases, without having to account for his actions to anyone, simply because it is his business. When a person is not free to do as he pleases with his own property, in this case his business, his liberty has been violated. It would be an unavoidable contradiction to refer to such a person as free.

Milton Mueller, in an article in *The Libertarian Review*, put the affirmative-action issue in proper perspective, noting that "affirmative action is the last gasp of a crumbling economic system." Mueller went on to say that:

> . . . *if special exceptions and special laws are necessary to bulldoze minorities into the system, then something is clearly wrong with the system. If the regulations that burden the economy are so intrinsically racist that quotas are the only way to get minorities in, then something is wrong with the regulations. . . . A government-controlled economy is a static economy—the people on the bottom stay there. If the energies of a free, unrestricted economy are released, if the roadblocks are blown away, then minorities—and the rest of society—can advance.*

Eminent Domain

Back to the question of property rights once again. If the government decides it wants your property, all other considerations are irrelevant— including the number of years you have owned your home or land, the emotional value it may have to you, and even what you believe it to be worth.

When the government takes your property, it pays you a price that it deems to be fair, but that does not change the fact that your rights have been violated. If someone comes up to you on the street and demands your watch, then pays you what he deems to be a fair price in return, such payment does not change the fact that a theft has occurred.

As with all other victimless-crime laws, however, you will be arrested and punished if you refuse to do as you are told by authorities—in this case, sell them your property. And if you try to defend your property, you will either end up in jail or lose your life in the process.

History is filled with cases like that of Stephen E. Anthony, who refused to give up his half of a house to the government. Local politicians wanted to make room for a Hollywood film museum on his property. Anthony, who protected his property at gunpoint, eventually was arrested and put in jail for six months. A few months after his house was razed, the museum project was abandoned and the site of his former home became a parking lot. Here again, the only victim in this victimless crime was the person victimized by the government itself—for refusing to give up what was rightfully his.

Seat Belts, Helmets, and Other Protective Devices

However wrong you or I may believe them to be, many people do not want to wear seat belts and therefore do not want to pay for them when purchasing a new car. Government, however, does not give the public an option on this extra. Everyone must pay for seat belts even if they never use them.

Helmets and all other mandatory safety devices involve the same type of control over people. They force individuals to do what others believe to be in their best interests, even if they do not agree. Many motorcycle riders, for example, feel that helmets cause accidents by obstructing peripheral vision. But the motorcyclist is no different than anyone else: The government owns his life.

Because of their desire to capture the votes of consumer-safety advocates, helmet manufacturers, and anyone else who may be in favor of the compulsory use of safety devices, politicians feel obliged to burden citizens with the cost and inconvenience of expensive equipment "for their own good."

Prohibitive Victimless-Crime Laws

Prohibitive victimless-crime laws are those that make it illegal for you to do certain things that you may want to do. The same basic principle applies here as with compulsory victimless-crime laws (i.e., government prohibits your acting according to your will). Like compulsory victimless-crime laws, prohibitive victimless-crime laws involve external control and are therefore a form of involuntary servitude. Following are some examples.

Gun Control

Through the years, there has been a great deal of heated debate over so-called gun-control legislation. All arguments that favor gun control are invalid on the basis of logic, fact, and morality, and even those who are against gun control usually miss the real issue: freedom.

A person has a right to own a gun for the same reason that he has a right to own anything. The corollary to this is that the government has no right to forbid anyone to own a gun, for the same reason it has no right to forbid anyone to own *any* item. Gun control, therefore, is a misnomer. When politicians talk about gun control, they really are talking about people control.

Those who insisted on the Second Amendment to the Constitution— "the right of the people to keep and bear arms"— had important reasons for wanting this protection. Having been tyrannized by the government of Great Britain, they saw the right to bear arms as not only a means of protecting one's life and property from other citizens, but also a last resort of defense against an oppressive government. That is precisely why it is in the best interest of today's government to disarm the population. It has cleverly masked this violation of a Constitutional and natural right by appealing to the emotions of a fearful public.

Owning guns has nothing to do with crime. If anything, it has to do with preventing crime. Notwithstanding their continual efforts to build a case against gun ownership, government legislators have failed in their attempts to show that gun control lowers crime rates. On the contrary, the results of numerous studies have shown the opposite to be true.

The old slogan "if guns are outlawed, only outlaws will have them," is all too true. Today, it is illegal for most private citizens to carry concealed weapons; thus, millions of law-abiding people walk around unarmed. At the same time, criminals in every city in America are walking the streets carrying concealed weapons. In other words, gun-control laws have the very real effect of giving criminals an advantage over non-criminals.

The view of government toward a citizen is that of a parent toward a child: "You mustn't carry guns because you might accidentally hurt yourself or others." The assumption is that just because something can be used to harm someone, it will be used for that purpose.

Approximately 8,000 people a year are killed by handguns in the United States, and, to be sure, each of these deaths is a tragedy. Nevertheless, this is only about 20 percent of the number of people killed every year by automobiles. Yet, the large number of automobile deaths is not sufficient cause to deny sensible, responsible individuals the use of automobiles. Should not the same logic be applied to guns? Just because some people use guns negligently or for criminal purposes is no reason to deny responsible, law-abiding people the right to own them.

Guns are a form of self-defense, and by removing a tool of self-defense from an individual, government not only violates his rights, but also endangers his life. A gun is an individual's ultimate means of preserving his freedom. It may well be that there is a direct connection between government's stepped-up efforts to eliminate private ownership of guns at a time when government itself is increasingly guilty of violating human rights.

As Morgan Norval put it in an article in *Reason* magazine: "'Order' may be the excuse; 'law' may be the argument; 'keeping someone else in his place' may be the emotional rationale; 'supporting the police' may be the civic slogan; 'ending violence' may be the dream—but the nightmare of reality is total tyranny of the state."

The right to bear arms should be defended to the bitter end. Because in the bitter end, as the American Revolutionists discovered, it may very well get down to a matter of whether people have arms.

Zoning

Remember, one of the true tests of ownership is whether you can do any-thing you want with your own property. If you have to get government's permission to build the house of your choice, or to do remodeling, or put up a fence, how can you be called the owner of your property in the truest sense of the word?

Aside from the moral implication of others telling you what you can and cannot do with something you own, the whole concept of zoning is based on the mythical vision of an avaricious entrepreneur building a slaughterhouse adjacent to someone's $250,000 home.

Common sense is in order here. For obvious economic reasons, this would never occur. Why would someone want to pay an enormous price for residential land to build a slaughterhouse when he could choose an industrial location at a fraction of the cost? Land prices negate the practical need for zoning laws. The beautiful city of Houston, with virtually no zon-ing laws, is living proof of why such laws are an unnecessary intrusion of privacy.

Usury

The major effect of usury laws is somewhat analogous to the effect of minimum-wage laws. Minimum-wage laws force people to be unemployed; usury laws force people out of business. Because some voters believe that usury (i.e., interest rates they deem to be too high) is immoral, poli-ticians have burdened the public with yet another nuisance. They must protect the innocent citizen from being victimized by unscrupulous lenders—with the exception, of course, of their banking pals in the credit card business who are allowed to rape and pillage at will.

Gambling

Many voters consider gambling sinful, which gives politicians yet another opportunity to preach about public morals. Gambling, of course, puts government in a hypocritical position, because it does allow selected entities—who give government a cut of the take—to conduct gambling operations.

Horse racing is licensed in most states, but only to privileged operators. This licensing arrangement contributes enormous revenues to state-government coffers. And, of course, state-run lotteries, which suck billions of dollars from those who can least afford to lose their money, are the ultimate government hypocrisy.

The implication is that gambling is immoral unless government is involved. Because every person who gambles loses money in the long run (and, usually, in the short run), I guess the reasoning is that citizens are protected so long as the government is the one who ends up with their money. Interesting logic.

Pornography

This is a tough one for libertarian-centered conservatives. Exactly what constitutes pornography is subjective, which is why a liberty advocate must question why government should involve itself in this area. The libertarian approach here (though not the approach of most hardcore conservatives) is the same as with all victimless crimes, and was best expressed by Murray Rothbard:

> *The good, bad, or indifferent consequences of pornography, while perhaps an interesting problem in its own right, is completely irrelevant to the question of whether or not it should be outlawed. . . . It is not the business of the law . . . to make anyone good or reverent or moral or clean or upright.*

Nevertheless, as I said earlier, common sense must prevail in the area of pornography. Civilization cannot exist without a generally accepted code of conduct. The harsh reality is that the United States has devolved into a moral cesspool—one of the many unpleasant results of progressive relativism—so I believe that ongoing, rational debate is called for in this area. There is no reason why people of goodwill, on both sides of this issue, cannot keep a healthy balance between liberty and restraint, always striving, of course, to err on the side of liberty.

Sexual Behavior

Government interference in the sexual behavior of consenting adults is one of the most flagrant violations of individual liberty. The idea of the government having a right to say what goes on in your bedroom should give even the most apathetic individual cause for concern.

To argue for the rights of people to engage voluntarily in sexual acts of their choosing dignifies the incredible gall of absolute moralists who believe they should have a say-so in the most private affairs of others. Anyone who believes in personal freedom would be on shaky ground trying to argue that the sexual conduct of consenting adults is in any way the government's business. Big Brother has no place in the regulation of *any* kind of private conduct—period.

Drugs

Another tough issue for libertarian-centered conservatives to face up to is the legalization of drugs. In fact, probably no other promoting-the-general-welfare function of government causes so many innocent people (including nonusers of drugs) so many problems. As happens with virtually all outlawed products and services, government, by prohibiting the use of certain drugs, creates a black market for them.

As soon as something is outlawed, criminal elements will gladly jump in and provide the illegal product or service at substantially increased prices. The higher prices are due not only to the scarcity of the product or service, but also the seller's need to be compensated for the government-created risks involved. These higher prices motivate some consumers of such products and services, particularly drugs, to commit crimes against innocent people to raise the money needed to obtain them.

Aside from the fundamental issue that it is not the government's business to run around protecting people from hurting themselves, as with pornography, harmful drugs cannot be conclusively defined. Marijuana is outlawed in most states, though many experts believe it to be relatively harmless—even medically helpful to some. Yet, people can consume all the caffeine they want, even though it is a drug considered extremely harmful by many doctors.

Alcohol is another substance that is much more harmful than many others that have been outlawed, and, indeed, government once spent billions of dollars of taxpayers' money in a vain effort to stop people from consuming it. The result, of course, was that people drank more during Prohibition than at any other time in U.S. history.

Now people are free to put as much alcohol as they want into their bodies, and some may even consume so much that they virtually kill themselves in the process. But the reality is that people also kill themselves by consuming too much cholesterol. Does this mean that the government should outlaw foods containing cholesterol? Don't laugh. It's precisely the kind of thing that the power-holding progressives are discussing today in Washington. Where does it end?

I have no personal ax to grind regarding any of these substances, because I'm not even an occasional social drinker and have never taken so much as a puff of marijuana. These are products that happen not to be of interest to me. But, just as I do not go running to the government over the quality of television programming, neither do I insist that government stop others from harming themselves by the use of certain substances.

Being against restrictions on the use of drugs does not mean that one approves of the use of cocaine, heroin, or any other substance. On the contrary, I consider it unwise and unhealthy to use such substances indiscriminately. But the fact is that their use is not a political matter; it is a private matter.

Who would protect children from the harmful use of drugs in a free society? The same people who are supposed to protect them from touching a hot stove or getting run over by a car: parents.

The only thing we know for certain about the outlawing of drugs is that government does a very poor job of it. The fact is that the finest work done in the area of drug rehabilitation has been accomplished, as one would expect, by private charitable organizations. Individuals can solve problems just fine if left alone to do so on a non-coercive basis.

It's time for politicians to get out of our private lives, get off our backs, and let us fend for ourselves. Self-responsibility was once an integral part of the American Dream.

Smoking

Most of the same points made about antidrug laws are equally valid for antismoking laws. There is, however, one additional twist to antismoking laws: Some nonsmokers claim they do not care if others smoke, so long as they do not do it in a public place.

The problem here is the latitude people use in defining the term *public place*. A restaurant is one commonly used example, yet a restaurant is a privately owned establishment. As such, its owner should have the sole right to decide whether to allow people to smoke on his premises. If he chooses to allow smoking, and a nonsmoker (like me) is bothered by the smoking, the nonsmoker can take immediate, non-coercive steps to do something about it—on his own—by simply not frequenting that restaurant in the future.

On the other hand, if the owner does not allow smoking, a smoker can either refrain or take his business elsewhere. There is no need for the heavy hand of government to become involved. Free individuals can settle differences by respecting each other's rights—especially property rights.

The U.S. Surgeon General may believe that smoking is dangerous to your health, and government can even force tobacco manufacturers to put warning statements on cigarette packs, but apparently millions of people still prefer to make their own decisions regarding their own well-being.

Should antismoking crusaders ever succeed in getting smoking out-lawed, look for organized crime to set up an elaborate black market in cigarettes that will pretty much mirror the days of Prohibition and illegal drug use. Smokers will continue to smoke; you can be sure of that. The only question is whether smoking will be controlled by private industry or organized crime.

Privacy: Lost Forever?

As is true of the first two government functions, the aggression couched under the benevolent guise of promoting the general welfare continues to grow each year. Over the past several decades, people have become ever more complacent, accepting government interference in their lives as normal. And the new socialist regime in Washington has made it clear that its goal is to secure complete control over every citizen's life.

I don't believe that this is what our Founding Fathers had in mind when they threw out those oppressive rascals from England. In fact, they had just the opposite of government function number three in mind when they signed the Declaration of Independence.

Can these violations of freedom be stopped? Not unless a majority of Americans are willing to spend the time to learn the Constitution and work with others to organize mass protests. So long as millions of citizens play into the government's hands and demand that their expedient moral desires be met, the number of victimless-crime laws—under the mask of promoting the general welfare—will continue to increase, along with the invasion of privacy, which will result in a decrease in freedom.

Since the fateful presidential election of 2008, far from stemming the tide of this coercive government function, it appears that things are now moving at mach speed in the direction of more government control over our lives—all, of course, under the guise of promoting the general welfare.

CHAPTER 7

How the Bill Is Paid

Finally, it comes time to pay the bill. The government functions created by the calamitous combination of expediency factors and the vote now represent an annual deficit in the area of $2 trillion and long-term, unfunded liabilities of more than $100 trillion. (The truth is that no one knows the exact amount because there are so many variables that it's impossible to calculate precisely.)

It turns out, then, that government's overall objective to help people fulfill their desires is just a bit on the expensive side—and getting more so each year. Because governments have no way of producing wealth, such generosity must be paid for with wealth produced by others. Governments, as previously noted, exist off the surplus wealth of citizens, which necessitates violating the rights of those who do produce wealth. This comes about through a well-structured process of expropriation of assets.

This process, referred to for thousands of years as *taxation*, presents a philosophical dilemma for millions of well-meaning citizens. It is instructive to note that one dictionary definition of a *tax* is "a heavy demand; a burden; a compulsory payment of a percentage of income . . . or the support of a government." All this sounds rather unpleasant, but the real heart of the matter, and what causes the philosophical dilemma, is the word *compulsory*.

If something is compulsory, it means you are forced to do it. And the use of force is a violation of Natural Law, because it means aggressing on the natural rights of individuals. While one may believe, however irrationally, that the end (that for which taxes are used) justifies the means (taxation), it does not change the fact that taxation is an act of aggression.

The philosophical question then becomes one of morality. And that takes us back to the early part of this book and Natural Law: Personal integrity demands that one's belief in Natural Law not be betrayed on an emotional whim. Just as all government functions we have discussed violate human rights, so, too, does the means of paying for these functions.

No matter how much good certain people may believe is accomplished with money collected through taxation, the good can never negate the immorality of using force against people who are not harming anyone. You cannot change the nature of taxation simply by explaining that it is a patriotic means of raising revenue.

To argue that government gives people services in return for the money it expropriates from them is, of course, irrelevant for the same reason explained in conjunction with eminent domain in the previous chapter. If someone takes your money at gunpoint in an alley, but gives you something in return that you either do not want or did not bargain for, it does not make him any less of a criminal.

Of course, street robbers never give you back anything in return, which is somewhat of an advantage over government. When a thief puts a gun to your head in an alley and says, "Your money or your life," he does not pretend, like the government, to be doing anything but robbing you. He does not claim to be your protector or offer you services you did not ask for and do not want. He goes away and leaves you alone. He does not insist on protecting you or demand that you be loyal to him. He does not try to impose his moral standards on you or forbid you to do anything. If you do not obey him, he does not call you unpatriotic or apathetic.

One of the emotional arguments of the patriot is to insist that the government does not go around sticking guns in the ribs of taxpayers. And he's right. That's because most people either have been conditioned to accept taxation as a way of life or realize it is futile to resist. Therefore, there is no need for the use of guns.

If, however, you suffer from the delusion that the government will not use guns to force you to hand over what it deems to be your fair share of the bill, try defending your assets to the absolute end. By *absolute end*, I mean using literal self-defense to protect your assets.

If you refuse to pay, you will receive notices at first, which will get progressively more threatening if you do not respond. Assuming you do not have property on which the Internal Revenue Service (IRS) can file a lien (which is, in itself, an act of aggression), the IRS ultimately will pay you a visit. If you refuse to talk with the IRS agents when they appear at your door, they will obtain a court order for your arrest. And that in turn will bring people with guns to your front door. If you try to use physical force to defend yourself against such aggression, these men will—if necessary—kill you, just as they killed John Singer, who tried to defend his right to educate his children.

Never deceive yourself about the gun power that stands behind taxation. Were it not there, governments would be powerless to continue taxing their subjects. Of course, because the physical force behind taxation was established long ago, it rarely needs to be used—or even discussed. Instead, politicians can concentrate on dressing up taxation's image by inundating citizens with slogans like "pay your fair share."

The person who believes it is patriotic to pay taxes (Joe Biden, for example) either has forgotten the American Dream or is too young to have experienced it. The American Dream was not about government's taking huge sums of money from citizens by force. The American Dream was not about government's "using all its power and resources to meet new social problems with new social controls."

The American Dream was about people, not government. It was about people who, for the first time in history, declared that they were *above* government. It was about individualism and the opportunity to achieve success without interference from others. Most of all, the American Dream was about freedom.

On the contrary, the last thing in the world that the American Dream was about was taxation.

Who Pays How Much?

When the Sixteenth Amendment to the Constitution became law in 1913, an important step was taken in laying the groundwork for the destruction of the spirit that had made America the freest, strongest, and most prosperous country in history. We need not go into the technical aspects here except to point out that the power holders of that day arbitrarily decided to take away a right guaranteed by the Constitution.

The key element in the Sixteenth Amendment was that it gave government the power, for the first time, to levy taxes against incomes. Just as important, it left the interpretation of the word *income* up to the courts, which meant from that point on the rules could be changed at the discretion of the government.

As taxes mounted and the something-for-nothing attitude of the 1920s began to destroy productivity, the Great Depression befell America. That, in turn, brought us Franklin D. Roosevelt, who took the next giant step in helping to destroy the American Dream. This was accomplished through implementation of his politically expedient soak-the-rich policy of taxation. The result of this policy was the birth of the anything-goes attitude so prevalent in our society today, as well as the economically destructive idea of cradle-to-grave security.

Lyndon Johnson put the final cornerstone of the FDR philosophy in place, assuring us that we could have guns, butter, and anything else we desired—without having to work for them. How could we resist? At long last, the American Dream had been replaced by the Great Society Nightmare.

Like Roosevelt, Johnson did not live to have to face today's taxpayers. And very few Americans understood that they, not Roosevelt or Johnson, were going to have to pay the bill some day. In fact, only a handful of the most economically sophisticated individuals realized that a bill was even accumulating. After all, no one had bothered to tell them. Now, as the expediency factors of irate voters motivate them to scramble for an ever-larger share of government largesse to keep up with their neighbors, government expenditures at the federal, state, and local level continue to rise faster than ever, notwithstanding the threat of complete economic collapse.

Today, though politicians still love to preach about the injustices of our tax system, the fact is that the top 1 percent of taxpayers pay about the same amount of federal individual income taxes as the bottom 95 percent.

Income taxes, of course, are only part of the story. The wild scramble among politicians and voters to increase government functions would be impossible to sustain through income taxes alone—particularly because the payment would be too visible to voters. So, along the way, government has thought up a few other methods by which to tax people, many of them very subtle and thus not apparent to voters.

Some of these other methods include excise taxes, sales taxes, amusement taxes, gasoline taxes, liquor taxes, cigarette taxes, real estate taxes, Social Security taxes, inventory taxes, capital gains taxes, inheritance taxes, corporate income taxes, excess-profits taxes, gift taxes, and estate taxes.

Then there are the *very* subtle taxes. A tariff is just one example. When you buy an imported product, you indirectly reimburse the exporter of the product for the tariff (tax) he was forced to pay on it.

An even more subtle tax is the free labor contributed by every taxpayer in complying with government tax forms and, in the case of employers, extracting taxes from employees on behalf of the government. In the original edition of this book, I pointed out that the U.S. Controller's office estimated that it took about 613 million man-hours a year to comply with its requirements for recording and reporting tax information. Today, thirty years later, that figure has grown to more than 3 trillion man-hours! It might be appropriate to call it a hidden slave-labor tax.

In discussing who pays for Washington's irresponsible spending sprees, it is important to point out one other reality: Business taxes (including the cost of complying with tax forms and filing) are, for the most part, paid for by consumers. Businesses merely pass along tax increases to consumers in the form of higher prices—and for good reason: If they did not do so, they would soon go broke. Business taxes are a great scheme for politicians because they are really hidden consumer taxes. As a result, the average person blames greedy businesspeople for increasing prices, not realizing that those prices carry a hidden tax on him.

All these subtle and hidden taxes are impossible to calculate, so no one can be certain just how much any given individual is paying to support government functions. But there are enough data available to give you at least a rough idea of where you stand. The average American worker pays about 45 percent of his income in direct taxes of various kinds and works until well into May each year for the government—or approximately one-half of his working life—without compensation.

No matter what one's opinions regarding the necessity of government functions, how can 20 years of labor without pay be called anything but slavery?

Protecting Your Assets

Is there any way to stop economy-killing, job-destroying taxes? With the massive budget deficits now in place in Washington, the outlook for putting an end to confiscatory taxation is grim.

That said, while it is true that you have a moral right to protect the fruits of your labor from confiscation, prudence dictates that tax evasion is an unwise move. The question here is not one of morality, but of practicality. The IRS does not hesitate to check private records (such as bank accounts), search offices, threaten, and, ultimately, institute physical force, if necessary.

Though the entire system of taxation is an extreme transgression of human rights, I would strongly advise anyone against resorting to so-called tax evasion (i.e., trying to protect the government from taking your assets). Tax evasion is particularly dangerous for high-income earners because the IRS monitors such people more closely than most.

It goes without saying, however, that one is morally obligated to himself and his family to use every available legal method to avoid paying more taxes than necessary. Notwithstanding Joe Biden's ignorant statement to the contrary, you are not unpatriotic for paying the minimum amount of tax legally required of you. You have every right to protect as much of your earnings as possible by taking advantage of all legal deductions.

In our upside-down culture, where giving up a substantial portion of your income has come to be accepted as a moral act, people are often chastised for using a loophole or receiving a windfall when they protect their assets by playing by the very rules created by the government. Again, however, tax evasion, as defined by the IRS, is an unwise course of action.

Had the average American taxpayer read the works of Lysander Spooner, perhaps he might have thought twice before being so trusting. Said Spooner, "Whoever desires liberty should understand . . . that every man who puts money into the hands of a 'government' (so called), puts into its hands a sword which will be used against himself, to extort more money from him."

Observing the effects of tax cuts over the years has led me to coin a hypothesis I refer to as the Tax-Cut Illusion Theory, which states: All tax cuts are illusions. There is no such thing as a tax cut; there is only a change in the manner in which money is extracted from taxpayers.

All tax cuts turn out to be illusions based on the realities of the system, as discussed in Chapter 2: The government needs more money each year to keep up with its expedient promises to give more of everything to everyone without their having to work for it.

I should also mention here a type of tax rebellion that is the most commonly practiced, though most of those who engage in it are not consciously aware of it. It is also the method most destructive to our economy. I refer to it as the loss-of-incentive tax revolt. As taxes become an ever-increasing burden on producers, they lose incentive. They opt to produce less and enjoy life more. And when a person lowers his ambitions, he lowers his income, which lowers government revenues. This is the taxpayer's last-resort for keeping government confiscation to a minimum. Short of the institution of a police state, government has no way of making people work harder or longer hours.

This increasing phenomenon in the United States can be viewed in its more advanced stage in socialist countries such as Sweden and France. Swedes commonly refuse promotions, but take more vacation time. Why? Because taking vacations and enjoying life are not taxable.

This latter type of tax revolt is devastating to the economy not only because an increasing number of people produce less, but also it prompts government to increase taxes on those who continue to produce. Back to the drawing board: Higher taxes mean lower profits and/or higher prices, which decreases demand, which decreases production, which decreases employment, and so on. Since the 1980s, we have commonly referred to this phenomenon as "The Laffer Curve" (so named after supply-side economist Arthur Laffer), but regardless of what you call it, the laws of economics never change.

Plain and simple, the libertarian-centered conservative believes that taxation is a violation of property rights, which means a violation of human rights. Politicians love to prate on about tax abuses, and I agree with them. Taxes *are* an abuse, which is why the tax structure should be dramatically revised (perhaps a flat tax or fair tax?) and lowered.

The Red-Ink Sea

Believe it or not, if the taxation just described were our only problem, we might make it. We still would not be a totally free people, but we probably could continue stumbling along with remnants of the American Dream to sustain us. Unfortunately, however, taxation is not the only problem when it comes to paying the bill. It is not even the worst problem.

A far greater problem is that government not only refuses to make serious cuts in its benefits programs, but with the stranglehold progressives now have on both the legislative and executive branches, taxes cannot hope to keep up with spending. The wealthiest Americans already pay most of the taxes, and too heavy a tax burden on the middle and lower classes would cause a revolt—especially because our illustrious president has already made it crystal clear that he will never raise taxes on anyone making under $250,000.

The result is a massive sea of what accountants refer to as *red ink* (i.e., deficits). A deficit, plain and simple, means that an individual's income is less than his expenses. If such an individual continues to run up expenses in excess of his income, he is guilty of a practice known as *deficit spending.* Everyone I know who has tried it has gone out of business. But this does not deter government. Why? Because deficit spending is a way for politicians to support programs that are popular with voters—without raising taxes.

Deficit spending has always been used by politicians, but usually with some degree of discretion (perhaps *sanity* would be a more appropriate word). As previously noted, however, Lyndon Johnson got carried away with his delusions of a "great society"—a society so great that it could spend $200 billion on a no-win war in Vietnam, feed the poor at home, and satisfy the expedient desires of virtually everyone in America, all without producing anywhere near an equivalent amount of wealth. Johnson started the momentum of a new era of pre-election deficit spending the Founding Fathers could never have imagined.

I use the term *pre-election deficit spending* because initially it was a scheme designed to ensure reelection for an incumbent president. Deficit spending has the short-term effect of stimulating the economy, which makes the reigning administration look good. But it's an illusion. What people actually experience from deficit spending is false prosperity. They do not understand that the goodies they receive have not been paid for (i.e., that they have unknowingly accepted goods and services on credit).

As Morgan Maxfield said in *1929 Revisited,* Johnson started the ball rolling with an unprecedented pre-election 1967–1968 deficit of $34 billion. After a $.4 billion surplus in 1969–1970 (post-election years), Richard Nixon went all out in the pre-election years 1971–1972 with a $46 billion deficit. By that time, people had already gotten hooked on false prosperity and did not want to hear about economic realities.

As a result, even in the post-election years 1973–1974, the deficit was $17.8 billion. Even so, expediency-minded voters screamed bloody murder at the new president, Gerald Ford. How dare he cut back on handouts?

So Ford, the theretofore fiscally conservative politician, let loose with a pre-election spending barrage in 1975–1976 that just about sealed our fate—an unheard-of $110 billion.

With this record-breaking injection of false prosperity, deficit spending had developed into an incurable disease. What started out as a pre-election-year scheme had become a year-in, year-out political necessity. Americans were addicted. They needed their fixes on a regular basis. As a result, Carter came right out of the starting gate in 1977–1978, topping even Ford's pre-election effort by running up another record-high deficit of $118 billion. And it now appears as though few politicians have the courage to seriously challenge the desires of the heavyweight spending champion of the world, Barack Hussein Obama.

Obviously, no entity can continue in business indefinitely without paying its debts. So how does government cover these massive deficits? They cannot be paid through direct taxation because voters already are rebelling against onerous taxes. Thus, government is left with only two ways to cover the trillions of dollars in deficit spending that the progressives have already set in motion.

Ponzi Scheme II

Earlier, I pointed out that the Social Security system is but a sophisticated version of the so-called Ponzi scheme. But in addition to Social Security, government also employs the Ponzi scheme to cover its deficit spending. The U.S. Treasury sells securities (usually in the form of bonds) to raise as much capital as possible to offset each year's deficits. There is no plan whatsoever to pay off these securities, other than through the sale of new securities. In the meantime, the interest obligations (particularly to China) keep rising, so it does not take a degree in advanced mathematics to figure out that at some point in time the interest payments alone will exceed the total wealth-producing capacity of all U.S. citizens and businesses combined.

On top of all this, there is a side effect to this Ponzi scheme that hastens the economic day of judgment for the United States. When the government sells bonds to the public, it drains funds from the capital markets. Much of this money would have been used to finance new plants, equipment, and research and development. Thus, the effect of government borrowing on the economy is that it removes the lifeblood (capital) that is essential for production and employment.

The figures here, too, are astounding. Between 1946 and 1966, the government was borrowing an average of a little over one-half of 1 percent of the funds available in the capital market, or about $500 million a year. By 1975–1976, the government was draining about 150 times as much from the capital markets—38 percent, or about $74 billion a year. Now, with U.S. deficits projected to be in the area of $10 trillion over the next ten years, it will be impossible to sell enough new bonds to pay off old ones—not to mention paying the annual interest obligations on the national debt. But, even worse, increasing government bond sales will prevent the economy from producing the wealth necessary to avoid a total financial collapse.

I hope all this has not upset you to the point where you can't take any more bad news. Because, hard as it may be for you to believe, the worst is yet to come. The government is not able to sell all the bonds it would like to sell in the open market, so it still comes up short on cash. That's right, even after exhausting the capital markets, the government does not raise enough money to cover its massive deficit spending.

Of course, Congress and the president could choose to end the policy of deficit spending (i.e., stop spending more money than it can raise through taxation and borrowing), but it's far too late for that. The expedient desires of politicians to stay in office and the expediency factors of more than 300 million Americans have hooked up to form an economic weapon of mass destruction. The charade of false prosperity must go on, regardless of the long-term consequences.

After taxing and borrowing to the maximum of its capacity, there is only one place left for politicians to turn to cover the remainder of government's unpaid bills: the printing presses.

The Inflation Swindle

The remaining portion of the federal deficit each year is paid for by a process that sounds like it's right out of Aesop's Fables: Government simply prints up pieces of paper and uses them as money! But that's getting ahead of the story. To understand the mechanics of this sinister act, and to be fully aware of what this fairy-tale approach to monetary policy really means, it is first necessary to explain some basics.

At the outset of this book, I said that I could not resist the challenge to reduce the truths about big government to components simple enough to be easily understood by virtually everyone. And inflation is the one government scheme, above all others, that must be demystified if the American Dream is to be restored. Unfortunately, a significant percentage (probably a majority) of the population has almost no understanding of what inflation really is and what causes it.

It is my sincere belief that if a majority of citizens in this country do not soon understand the truth about inflation (which is virtually the opposite of what most people have been led to believe through government propaganda), our country will, in the near future, experience a total financial collapse, which in turn will result in the loss of most, if not all, of our remaining freedoms.

No one can predict the exact timing of such a collapse because government has the power, unlike a normal bankrupt business, to institute one illegal measure after another to postpone the day of reckoning. That is precisely what it has been doing for decades via the printing of counterfeit money and the passage of laws that keep changing the rules of the game. These rule changes are specifically designed to shift the blame from the real culprit—government—to innocent parties.

"Inflation is the biggest killer of civilizations," says John Hospers, "even more than war itself." From the Sung dynasty in China a thousand years ago to the infamous German runaway inflation of the early 1920s, the real executioner was inflation.

Again, it is not so much that people do not learn the lessons of history; it's more a matter of their not understanding the lessons. "Each generation and country," said Henry Hazlitt, "follows the same mirage. Each grasps for the same Dead Sea fruit that turns to dust and ashes in its mouth. For it is the nature of inflation to give birth to a thousand illusions."

As a final preface to my explanation of this universally misunderstood subject, I offer a description by Pearl Buck of the devastation wrought upon the German people by the runaway inflation of 1923. (Buck's report was quoted in Fritz Ringer's *The German Inflation of 1923.*)

> *The cities were still there, the houses not yet bombed and in ruins, but the victims were millions of people. They had lost their fortunes, their savings; they were dazed and inflation-shocked and did not understand how it had happened to them and who the foe was who had defeated them. Yet they had lost their self-assurance, their feeling that they themselves could be the masters of their own lives if only they worked hard enough; and lost, too, were the old values of morals, of ethics, of decency.*

Like all other financial collapses brought about by inflation, the German hyperinflation brought with it a strong-willed savior—Adolf Hitler—who ended the resulting chaos by clamping down on freedom. Likewise, the French assignat inflation of the late 1700s helped bring to power another ironfisted dictator, Napoleon Bonaparte.

I have no desire to live under a totalitarian regime headed by anyone—certainly not an American politician. That is my inspiration for writing this book and my inspiration for writing this chapter.

Paul Johnson, in *A History of Christianity*, has formulated Goebbels' law in a way that fits the inflation swindle perfectly: "The louder the abuse, the bigger the lie." The lies that government has spread about inflation are both ingenious and galling. Which is why this gigantic swindle is the world's best-kept secret.

The Necessary Ingredient

One cannot understand inflation without having at least an elementary understanding of money, for money is what makes inflation possible. Early men bartered with one another for goods and services (i.e., one man would give another his product as payment for a product or service he desired).

As we can imagine, this would have been a rather cumbersome procedure. It was the advent of money that simplified this bartering process. The purpose of money was, and is, to facilitate exchange. Men could now exchange their goods and services for money, then use the money at a later date in exchange for other goods and services.

Since the beginning of civilization, almost anything one can think of has been used as money at one time or another. In earlier times, this included such items as ornaments, weapons, horses, hunting knives, and even wives. As civilization advanced, mining brought metals to the fore, with silver and gold eventually emerging as the most desirable forms of money.

What caused gold and silver to become the most acceptable forms of money were their features. They were durable, easily transportable, subject to precise division by weight, and scarce enough so that they could not be obtained in great quantities without considerable effort. Gold and silver, in other words, were not arbitrarily chosen commodities. They evolved as a result, and survived the test, of supply and demand over the centuries.

Money, then, is nothing more than a commodity. But it has one great distinguishing feature: It is highly acceptable to most people as a medium of exchange. For people to accept money in exchange for goods and services, they must have confidence that others will, in turn, accept it from them in exchange for things they subsequently will want to acquire.

Money, therefore, is not wealth. It is only a medium of exchange. Wealth is goods that you possess or desire. A refrigerator, for example, represents wealth. Money is a commodity that the owner of a refrigerator will accept as payment for the refrigerator, provided he believes he can use that money to buy other products and services he wants.

There are basically three kinds of money. One is *commodity money*, which I have just described (i.e., money such as gold coin) that is in demand because of its durability, transportability, and other features, and that usually has a utilitarian purpose as well (such as for manufacturing or ornamental use).

A second kind of money is *credit money.* Essentially, credit money is when a person gives someone an IOU in exchange for something of value (i.e., he promises to pay for the item at a later date).

Finally, there is *fiat money.* Fiat money is anything that a government, unilaterally and arbitrarily, decrees to be money. The normal way that fiat money comes into use is for a government simply to print pieces of paper and proclaim that they are "legal tender," with complete disregard to the factors that make money acceptable to people.

So, what does all this mean in practice? To simplify what actually occurs, let us assume that a shoemaker has made one pair of shoes and a hatmaker has made one hat. The shoemaker needs a hat, but the hatmaker does not need a pair of shoes. Assuming there is no government fiat money involved, there are two ways these men can trade with one another.

The shoemaker can give the hatmaker an amount of gold or silver (or some other commodity acceptable to the hatmaker) that the hatmaker feels is adequate compensation for his investment of time, labor, and materials. He must, however, feel confident that he can later use the commodity he receives to buy something that he believes to be of equal value.

The other possibility is for the shoemaker to give the hatmaker an IOU, promising to repay him a specified product, service, or commodity at some specified later date. The hatmaker's willingness to accept the shoemaker's IOU will depend on his faith in the shoemaker's ability to make good on his obligation.

We will leave the story of this hypothetical transaction for now and return to it later for reasons that will become obvious at that time.

The Government Enters the Banking Business

For many centuries, there existed well-established private coin minters and gold and silver warehouses. (For the sake of simplicity, we will restrict our discussion to gold from this point forward.) People would bring their gold to a private minter of high repute, who would form the gold into coins and stamp them with his official seal (which included a guaranteed designated weight for each coin). For this service, the minter would charge a fee, as would any other service business.

It is important to point out here that weights of gold were described by various terms in different countries. The word *dollar* came to be used as the term for 1/20th of an ounce of gold. The dollar itself was not money; it was simply the name given to a certain quantity of money. Therefore, not only was money not wealth, but also a dollar was not even money. Similarly, other countries used words such as *franc* and *mark* to describe various weights of gold.

Gold warehouses came into existence to accommodate people who did not want to be burdened with carrying gold around to make their purchases. Like a warehouse keeper of any other product, the operator of a gold-storage warehouse would agree to store someone's gold for a set fee and would give the owner of the gold a receipt for his stored merchandise. Whenever the owner desired to redeem his gold, he would simply bring in his receipt and the warehouse keeper would hand it over to him.

These early warehouses were the first banks. Their deposits were gold, and the receipts they gave to its owners could be used as a substitute for money in most transactions. The receipts were acceptable to the sellers of goods and services to the degree that such sellers had faith in the integrity of the warehouse keeper (i.e., to the degree they had faith that the receipts could be converted into gold on demand).

But private minters and warehousers were a problem for governments. Throughout history, and particularly modern history, governments have realized that the most essential step in gaining control over a populace is to establish monopolistic control of the money system. The monetary system is the jugular vein of the power game. Karl Marx, in *The Communist Manifesto*, made this very clear, stating that one of the most important aspects in achieving communist control was "centralization of credit in the hands of the state, by means of a national bank with state capital and an exclusive monopoly."

Until a government can eliminate private minters and gold warehousers, it cannot use the money system to achieve the kind of control made possible through a monopoly. In the United States, the history of achieving such a monopoly followed the same creeping-control pattern government has used in all other areas of our lives.

The first step toward the ultimate goal of a money monopoly was Article I, Section VIII, Clause V of the Constitution, which gave Congress the power "to coin money, regulate the value thereof, and of foreign coin, and fix the standard of weights and measures." So as early as 1789, just thirteen years after the British had been overthrown and the American Dream of near-total freedom had been born, new power seekers were beginning to take control.

This was one of the earliest indications of how men of power would operate under the experimental democracy set up by our Founding Fathers (i.e., they would achieve control gradually, over a long period of time). The rugged colonial individualists were too independent to have tolerated abrupt tyranny. So Article I, Section VIII, Clause V of the Constitution was a subtle way of opening the door for the new government's entrance into the money business. Keep in mind, however, that this first step only allowed government to compete with other minters and warehousers.

It took government nearly seventy-five years to take the next significant step, the enactment of the National Bank Act of 1863, which, in effect, outlawed its competition. It is interesting to note here how the passage of time can be used effectively to make people lose sight of what has taken place.

Few, if any, of the citizens who saw government pass an arbitrary law in 1789 allowing it to compete in the money business were around to see it take monopolistic control of the entire system in the mid-1800s. Americans just after the American Revolution were distrustful of government, but by the middle of the next century, government involvement in many areas, including the country's monetary system, had come to be accepted as normal.

It is important to note that even though government outlawed its competition and took full control of the money system, it did not try to change the system itself for more than another half century. The term *dollar* continued to mean 1/20th of an ounce of gold, and the United States remained on a fairly strict gold standard until 1914.

People had been taking their gold to government banks for years, either receiving minted gold coins or gold receipts in return. As time passed, however, it became less common to keep gold and more common to use gold receipts (money-substitutes) as money because it was not practical to carry gold around. Again, it was the passage of time that made this possible. People, influenced by government's encouragement to keep their gold safely on deposit with banks, erroneously began to refer to government receipts for gold as *dollars*.

This clever transition in semantics became very important in later government monetary schemes. The receipts, of course, were not dollars. They were receipts for a specified weight of gold, that weight being defined as a *dollar-weight* (1/20 of an ounce of gold). The slowly evolving practice of referring to government gold receipts as dollars was a subtle but critical maneuver by government in carrying out its long-term inflation swindle.

December 23, 1913, was a day of infamy for our country. On that day, government passed the insidious Federal Reserve Act, which provided for the establishment of Federal Reserve Banks, gave government power to print notes (which it referred to as *currency*), and established a system for member banks to exchange their gold deposits for government currency, and a long list of other measures that pretty much gave government carte blanche to do as it pleased with the country's money system.

From that point on, banks encouraged people to accept government currency when they wished to withdraw their money, assuring them that their gold was safer in the hands of the government. Gold, after all, was old-fashioned. Government's paper currency became the reserves of member banks, while the Federal Reserve Bank retained everyone's gold as its reserves. A nice little piece of maneuvering, to say the least.

Since then, of course, people have been fed a continual diet of government propaganda about the need for a Federal Reserve System. (Which begs the question: How did the United States get along so nicely—and freely—prior to 1913?) It is disheartening that many college professors teach students that the Federal Reserve System is necessary to prevent panic and disorder in banking. Few people stop to realize that the Federal Reserve was established sixteen years before the financial collapse of 1929!

It's true that the Federal Reserve Act put government in a position to prevent runs on banks. But such prevention is not protection—it is aggression. If people flock to banks to withdraw their money, it's because they have lost faith in those banks. It means they want their property back. All the Federal Reserve Act and other related banking laws have done is guarantee that government will use force, if necessary, to prevent people from getting their money back. Some protection!

(If private banks were allowed to exist, they would rarely experience runs because they would know that if one bank failed, it would be bad for the entire banking industry. Therefore, not only would they be forced, by the free market, to operate prudently in handling depositors' money, they also would be apt to bail each other out simply because it would be in their best interest to do so.)

Having taken firm control of the money reins, the government did not wait as long for its next major move. In 1917, it set the minimum reserves that a member bank needed to keep on deposit with the central bank at 10 percent. The 10 percent was retained by the Federal Reserve in gold, but the reserve ratio meant that banks could loan out ten times as much in paper money (notes, currency, etc.) as they actually had on deposit with the Federal Reserve in gold. In other words, 90 percent of the receipts banks could loan out were fraudulent! (Keep in mind that Federal Reserve notes, or "dollars," technically were only receipts for gold owned by others.)

The government arbitrarily printed these receipts and allowed member banks to lend them to unsuspecting individuals as though they were money. People, in effect, were paying interest on counterfeit receipts—receipts for gold that did not exist. The evolution toward paper money was well under way.

The next step? In the early 1930s, government went off the gold standard. Gold receipts (which by this time were referred to by everyone as *dollars*) could no longer be redeemed for gold. Not only were the gold receipts not redeemable, the government stopped printing them altogether and replaced them with Federal Reserve notes. Once again, government arbitrarily passed a law, this one forcing people to recognize Federal Reserve notes as legal tender. People were forced to accept pieces of paper—fiat money—as the only legal money that could be used in transactions.

Governments go off the gold standard because it allows them to increase the supply of paper money more easily. People become confused because there is no way to judge the value of the paper money. But experts are not confused. As soon as we went off the gold standard, the price of gold in the open market zoomed upward. This is because financial experts realized that gold was far more valuable than paper money.

In less than 150 years, consider what had taken place: Government entered the money business, in competition with other minters and warehousers; government then outlawed all competitors and claimed a monopoly on the money system; government established a so-called Federal Reserve System, which, among other things, gave it the power to hold everyone's gold in its vaults and issue receipts far in excess of the gold it had on deposit; and, finally, government made it illegal for people to get their own gold back and declared paper money (as opposed to receipts for gold) to be the legally recognized money of our country.

It was the most protracted theft in history, but it certainly made a case for advocates of gradualism. It had taken 150 years for government to complete the theft of the American people's gold. But from that point on, the government was in a position to speed things up considerably. It now had all the gold, it could print paper money at will, and it was in total control of the money system.

Almost immediately after going off the gold standard, government devalued the currency by about 40 percent. It is significant to point this out, because a currency devaluation is an admission of bankruptcy. What the U.S. government was telling foreign countries (who, unlike American citizens, still had the right to redeem dollars for gold) was that each receipt they held was now worth only 60 percent of the amount of gold it originally had promised them. Devaluations, of course, are always couched in terms designed to make people believe that some brilliantly conceived fiscal miracle has been achieved. What, in fact, has occurred when a government devalues its currency is that it has announced it is reneging on its debts.

Nations, however, are much more powerful than individuals, and they do not take kindly to the news that the pieces of paper they are holding are counterfeit. As a result, countries holding large quantities of U.S. dollars began increasingly to cash them in—a sort of international run on the central bank of the United States.

Out of desperation, Richard Nixon, on August 15, 1971, threw in the towel and, in effect, admitted to nearly 200 years of fraud when he told foreign governments that they no longer could redeem their dollars for gold. From that point on, no one—not even foreign governments—could redeem U.S. currency for real money (i.e., gold). We were now a 100 percent paper-money country.

Fire up the printing presses—full speed ahead!

To rub salt in the wounds of American citizens, the government then began selling gold in the open market. You've come a long way when you enter the game as just another competitor, force everyone else out of the business, steal billions of dollars in gold through outright fraud, and then, finally, turn around and sell that same gold to the people from whom you confiscated it.

The World's Best-Kept Secret

The fantastic gold scam just described is, unfortunately, only a small part of the overall inflation swindle. Everyone agrees that inflation is a big problem, and most people want the president and Congress to bring it under control.

There is only one problem with this: The vast majority of people who pledge their support to inflation-fighting politicians and decry its ravaging effects have absolutely no idea what inflation is, let alone what causes it. Almost without exception, the politician who gains public support for his inflation-fighting measures proposes actions that will make inflation *worse*.

If I were asked to name one thing, above all else, that I would want readers to understand and remember from this book, it would be this: Increased wages and prices do not cause inflation; in fact, they do not even contribute to it. Inflation is caused by only one thing: an increase in the supply of money. It is this increase in the money supply that causes wages and prices to increase. In other words, wage and price increases are a *result* of inflation. (Of course, in a free market, prices may also rise if demand exceeds supply, but such rises are natural. Market prices will always adjust to the ratio of supply and demand, which is a good thing.)

This means that virtually everything politicians, government bureaucrats, a majority of economists, and most members of the media tell Americans about inflation is not only false, but the exact opposite of what is true. Big business does not cause inflation; big labor does not cause inflation; it is big government that causes inflation—and it is the *only* cause. Government accomplishes this through the indiscriminate printing of paper money, and it is the only entity that has the power to increase the money supply.

I really should go one step further and correct my own explanation of inflation. I said it was *caused* by an increase in the supply of money. Technically speaking, inflation *is* an increase in the supply of money. Even more technically, it is an increase in the supply of money-substitutes, that is receipts, over and above the supply of actual money (such as gold). I refer to the inflation swindle as the world's best-kept secret for good reason. Had every American in history simply taken the trouble to open a dictionary and read the definition of *inflation*, the government would have been caught red-handed. Though many dictionaries have updated their definitions of inflation, as recently as 1975 Webster's *New World Dictionary* still defined *inflation* as "an increase in the currency in circulation or a marked expansion of credit, *resulting* in a fall in currency value and a sharp rise in prices." [Italics added.]

Just as government cleverly succeeded in getting people to call gold receipts *dollars*, which led to future generations believing that the receipts themselves, rather than the gold they represented, were money, so, too, did government succeed in getting people to refer to an increase in prices as *inflation*, which took their attention off of real inflation: government's printing of fiat paper money.

Thus, when most people talk about inflation, they use a misnomer. What they really are referring to are high prices. It also would be technically correct to refer to an increase in prices as *price inflation*. When government puts out propaganda about the inflation rate, it is really talking about the so-called consumer price index.

It also should be noted that the consumer price index is a misleading indicator of overall prices because it covers only a few hundred items out of thousands, and many of those thousands of items may play a bigger role in your life than in the lives of others. More important, however, is that the so-called inflation rate really does not tell you the rate of inflation at all. The rate of inflation, once again, is the rate at which government increases the supply of money. However, by referring to an increase in the consumer price index as the inflation rate, government avoids discussing its irresponsible and fraudulent increase of the money supply.

Why is this little game of government-engineered semantics so important? Because it is so confusing that all but a small percentage of the population do not understand what causes prices to rise. And it is rising prices that people are concerned with (i.e., they are concerned with the *results* of inflation). It is inflation of the currency that falsely increases prices. If most people understood this one simple fact, they undoubtedly would revolt against government's printing of money. That is why the semantics charade—and the resulting confusion—is so important to politicians. So long as people can be led to believe false explanations of what causes prices to rise, they can be made to believe in false solutions.

Again, men are most apt to believe what they least understand.

Mechanics of the Swindle

Why do prices rise when government prints too much money? Remember, money is not wealth; money is only a medium of exchange. Wealth is what you exchange the medium for (television sets, automobiles, etc.). Wealth in turn can be produced only by labor. Today's money, on the other hand, is produced merely by printing pieces of paper.

The result is that when the Federal Reserve prints up money faster than people can produce wealth (i.e., products and services), the ratio between available money and available products and services increases. The supply of money, increasing faster than the production of goods and services, increases the demand for the available goods and services, which, as per the law of supply and demand, stimulates prices to rise.

Whence comes the saying that inflation is "too much money chasing too few goods." Rising prices (what people think of as inflation) are caused primarily by the money supply's increasing faster than the supply of goods and services.

Now, let's get back to our shoemaker and hatmaker mentioned earlier in the chapter. If you recall, the shoemaker gave the hatmaker an IOU for the hat he purchased. The hatmaker accepted the IOU because he believed the shoemaker to be creditworthy. He felt confident he could use the shoemaker's IOU to purchase another product from someone else, or, if he later decided he needed shoes, he could redeem the IOU for a pair of shoes directly from the shoemaker.

In the meantime, however, two things have occurred, and the hatmaker is unaware of both of them. First, the shoemaker has stopped making shoes (i.e., he has ceased to produce wealth). Second, he has discovered that he can persuade other people to accept his IOUs, which has motivated him to go on a drunken orgy of spending.

The shoemaker has passed out an additional ninety-nine IOUs since he gave that first IOU to the hatmaker. None of the 100 people realizes, however, that the IOU he holds is not the only IOU that was given out by the shoemaker; hence, each one believes that his IOU is as good as gold (i.e., as good as the pair of shoes behind it).

The problem arises when each of these hundred people tries to spend his IOU. Merchants, sensing the sudden increase in the demand for their goods, raise their prices. Due to the shoemaker's printing of excess IOUs, the hatmaker, who accepted the shoemaker's original IOU in good faith, theoretically (and, most likely, in reality) has had the value of his IOU reduced by 99 percent.

To compound the problem, sellers of goods, realizing that an excess of IOUs has been distributed by the shoemaker, become leery of the value of his IOUs. As a result, they raise their prices even higher to compensate for what they deem to be a bad risk in accepting the shoemaker's IOUs at all.

Of course, this situation would correct itself rather rapidly in a free market, with no government involvement. What would happen at a very early stage is that the community would realize what the shoemaker had been doing, and would not only stop accepting his IOUs but also demand that he make good on those he had already distributed. This probably would result in his having to go to work to produce more shoes to pay off his debts.

When government becomes involved, however, it destroys the smooth workings of the marketplace. Government, in effect, legalizes the shoemaker's theft and, worse, allows the theft to go on indefinitely. It accomplishes this by forcing everyone to use government IOUs as money. (Technically speaking, they are warehouse receipts, payable on demand. As already explained, however, they can never be redeemed for anything.) With government in the picture, the shoemaker simply would have given the hatmaker a government receipt, rather than his own, in exchange for the hat he purchased.

Now, with the government controlling the situation, what happens when the shoemaker stops working? The government continues to print up receipts (i.e., paper money) and gives the shoemaker a new supply of these receipts each week, referring to such handouts as welfare or unemployment benefits. In fact, government gives large quantities of this paper money to many other people in the community, for a variety of reasons, ranging from unemployment to grants for special projects. But what about the hatmaker, who accepted the government receipt in good faith as payment for the hat he produced?

He has been the victim of inflation!

Every paper dollar the government prints up and arbitrarily passes out to the hatmaker's neighbors decreases the value of his paper dollar. And all of those newly printed dollars, with no wealth behind them, compete with the hatmaker's dollar for the available goods and services in the community. This, as already explained, causes prices to rise, the result being that the dollar the hatmaker was paid no longer has the purchasing power it had when he accepted it. The problem is that he knows absolutely nothing about government's money-printing scheme, so he hasn't the vaguest notion as to why prices are rising all around him while he still has only one paper dollar.

Again, government would like you to believe that its mysterious-multiplier concept applies here, and for good reason: The marketplace each day involves billions of individual transactions of every conceivable kind. If one can be led down a path toward this confusing maze of transactions, thereby directing his attention away from the one, real, and only cause of inflation, he can be made to believe that inflation is an impossibly complex problem that only politicians and government bureaucrats can understand.

Why Governments Love Inflation

Now let us return to where we left off with government's deficit-spending dilemma—its problem of having spent more than it could raise through taxation and the sale of government securities. Presto! Through Gutenberg's invention, all things are possible. Just turn on the printing presses and the money to cover the deficit can be created in no time.

Now you can see why it was so crucial for the government to gain monopolistic control of the money system and extricate itself from the gold standard as soon as possible. Once money was not tied to gold—once gold had become old-fashioned—government was free to print money in any quantities it desired.

This practice of indiscriminately increasing the money supply—inflation—gives politicians the ability to have their cake and eat it, too. They are cautious about raising taxes too fast for fear of revolt, which could result in their failure to be reelected. On the other hand, we know that the surest way to be voted out of office is to fail to respond to the expediency factors of voters, so vote-conscious politicians certainly cannot afford to cut back on government handouts.

Thus, inflation provides politicians with a way out, because it is a hidden tax. By printing up enough paper money to, in effect, cover the remainder of each year's deficit, Congress and the president get off the hook. As a result, individuals see prices rising, but they do not understand why. So, not understanding what is happening, they not only do not revolt against Washington, they take up the government's battle cry to fight inflation, following its lead in pointing a guilty finger at all the wrong parties. It's tantamount to a bank robber shouting to a bunch of depositors, "The culprits went thataway. Let's get 'em."

Neither Charles Ponzi nor Bernie Madoff could have done better. The victims not only have been taxed without realizing it, they look to the tax collector to help them solve what only appears to be the problem—high prices.

Results of the Swindle

The hidden tax of inflation allows the government to continue its politically expedient, redistribution-of-wealth policies and other non–wealth-producing programs with virtually no restraints. In the earlier stages of a prolonged inflation, most people are fooled into believing that the government has stimulated the economy. Many economists, in fact, still believe in the Keynesian philosophy that inflation of the currency increases employment and production and improves the health of the economy. They not only totally ignore the long-term effects of inflation, as well as the moral implications (fraud and theft), but also naively believe that politicians will stop increasing the money supply once the economy is again healthy.

There are many fallacies in such thinking, but I will point out only a couple of the more obvious ones. First, the inflation spiral causes voters to continue to clamor for higher wages and more handouts to keep up. Second, that old reality, the vote, motivates politicians to satisfy voter demands, which means more inflation of the currency, which, in turn, leads to still higher prices. Third, because the economy is to a great degree artificial (in that it is supported by deficit spending and valueless paper dollars), it is only a matter of time until the laws of economics set in: Higher prices and lower purchasing power leading to less production; less production leading to still higher prices and less employment; and so on.

From a politician's standpoint, the nice thing about inflation is that deficit spending (which is what necessitates an increase in the money supply) creates short-term, artificial prosperity, designed to win votes. It can take a year or two for prices to rise enough to make voters angry, but by that time, the election, hopefully, has been won. When deficit spending was merely a pre-election scheme, the new administration would cut back on spending once the election was over. As noted, however, this is no longer possible, because voters are hooked on government benefits, and the last thing in the world they want to hear about is cutbacks.

In the meantime, the purchasing power of the dollar continues to erode. Since 1975, the value of the dollar has decreased by close to 75 percent. This means that if you are not making at least four times as much as you were thirty-five years ago, you are not living as well now as you were then.

One of the things that commonly confuses people who try to understand inflation is that, theoretically, it is true that the quantity of money in circulation makes no difference. In other words, if government handed everyone double the amount of money he now has, prices and wages roughly would double in a short period of time and no one would be any worse off. Likewise, if government took 50 percent of the currency out of circulation, prices and wages generally would fall by 50 percent, and no one would be hurt.

But that is not what happens with inflation. Everyone does not get a proportionate percentage of the new money, nor do people get equal quantities of the new money. In addition, it is those who receive the newly printed paper dollars earliest who gain the most from them. People who receive them the latest are the losers, which means they have been taxed without realizing it. This is so because by the time the new money circulates to them, prices have already risen considerably; thus, they are victims of the inflationary spiral (i.e., they are at the bottom of the spiral).

The person who gets caught at the bottom of the spiral is likely to demand higher wages to keep up. His increased wages, in turn, help increase prices, thus the upward spiral continues. But his increased wages did not cause the increase in prices. The real cause was the increase in the money supply, which decreased his purchasing power (i.e., he was taxed so high that he needed higher wages just to keep up with rising prices).

Remember, the cause of the increase in the money supply was an increase in government spending. And when government spends, most people lose in the long term. That's because government takes money from them to support its politically expedient functions.

Therefore, the higher wages most people continue to receive are an illusion. Inflation is just another redistribution-of-wealth scheme. When someone else receives dollars without producing wealth, his dollars compete with your dollars for available goods and services. The result is that you see prices rising in relation to your income, which is a manifestation of government's increasing your taxes without telling you.

Inflation, in fact, can cause you to be taxed in three ways. First is the hidden inflation tax itself. Second, if your wages are increased as a result of overall wage-and-price increases, you will pay higher income taxes on your increased income. Third, your wages may increase enough to push you into a higher tax bracket, which means, in addition, that government taxes you at a higher rate.

Inflation, then, encourages the free-for-all spirit among individuals and special-interest groups of trying to get more from the government than their neighbors. Henry Hazlitt noted that inflation fosters "the illusion in the great majority of voters that they will somehow get the better of the swindle, and profit at the expense of a few unidentified victims."

Long term, however, everyone loses unless inflation is brought under control. This is so because the continued onslaught of valueless paper money disrupts the market and causes confusion, apprehension, and, eventually, panic. People are afraid to enter into long-term agreements because they have no idea what money will be worth in the future. Businesspeople decrease investments in new plants and equipment because they do not know if their real profits will be worth the risk. The latter causes shortages, which leads to even higher prices.

Worst of all, everyone puts the blame on everyone else. Business blames labor; labor blames business; everyone points a finger at the other guy, yet the truth is that none of those accused is responsible for the higher prices.

If inflation is not eventually curtailed, a final collapse of the economy begins when people start to guess what future prices will be. This sets off a chain reaction by which sellers increase prices even faster than the increase in the supply of money (i.e., panic eventually pushes prices up faster than government's inflation of the currency). At that point, government faces its last chance to avoid a total collapse of the economy. As Henry Hazlitt explained, "Every inflation must eventually be ended by government or it must 'self-destruct.'"

The self-destruction Hazlitt described is what has happened to nation after nation throughout history. The one most of us are familiar with is the German runaway inflation of 1923. If you doubt the ultimate results of a policy of continued inflation of the currency, consider these figures: Between 1914 and 1923, the German government issued an additional 92.8 quintillion (92,000,000,000,000,000,000) paper marks, a 245 billionfold increase in the money supply. Prices, in turn, rose 1.38 trillionfold. Interest rates rose as high as 10,000 percent per annum on some debt instruments.

As you would guess, people eventually refused to accept paper money in exchange for goods and services. The economy collapsed; chaos and crime ensued; and waiting in the wings, preparing hysterical answers for hysterical people, was a man—Adolf Hitler—who understood all too well that only an authoritarian police-state regime could restore order.

Can It Be Stopped?

The question of whether inflation can be stopped avoids the real question. Of course inflation can be stopped. All the government needs to do is turn off the printing presses. The real question is whether those in power will stop it. And that can best be answered by yet another question: Will enough people ever sufficiently understand the real cause of inflation and have the courage to demand those in power stop the printing presses?

Realistically, given that their livelihoods and power depend on the vote, it is wishful thinking to believe that politicians will ever stop inflating the currency voluntarily. The best hope is that a majority of Americans will come to understand the colossal inflation swindle for what it is and insist upon reform. Admittedly, that's a long shot, but in this day and age of the tea-party people, it's at least a possibility.

Education of the public is an uphill battle. Politicians and government bureaucrats, more so than ever today, have virtually unlimited access to the mainstream media on a daily basis. This means that the public is fed a continual diet of false remedies for inflation, based on a continual flow of false ideas about what inflation actually is.

Even many respected conservative economists have capitulated to government's logic-twisting and now accept some inflation of the money supply as normal. Instead of talking about putting an end to inflation, such economists now argue the academic advantages of varying degrees of inflation.

But, as Henry Hazlitt pointed out decades ago, inflation is either good or bad. If it is good, why not inflate the currency 100 percent a year instead of just 5 or 10 percent? If it's good, we may as well have lots of it. But if inflation is bad, we should get rid of it altogether so that everyone (except politicians) can be better off.

Five percent a year, for example, may sound like a realistic inflation target, but even that seemingly harmless rate of inflation reduces the value of your dollars by 50 percent every fifteen years—without giving any consideration to inevitable panic and subsequent runaway inflation.

People must start to ignore government ploys of treating the symptoms rather than the disease. When politicians vow to fight inflation, they lie. They are not talking about putting an end to the printing of money. Usually, they are talking about intimidating "greedy" businesspeople into not raising prices.

And *intimidate* is the right word. Profits, the centerpiece of the capitalist system, are constantly derided by populist politicians. But what happens when Atlas finally shrugs and says, "You're right, profits are evil. I'm not going to waste my time earning them anymore. I quit." Then where does government turn to raise money for its vote-oriented functions?

All this finger-pointing at the key source of the country's wealth—business—is nothing but an excuse to institute action intended to lead the public still further away from the real cause of higher prices. The action I am referring to is known as "wage-and-price controls," which were discussed in Chapter 5. These controls are but another scheme to erroneously shift blame to business.

Wage-and-price controls have never worked—and never will, mostly because, short of an outright dictatorship, it's impossible to control the price of everything (land, housing, health care, interest rates, and oil are just a few examples). The result is that people will spend their excess money (such excess having been brought about by controls on the prices of certain items they want) on those goods and services that are not controlled, which will disproportionately raise the prices of the latter. Further, as history has repeatedly demonstrated, when controls eventually are lifted, prices shoot through the roof on the controlled goods and services to compensate for their previous artificially low levels.

Finally, there is the dumb act. It is imperative that every president foster the illusion that inflation is a complex natural catastrophe, much like earthquakes and tornadoes, which man has not yet conquered. The result has been a procession of presidential faces on our television screens, each one espousing inflation-fighting methods that would make witch doctors envious.

Perhaps the most famous solution to this occult force was Gerald Ford's W.I.N. (Whip Inflation Now) buttons. It was yet another example of how much politicians look down on the intellect of the American public. People may not know what inflation is, but they have enough brainpower to realize that wearing badges does not make anything go away.

Jimmy Carter should have won an Oscar for his inflation-fighting speech in October 1978. With a straight face, he appealed to his victims to cooperate. Cooperate how? By not objecting to the government's printing more money? He talked about business cooperation; he talked about labor cooperation; he talked about everything except the massive deficit spending incurred during his first two years in office and the resulting massive increases in the money supply. At a later date, he outdid his October statement by saying that "a preoccupation with private pursuits and private gain at the expense of public purpose" was "a troubling challenge to efforts to control inflation."

It was as though Carter was trying to convince the American public that inflation was a mysterious force from outer space that was menacing planet Earth and that no one was sure how to combat this extraterrestrial plague. Sadly, many intellectuals rushed to the fore and pleaded with citizens to give President Carter's program a chance.

What program? Had Carter appealed to Americans to give him a chance to stop printing worthless money, you can be sure I would have been front and center urging the public to give his program a chance. But, like all political inflation fighters, Carter merely swayed back and forth between irrelevant issues and the dumb act.

I bring up these two examples from the distant past because over the past twenty-five years the dollar has lost only slightly more than half its value. The Reagan pro-business years, followed by the advent of the hi-tech revolution, China as a major producer of low-priced goods, *and* China as a major source of borrowing, worked together to slow the debauchment of the U.S. dollar.

The Real Solution

Unfortunately, the long-term solution to inflation is an unrealistic one, given today's climate: Get government completely out of the money business and repeal the legal-tender laws. If the money business were returned to private minters and warehousers (i.e., banks that are not in any way connected to government), printing of false warehouse receipts (money-substitutes) would be controlled by the same forces that control all free-market activities.

Banks that were guilty of irresponsibly inflating their warehouse receipts would soon lose their customers when word of their fraudulent actions became common knowledge. Originally, this is what inflation entailed—printing of excess gold receipts over and above the amount of gold being stored in private warehouses.

The power holders in Washington, however, are not likely to give up one of their most effective tools for controlling people's lives, especially when one realizes that it took them nearly 200 years to gain monopolistic control of the money system, confiscate people's gold, get completely off the gold standard, and, finally, maneuver themselves into a position to inflate the currency at will for political purposes.

Thus, the only way to stop inflation is to find a way to motivate politicians to dramatically cut back on spending and in turn lessen the need to increase the money supply. The problem is that the only thing politicians respond to is the vote. So, with that in mind, let's start with the result—high prices (which, again, is not inflation)—and see if we can work backward to a solution:

- Higher prices are a result of inflation of the currency.
- Inflation (an increase in the money supply) is a result of deficit spending.
- Deficit spending is a result of too much government spending in general, and, more specifically, that portion of government spending that is not covered by taxes.
- Government spending is the result of politically expedient actions—the desire of politicians to capture the vote.
- Politically expedient actions are the result of the expediency factors of voters.

So the story has a surprise ending: It is the voters who are responsible for inflation! The focus of most voters' expediency factors is on their short-term well-being, which manifests itself in an attitude of wanting to get all they can from the government. This penchant for artificial prosperity is what led to massive deficits and brought the insidious American progressive movement to power in 2008.

Everybody wants something done about high prices, but nobody wants to be the one to get stuck at the bottom of the inflation spiral. So, the question becomes, who will take the first step to stop this financial suicide?

We have two choices:

1. We can all take our lumps together, let the deflationary crash come with all its fury, allow wages and prices to settle to their normal market levels, and get back to living the real American Dream that gave us our original freedom and prosperity; or

2. We can continue to fight for all the short-term benefits we can get, which will continue to fuel government spending, which will continue

to fuel inflation, which must ultimately lead to a total collapse of the economy, which could lead to anarchy, which could bring about a call for a dictatorship to reestablish stability in America.

The mere mention of a dictatorship suddenly makes the first option not sound so bad. Everything is relative. We've been so busy grabbing for free material benefits that we have forgotten all the material wealth in the world is useless without freedom. Great wealth can be produced only if men are free. If men are not free, then slaves produce wealth for those in power.

The Bottom Line

The bottom line is that the bill for government functions is paid, in one way or another, by the only source of wealth that exists: those who produce. The producers pay the bill for government spending through either regular taxation or the hidden tax of inflation. Those who produce more than they receive from the government are net-tax producers. In reality, it is they who pay the bill for everyone else. Those who receive more from the government than they produce are net-tax consumers, and it is they who benefit most from government's redistribution-of-wealth policies.

Because politicians and government intellectuals have done such a masterful job of masking over the real issues, it is hard for most people to see that the only workable solution lies in the simple explanation just given. For example, some politicians pose as crusaders against government waste. However, waste is but a byproduct of the real problem: government spending. To cut down on government waste, you have to cut down on government spending. And to cut down on government spending, you have to cut down on government income (i.e., both direct taxes and inflation taxes).

Another issue for ambitious politicians is the drive for a balanced budget. It sounds great, but a so-called balanced budget, of and by itself, is meaningless, because all you need to do to balance the budget is raise taxes. The alternative politicians never bother to discuss is lowering both direct taxes and inflation taxes, which forces them to cut spending to balance the budget.

Finally, there is the argument that inflating the currency is okay so long as it does not exceed the country's overall productivity rate. The implied attitude is as follows: The confiscation of our ancestors' gold, like the injustice of black slavery, is a great unchangeable fact. Let's just forget about it and concentrate on keeping current inflation of the currency in line with the rate of wealth being produced; thus, future prices will tend to rise pretty much in line with the increase in the money supply, and no one will be hurt.

But if inflation is really just a hidden tax, someone has to be paying the inflation tax and someone has to be receiving it, no matter what the productivity rate is. Thus, the hidden tax must in some way be paid by net-tax producers (i.e., those who produce more than they receive from the government).

If, say, the productivity rate of the nation as a whole increased 3 percent a year, and there was no increase in the money supply, then, generally speaking (because there are so many variables, we can only talk in generalities when dealing with an entire nation), prices would decrease by 3 percent a year. Prices would decrease because more goods and services would be produced, yet there would be no corresponding increase in the amount of money in circulation.

However, if the money supply also was increased by 3 percent a year, as advocated by those who believe that an increase in the money supply is okay so long as the increase does not exceed the productivity rate, prices would not decrease. They would stay approximately the same. Therefore, net-tax producers (again, those who produce more than they receive from the government) would be taxed through inflation by the amount that prices did not drop. Part of their wealth would be siphoned off through inflation, with the recipients of the inflation tax (net-tax consumers) being the winners, just as they are today on a larger scale.

While I will certainly agree that inflating the currency somewhat in line with the productivity rate is better than inflating it far in excess of the productivity rate, the only difference lies in the degree of redistribution of producer income. All inflation (beyond demand receipts that are 100 percent redeemable in gold) is taxation. No matter what the productivity and inflation rates are, if you are a net-tax producer, you help pay the bill, which means that part of your income is given to net-tax consumers.

Of course, none of these facts will ever budge "humanitarian" progressives, who may say in rebuttal: "Okay, so you've caught on to our schemes. But helping the needy (i.e., those whom *they* deem to be needy) is an end that justifies the means."

But their arbitrary justifications for committing aggression do not alter my main point: What good is redistribution of the wealth to anyone if it causes economic chaos, which results in a loss of freedom? Those who advocate fiscal responsibility and morality are not the ones who are callous to the needs of the poor. On the contrary, it is fiscally irresponsible social progressives, who cry out for government to spend ever-increasing sums of other people's money on programs they deem to be desirable, who are callous.

What could be worse than being poor *and* unfree?

One good thing that has come out of the far-left's monopoly on power is that more and more people are finally beginning to realize that there really is no such thing as a free lunch, however trite the term may be. No matter how high the tab goes, it must eventually be paid. Millions of people have, in fact, been making payments on the bill for many years, and the burden becomes more oppressive each day as direct taxation and inflation-taxation continue unabated. Let us hope that it is not our children and grandchildren who will ultimately pay the bill—especially if the payment is a loss of their freedom.

It is only fitting that I leave this chapter on a note from Henry Hazlitt, who had an exceptional understanding of what the long-term consequences of politically expedient spending really are:

Doesn't everybody know, in his personal life, that there are all sorts of indulgences delightful at the moment but disastrous in the end? Doesn't every little boy know that if he eats enough candy he will get sick? Doesn't the fellow who gets drunk know that he will wake up next morning with a ghastly stomach and a horrible head?. . . Doesn't the Don Juan know that he is letting himself in for every sort of risk, from blackmail to disease? Finally . . . do not the idler and the spendthrift know, even in the midst of their glorious fling, that they are heading for a future of debt and poverty?

CHAPTER 8

Keeping It All in Place

When one considers the daily violations of human rights carried out by government, particularly through its functions and methods for expropriating the wealth needed to pay for those functions, one wonders how the power holders manage to keep the system intact. What prevents people from rebelling against such massive injustices?

At the outset of Chapter 2, I said that the chief problem for those in power has been the same since the beginning of recorded history: What is the most practical way in which to maintain control over people?

As I also pointed out, democracy, though it has many disadvantages for power holders, seems to be the most practical way to maintain control because it gives the illusion of consent. If people can be made to believe they are free and that the government represents them, the energies of the ruling class do not have to be focused on policing measures. In addition, creating the illusion of consent has the advantage of rendering violent uprisings unlikely.

Even under a democracy or democratic republic, however, people cannot be held in check indefinitely. As evidenced by today's tea-party movement, as the truth about such things as majority rule, inflation, taxation, conscription, and other tyrannical measures become better understood, people grow angry in increasing numbers.

Therefore, wise rulers in any kind of democratic country employ backup measures for maintaining control in the event of an uprising. These tactics range from subtle to brutally straightforward. The most subtle of all methods, of course, has already been discussed: monopolistic control of the money system. But beyond the money-system scheme, government uses three additional techniques to ensure that the system is never seriously challenged.

Love of Servitude

A person may insist that he lives in a free country, but what good does his loyal statement do him if he is not free to do with his life as he pleases, despite the fact that he is not using force against anyone else? Can a person who feels overtaxed, overregulated, and overharassed really be free?

Sadly, I believe that most Americans do, in fact, believe this contradiction. They believe it because government, while increasing taxes and restrictions on our lives at an out-of-control pace, has been telling us for generations that we live in the freest country on earth.

When the original edition of this book was published in 1979, discussions about freedom had become almost passé—an attitude not new to history. Observed Etienne de la Boetie in the sixteenth century, "It is incredible how as soon as a people becomes subject, it promptly falls into such complete forgetfulness of its freedom that it can hardly be roused to the point of regaining it, obeying so easily and so willingly that one is led to say . . . that this people has not so much lost its liberty as won its enslavement."

The freest people in recorded history undoubtedly were the people of this country just after the American Revolution. Such freedom, however, is easily forgotten, particularly with the passage of long periods of time. Gradual change is desirable from the standpoint of governments because people are not aware of small changes on a day-to-day basis. Many generations have passed since the American Dream was born in 1776, and the civil libertarians of that era undoubtedly would shed many a tear if they could witness the present-day tyranny in America.

Creeping totalitarianism is effective because each generation views conditions at any given time as normal. One must objectively analyze where we began and where we are today to have a realistic understanding of what has transpired during a period of 234 years. The objective of the American Revolutionists was to make men free, to place them above government. Today's reality is that government has become firmly entrenched as the omnipotent, omniscient, omnibenevolent guiding force in people's lives.

Not a small part of government's achieving its position of superiority over the citizenry can be attributed to its success in teaching people to love their servitude. Control of men, as Machiavelli pointed out centuries ago, is much easier and far less dangerous if rulers can gain the cooperation of their subjects through mind control rather than by having to rely solely on the use of force.

The Word Spreaders

Adolf Hitler, probably the most successful political propagandist in history, was able to carry out unthinkable atrocities against mankind because he possessed an uncanny understanding of how to gain the support of the masses through logic-twisting and misrepresentation of facts. Said Hitler in *Mein Kampf*, "The German has no idea how much the people must be misled if the support of the masses is required."

But one cannot mislead millions of people on his own. Peaceful control of a nation is largely dependent on the efficiency of the government's propaganda machine. This entails the effective use of large numbers of intellectuals who have a vested interest in the outcome.

The vested interest to which I am referring is employment, status, security, and power. The demands of people in the market bid up the wages of plumbers, doctors, barbers, carpenters, and the like, but you will never see *intellectuals* listed in the classified-ad section of any newspaper. There simply is not a free-market demand for their services.

As far as government and intellectuals are concerned, theirs is a value-for-value alliance. While the government offers the intellectual employment, status, security, and power, the intellectual's task is to make the masses love their servitude. From government's standpoint, it would be ideal if intellectuals did such a good job at their task that using any other measures would be unnecessary. Said Aldous Huxley in his Foreword to *Brave New World*:

> *A really efficient totalitarian state would be one in which the all-powerful executive of political bosses and their army of managers control a population of slaves who do not have to be coerced, because they love their servitude. To make them love it is the task assigned, in present-day totalitarian states, to ministries of propaganda, newspaper editors and schoolteachers.*

To the degree today's intellectuals parallel Huxley's depiction of efficient control of people, they earn their keep. To the degree people ask too many questions, complain too much, or cause too many problems, intellectuals get a failing grade.

Inflation is a good example of an area in which government intellectuals have done an excellent job. As discussed in detail in the previous chapter, a majority of the population in the United States has been successfully taught to believe not only in false causes and false cures for inflation, but also that the result of inflation (high prices) *is* inflation.

The fact that so many people know so little about the real workings of government is certainly no accident. Government spends billions of dollars of taxpayers' money each year to help its intellectuals create illusions, mysteries, and confusion about scores of subjects important to politicians.

A critical factor in disseminating such propaganda is government's virtually unlimited access to the media—particularly since the progressives took full control of the government. What the president and other top politicians think and say continuously fills the pages of national magazines and daily newspapers. Their faces appear on television screens throughout the land, day in and day out. On top of the huge sums government invests in its propaganda programs, such media exposure amounts to untold billions of dollars in free advertising.

Do you think you might be able to succeed in getting people to accept your views if you were able to appear on television every day and have them printed daily on the pages of national magazines and local newspapers?

With its use of taxpayer money and free access to the media, government is in an enviable position to slant the news to its liking. As everyone with the slightest understanding of economics realizes, figures do lie. By presenting numbers out of context or failing to address certain consequential factors, subjects like the unemployment rate, as we have seen, can be presented in such a way as to mislead the public.

The creation of crises is another tool used by government intellectuals to keep people concentrating on anything other than their loss of wealth and freedom. Global warming (recently, and embarrassingly, transformed into *climate change*) and the government-created energy shortage are two good examples of this.

Then there are the intellectuals who control the compulsory-education process. There certainly is no moral virtue in compulsory education, so the objective, quite obviously, is to make certain that children grow up thinking the "right way." By the time young adults graduate from high school, it is essential to the government's aims that they understand that material wealth is evil, individual freedom is an archaic concept, and equality and security are far more important than liberty.

The government knows all too well that if children are allowed to learn the truth about such subjects, they will always know the truth. And once something is learned, it cannot be unlearned, as Thomas Paine explained in *Rights of Man*:

> *Ignorance is of a peculiar nature; once dispelled, it is impossible to re-establish it. It is not originally a thing of itself, but is only the absence of knowledge; and though man may be kept ignorant, he cannot be made ignorant. . . . It has never yet been discovered how to make a man unknow his knowledge.*

The proper teaching of history is especially important to power holders. "If all records told the same tale—then the lie passed into history and became truth," thought Winston in George Orwell's *Nineteen Eighty-Four*. "'Who controls the past,' ran the Party slogan, 'controls the future: who controls the present controls the past.'"

If one were to study American history in books published in, say, France or England, he might be quite surprised at the disparity between historical facts as presented in those books and as they appear in American history books. As an example of how history can be rewritten, think of some of the men most revered in our school texts.

Abraham Lincoln, we are taught, fought the Civil War to free the Negro slaves. But the truth is that the war was fought primarily because the Southern states, whom the Northern states had continually burdened with stifling tariffs and levies, wanted to secede from the Union. What Lincoln accomplished was to reestablish government's superiority over the individual (i.e., that individuals had to belong to the country whether they wanted to or not). After the North's victory, the issue of the federal government's authority over all people within its borders was never again seriously challenged.

The one good thing that came out of the Civil War was that blacks were given their freedom, but historical documents make it clear that this was not the key issue in the war. Two direct quotes by Lincoln, which, needless to say, are not found in public-school textbooks, make this clear.

In a letter to Horace Greeley in 1862, Lincoln wrote, "My paramount object in this struggle [the Civil War] is to save the union and it is not either to save or destroy slavery. If I could save the union without freeing any slaves, I would do it. If I could save it by freeing all the slaves I would do it; if I could save it by freeing some and leaving others alone, I would also do that."

And in a debate with Stephen Douglas, Lincoln stated, "I am not nor ever have been in favor of bringing about in any way the social and political equality of the white and black races. . . . There must be the position of superior and inferior, and I as much as any other man am in favor of having the superior position assigned to the white race."

Then there was Theodore Roosevelt, another legendary president. Because the slaves already were free by the time he took office, Roosevelt settled for Indians: "I don't go so far as to think that the only good Indians are dead Indians, but I believe nine out of every ten are, and I shouldn't inquire too closely into the case of the tenth. The most vicious cowboy has more moral principle than the average Indian."

So much for Abraham Lincoln; so much for Theodore Roosevelt; so much for American history. Indeed, "Who controls the past controls the future: who controls the present controls the past."

But the most important function of all for government intellectuals is to teach people either not to think at all (*nothink*) or to believe that the truth is the exact opposite of that which is true. In *Nineteen Eighty-Four*, George Orwell referred to the latter as *doublethink*. Orwell explained this as the ability of a person to maintain two contradictory beliefs in his mind at the same time and to accept both of them without conflict (the opposite of cognitive dissonance). Doublethink does not involve saying the opposite of what one believes, but thinking the opposite of what is true.

The ultimate in doublethink in Orwell's book was the party slogan: "War is peace; freedom is slavery; ignorance is strength." Current events make it clear that many people today literally believe in one or more of the contradictions of this supposedly fictional party slogan.

Americans today are products of several generations of heavy dosages of doublethink. Those who produce goods and services in the market are known as *exploiters*, while those who reap the benefits of the producers are known as the *exploited*; those who advocate suppressing individual liberty are called *liberals*; when our country entered into a political partnership with a regime in China that had killed upward of 50 million people and held nearly 1 billion people in bondage, it was celebrated as "a step in defense of peace."

Frederick Douglass, a self-educated slave of the pre–Civil War era, noted the importance of both nothink and doublethink in the maintenance of the plantation system of slavery when he observed that "to make a contented slave, it is necessary to make a thoughtless one [and] to annihilate the power of reason. He must be able to detect no inconsistencies in slavery, he must be made to feel that slavery is right."

And so it goes with government intellectuals. They teach us that majority rule is morally valid; that politicians can solve our problems better than we can; that government can do things better, cheaper, and more efficiently because of its mysterious-multiplier concept; that government interference in the marketplace stimulates free enterprise, prevents unemployment, and fights monopolies; that those who oppose government regulations are advocates of disease, poverty, and a dirty environment.

Combating Nothink and Doublethink

There is only one known antidote for nothink and doublethink: straight-think. Only the refusal to be intimidated by illogical or irrational thoughts, talking points, and slogans, only the insistence on using one's power to reason, can combat nothink and doublethink.

Too many Americans today have lost the spirit of individualism. As a result of continual admonishment by politicians, the media, intellectuals, and even peers, many among us seem incapable of thinking rational thoughts. Conforming to the wishes of an abstract entity known as "society" has become more important to them.

The only way out of such mental servitude is the use of reason as the starting point for every decision. Custom, law, and tradition must be rejected as a basis for argument. It is impossible to be committed to both truth and conformity at the same time. To seek truth, one must feel free to analyze, criticize, and question—to use his own mind.

It is not easy to practice straightthink when one has been bombarded by nothink and doublethink most of his life. It is frightening to many people when the things they grew up believing are suddenly exposed in a different light. Our fears, prejudices, preconceived ideas, and ingrained adherence to custom and tradition are the biggest obstructions to our understanding and seeking liberty for ourselves and others.

It is virtually impossible for some people to break through these mental barriers and take control of their own thought processes. Instead, they continue to believe the American Dream is in fine shape, that government is inherently good, and that "the world has always had problems." The latter view is especially dangerous because it ignores the evolution of our once nearly free country into a rapidly decaying socialist society. Making oneself believe that everything is fine is the worst possible example of nothink, and such cooperative refusal to face reality will only accelerate the decaying process. "Facts," said Ayn Rand, "cannot be altered by a wish, but they can destroy the wisher."

In today's doublethink environment, seeking and speaking truth can sometimes make one feel very lonely. Government intellectuals and henchmen have been extremely successful with the use of the put-down and the dismissal. When someone steps out of line, he and his ideas are likely to be publicly ridiculed. This is the psychology behind calling today's protesters birthers, teabaggers, astroturfers, and worse. The power holders have an endless arsenal of epithets with which to vilify, discredit, and dismiss their dissatisfied employers (i.e., the people who voted them into office).

The put-down and the dismissal are not just used against everyday people. On the contrary, intellectuals do not hesitate to wave aside the opinions of some of the most brilliant, high-profile people in this manner, for it is just such people who pose the greatest threat to mental control of the masses.

A good example of this technique involved a friend of mine during his college days. One of his instructors had asked each student to write a report on a philosopher of the student's choosing, and my friend did a critique of Ayn Rand. But when he handed in his paper, the instructor told him it was unacceptable because he "did not consider Ayn Rand to be a serious philosopher."

The casual dismissal of Ayn Rand as a serious philosopher by an obscure college professor does not affect her status in the eyes of the millions of people who have been positively impacted by her works. But it does affect her status in the minds of those who either have not read her works or fear being out of step.

A second example that comes to mind is an article that appeared in the *New York Times Magazine* about the brilliant libertarian professor, Robert Nozick. Nozick was out of step at Harvard, and in the intellectual community in general, because he believed in "antiquated" ideas such as individualism and freedom. The article explained that many of his peers simply dismissed his writings, maintaining that he must be pretending. Pretending? Anyone who has read his landmark book *Anarchy, State and Utopia* would have a hard time believing that Nozick was pretending when he wrote it, but government intellectuals hope that such a put-down will render rational and persuasive minds like his ineffective when it comes to influencing others to view life through the lens of liberty.

If government intellectuals have no qualms about dismissing the ideas of some of the world's greatest thinkers, it is not hard to see why the average person can be intimidated so easily by the "you-must-be-kidding" attitude of intellectuals. When an everyday libertarian or conservative talks about freedom, whether it be economic or social freedom, the easiest thing for the properly indoctrinated conformist to do is simply shrug him off as someone who is hopelessly out of touch with today's world. By so doing, the conformist conveniently avoids discussing the facts.

"Such ideas are outdated"; "he oversimplifies the problem"; "what would happen if everyone thought that way?" These are typical examples of statements intended to avoid rational discussion. When someone responds to you in this manner, it is almost always a sure sign that your thoughts are on a sound foundation, because it indicates that you've made a meaningful statement for which he has no logical rebuttal. And if that's the case, you should redouble your efforts to speak the truth—boldly. Too few people today have the courage to think, let alone speak out, as noted by Bertrand Russell:

> *Men fear thought as they fear nothing else on earth—more than ruin, more even than death. Thought . . . is merciless to privilege, established institutions, and comfortable habits; thought is . . . indifferent to authority, careless of the well-tried wisdom of the ages. Thought looks into the pit of hell and is not afraid.*

The Arsenal

The government has a seemingly endless arsenal of subjective, meaningless, and distorted words and phrases with which it mentally seduces the public. Here, too, government intellectuals have been extremely successful in their efforts. People accustomed to nothink and doublethink are perpetual victims. Only those who employ the power to reason can shield themselves from the mental control sought through the use of these intimidating words and phrases.

Examples of Government's Word/Speech Arsenal

The people, the public, society, and so on. These, of course, are abstract terms that refer to large numbers of individuals—usually millions of individuals. Wherever I have used these terms in this book, you should assume that I have been referring to large numbers of individuals, recognizing that the wants, needs, desires, and personal characteristics of each individual are unique.

When used by government propagandists or doublethinkers, however, the implication is that such terms refer to collective living entities capable of thinking, feeling, and acting human. Any reference to these terms in such a way as to intimate that they are living entities that have the power to reason should be totally disregarded.

Government. Again, wherever I have referred to government, I specifically have been alluding to individuals, namely those individuals in power (i.e., elected politicians and non-elected bureaucrats). If one thinks of government as a living entity, it tends to take on an aura of sanctity in his mind. And to think of government as a sacred entity is to believe that the human beings who comprise it are sacred. Hardly.

The subconscious tendency of people to think of government as a living entity is one of the factors that keeps them so passive in the face of government aggression. But a violation of your natural rights is not warranted just because it is committed by government (i.e., by those individuals who operate under the banner of government).

Country. A country is an even more curious abstract entity because it refers to a geographical area as well as to individuals. The point about only individuals having human qualities has already been made numerous times, but what about land? Land cannot think, feel, express desires, or experience emotions—and certainly does not have the ability to reason.

Therefore, all the same logic holds true for the term *country* that is applicable to terms like *the people, the public,* and *society.* Our country is not great. And neither is it good or bad. Only individuals are great, good, or bad. Some people in America are great, some people in America are good, and some people in America are bad.

Patriotic, apathetic, obligation, and so on. These are all words that politicians love to use in a distorted manner in an effort to lend respectability to immoral acts. One is considered patriotic if he unquestioningly supports his country. All of our Founding Fathers, therefore, were unpatriotic, because they did not support the government that was in power in their time. Likewise, anyone who challenges the authority of the present-day government to violate human rights—such as the tea-party people and town hall protestors—is referred to as unpatriotic by those now in power. It's not hard to see why the old adage "One man's anarchist is another man's patriot" lives on.

Though it may make some people wince, the truth is that whether you are patriotic depends on not only the eyes of the beholder, but also the time and place of your actions. The actions of the tea-party people and town hall protestors are mild compared to those of our Founding Fathers—and they were, and still are, considered patriots.

Then there is *apathy*, which has been popularized by government to refer to virtually any action or nonaction that may not be to its liking. For example, millions of people do not vote because they want to protest the lack of any significant difference between the handpicked major candidates. But politicians and intellectuals like to refer to such nonvoting protests as *apathy*, a convenient catchall word intended to shame people into going along with the status quo.

Obligation is one of the most intimidating words of all, due to the way in which our collectivist evolution has changed its meaning. Technically, an obligation is something one assumes. Once you voluntarily assume an obligation, then—and only then—are you responsible for it. Yet politicians, intellectuals, and absolute moralists insist on telling people it is their obligation to do things they have never agreed to do.

Duty, decent, fair, justice, and so on. Obviously, all of these words are totally subjective and have different meanings to different people. Much of the language government uses to control people's minds revolves around combining subjective words such as these with other distorted or meaningless words. What you end up with are such unintelligible and incoherent phrases as the following:

Public good, public property, social justice, public interest, and so on. Because the public consists of millions of individuals, each person has a different view of what is moral, good, or in his best interest. So, too, does each individual have a different view of justice. And public property simply refers to property controlled by those who control the government. Such property is available to private individuals only at the discretion of government officials, which means, for all intents and purposes, that government officials are the actual owners of the property.

Good of society, well-being of society, welfare of society, duty to society, obligation to society, and so on. Again, society, as an entity, does not exist. Society consists of millions of individuals, and the well-being and welfare of each individual in a society is different from that of his neighbor. What is good for him is not necessarily good for others. And because society does not exist as an entity, no one can possibly have a duty or obligation to it. (One can be obligated to a specific individual in a society provided one voluntarily assumes such an obligation.)

Good of the people, welfare of the people, rights of the people, the people have chosen, and so on. *The good of the people* and *the welfare of the people* have no meaning for the same reasons that *the good of society* and *the welfare of society* have no meaning. Because *the people* is not a living entity, *the good of the people* translates into that which fulfills the desires of those in power. Neither do the people, collectively speaking, have rights. Only individuals have rights, and each individual's rights are equal to those of every other individual. Such rights are framed in Natural Law, which I have previously discussed at length.

    The people have chosen is a meaningless statement for the same reason: Only individuals can choose. When this phrase is used to refer to the winner of an election in an effort to imply that the winner has received a mandate of the people, it is simply a falsehood (as discussed in Chapter 2).

Fair pay, decent living, your fair share, moral duty, and so on. All these phrases are meaningless because they involve subjective words. Another person's idea of *fair pay, decent living, fair share*, and *moral duty* may be quite different from yours. And you both have a right to your opinions. Neither of you, however, has a right to force your opinions on anyone else.

    The ultimate weapons in government's propaganda arsenal take the form of slogans. These are remarks intended to effect a knee-jerk response from citizens, which means they are intended to produce irrational thought and irrational action. Slogans of this kind rely heavily on nothink and doublethink.

Examples of Government Slogans

"And so, my fellow Americans, ask not what your country can do for you, ask what you can do for your country." This oft-repeated appeal by the late John F. Kennedy was brilliantly conceived, but does not stand the test of dissection.

    First, the statement refers to that same abstract word *country*, which in this case is a geographical area in which some 300+ million individuals reside. I personally have never asked 300 million people to do anything for me. How can I ask people to do things for me when I don't even know them?

"Ask what you can do for your country"? Does this mean asking each of the 300 million individuals within the geographical area known as the United States of America what you can do for them? Does it include the millions of murderers, rapists, thieves, and others who are guilty of aggression? If it does not include all 300 million Americans, then which ones does it include? In reality, Kennedy's statement was really encouraging people to ask what they could do for their *government*, meaning those people who control the reins of power.

Restated in translated form, then, it becomes: "Ask not what those in power can do for you; ask what you can do for those in power." Had Kennedy's statement been made in such a straightforward manner, without the use of abstract, misleading terms, it is doubtful that people would have responded so positively. Which is precisely why governments have compiled large arsenals of mind-twisters such as this.

Let me make it clear that I believe in being a responsible, contributing member of society, but I do not believe in blindly following government edicts that call for me to act immorally.

Love it or leave it. People who use this intimidating slogan imply that somehow they own the country and that you remain here only at their discretion. (In that case, perhaps the only people who might have a valid right to make such a demand are Native Americans.) What a person employing this slogan really is saying is that if you do not agree with his views on certain issues, you have no right to live in the United States.

In other words, you have no right to dissent—the exact opposite of the principle upon which our country was built. Must a person love everything about a country to have the right to continue to reside in it? I love many things about the geographical area known as the United States of America. Likewise, I love many people who live within that area. I have no desire to leave.

However, I also dislike many things about the United States. For one, I dislike the fact that other people, particularly politicians and bureaucrats, forcibly attempt to interfere in my life and impose their moral standards on me. I would like to see this type of aggression brought to an end and all people be allowed to live their lives as they please, so long as they do not commit aggression against others.

My feeling is that if anyone does not believe in the right of people to be free, perhaps it is he who has a problem. If someone does not like living in a country where people still have a right to voice their dissent, then it seems to me that it is he who should be looking for a new country. Perhaps he is the one who should "love it or leave it."

All power to the people. This abstract phrase is an old favorite of revolutionaries. We have already discussed the fact that there is no such living entity as *the people*. The problem, therefore, is that no one is ever sure who *the people* are. Am I a people? Are you a people?

Anyone who shouts this abstract slogan is really saying: "All power to those individuals whom *I* deem to be 'the people.'" And, as revolutions throughout history have clearly demonstrated, *the people* always turn out to be the handful of individuals who led the revolution. If it were to be taken seriously, "all power to the people" would mean that each individual would have power over his own life. What it really means to those who use it, however, is that some people should have power over the lives of others.

The Frills

While intellectually inspired propaganda, twisted words, and intimidating slogans are government's main psychological weapons for maintaining peaceful control of the masses, it employs other kinds of actions in an effort to appeal to the emotions of citizens.

One of these is the ceremony. This method has been used effectively in every known civilization throughout history. It is a call to one's emotions, which means an appeal to set aside one's reasoning power. Nonetheless, the time-tested effectiveness of the ceremony cannot be disputed. Eric Hoffer shed light on this subject when he said:

> *When faith and the power to persuade or coerce are gone, make-believe lingers on. There is no doubt that in staging its processions, parades, rituals and ceremonials, a mass movement touches a responsive chord in every heart. Even the most sober-minded are carried away by the sight of an impressive mass spectacle.*

Finally, there is tradition. The appeal to people to do things only because they have been done before is an appeal to override one's reasoning power. When people go along with actions just because they are steeped in tradition, they place a mysterious divinity on the passage of time that puts it above morality. The unquestioned acceptance of such immoral actions as the draft, compulsory education, and taxation are prime examples of this. Said Will Durant:

> *Time sanctifies everything; even the most arrant theft, in the hands of the robber's grandchildren, becomes sacred and inviolable property.*

Every state begins in compulsion; but the habits of obedience become the content of conscience, and soon every citizen thrills with loyalty to the flag.

It is remarkable how an immoral act gains an air of respectability with the passage of time. No one remembers that the Queen of England's ancestors were barbarians who conquered that land through savage violence. If one is to follow blindly the traditions of one's government, no matter how useless or immoral such traditions may be, then murder, theft, and enslavement could be justified on the grounds that such actions have been previously acceptable.

To build patriotic and unquestioned loyalty in the mind of every citizen—to make him love his servitude—is the most desirable method of control for any government. The U.S. government has been particularly effective at this, making slow but continuous strides toward the ultimate objective: total control of the populace through control of the mind. Whether this ultimate aim can ever be achieved is a question pondered by Erich Fromm: "Can human nature be changed in such a way that man will forget his longing for freedom, for dignity, for integrity, for love—that is to say, can man forget that he is human?"

Structure of Servitude

At present, it is unrealistic to believe that every citizen will cooperate with government's wishes, no matter how cleverly the tools of propaganda are used by those in power. Therefore, behind the mental control of any population, there must be a firm structure of law. The more effective the manipulation of people's thought processes, however, the less a government has to rely on laws to keep its system of rule in place.

Nevertheless, the law is an essential tool of control and can be used rapaciously when necessary. As Will and Ariel Durant put it, "Animals eat one another without qualm; civilized men consume one another by due process of law." The dependence on a legal structure to place forcible limits on the freedom of men is part and parcel to every government's system of control. Because all governments, including democracies, insist that citizens obey their laws, all governments are, to that extent, authoritarian (i.e., they demand unquestioning submission to authority).

Most libertarians and conservatives agree that laws that protect individuals from unprovoked force and fraud are justifiable. However, the vast majority of existing laws have nothing whatsoever to do with protection of lives and property. Most laws, as already discussed, do just the opposite (i.e., they validate the use of force against citizens). Victimless-crime laws, such as those discussed in Chapter 6, are prime examples of this.

Today, in addition to ongoing campaigns on the part of absolute moralists to pass more laws to further restrict the freedom of citizens, there are also many countercrusades to legalize various acts currently outlawed. The significance of the latter illustrates just how twisted the original concept of freedom has become. If people truly were free, why would anything need to be legalized? Free people have the right to do anything they please so long as they are not violating the rights of others. Natural rights do not have to be granted, because every human being inherits them at birth. If government is inclined to legalize anything, it should legalize freedom.

The Obstruction

It's amazing how many people do not know the difference between the Declaration of Independence and the Constitution—or even that there is a difference between the two. The Declaration of Independence, which was approved by the Continental Congress in Philadelphia on July 4, 1776, was the birth of the American Dream. It was not a set of laws and did not establish or authorize the formation of a new government. On the contrary, it was a document that, in effect, announced that men were superior to government and that the existing government had no moral right to rule them.

The Declaration of Independence was indeed an historic document, a radical experiment in freedom that stated, among other things, that men are endowed with "certain unalienable rights," including "life, liberty, and the pursuit of happiness"; that governments derive "their just powers from the consent of the governed"; and that "whenever any form of government becomes destructive of these ends, it is the right of the people to alter or to abolish it."

While it is true that the Declaration of Independence also stated that men have the right "to institute new government," it did not say that men were *compelled* to form or be ruled by a new government. The Declaration of Independence was by far the boldest statement in human history on the issue of individual freedom. It clearly was a temporary obstruction for those who aspired to control the lives of others.

The Structure

Beginning on July 4, 1776, the people of this country lived under circumstances never before experienced in the recorded history of mankind: a virtual absence of centralized control over the lives of individuals. This glorious fling of near-total freedom lasted almost thirteen years, until the passage of a set of manmade rules called the Constitution of the United States.

We have been told since we were children that the beauty of the Constitution lies in its flexibility. Doublethink. What the flexibility of the Constitution really means is that any rights arbitrarily granted by its original authors can be withdrawn at any time by those currently in power. A perfect example of this was the passage of the Sixteenth Amendment, which became law on March 15, 1913. As discussed in Chapter 7, this amendment made it legal for the government to use force to take a percentage of people's incomes, such percentage to be subject to change at any time at the sole discretion of those in power.

In addition, the Sixteenth Amendment nullified a guarantee made in the original Constitution. Article I, Section IX, Clause IV stated that no tax could be levied "unless in proportion to the census," meaning that no one could be taxed a greater amount than any other person. This reference to taxes, of course, was not a reference to income taxes, because taxes on income were unheard of at that time. But the Sixteenth Amendment simply washed away this guarantee by stating the exact opposite—that Congress *could* tax people "without regard to any census."

Such flexibility is quite convenient for politicians. Considering that it was also in 1913 that the government took total control of the money system through the passage of the Federal Reserve Act, you'd have to say that 1913 was a very good year for progressive government. These two actions made it possible for government to extract wealth from individuals and companies on a large scale and paved the way for future government functions that would help perpetuate the system.

As if the power to amend the Constitution were not bad enough, government itself also has the sole right to interpret the Constitution. And virtually all Articles and Amendments need interpreting because they are notoriously vague. Those in power decide what every word in the Constitution means.

Finally, there is the so-called elastic clause of the Constitution, inconspicuously hidden away in Article I, Section VIII, Clause XVIII. This is the clause that, in effect, renders all rights granted under the Constitution meaningless. The word *flexible* would be a drastic understatement here. The elastic clause gives government the right to "make all laws which shall be necessary and proper for carrying into execution the foregoing powers, and all other powers vested by this Constitution in the Government of the United States, or in any department or office thereof."

Translation: Government has the right to do anything! Does anyone who is not still in a post-election slumber seriously doubt this?

Mental control of the populace is instrumental in getting people to obey the law. Through years of conditioning, they have been trained to accept the law as gospel. In other words, people see the law as the premise underlying questions of morality.

This, of course, is completely backward. One does not prove that a law is moral simply by stating that it's a law. Laws can be moral, but they can also be immoral. For example, Article IV, Section II, Clause III of the Constitution not only condoned slavery, but also made it illegal not to turn in a runaway slave. If one were to insist on making a connection between morality and the law, he would have to be willing to state that, at least prior to 1865, slavery was moral.

But to a person who believes in Natural Law, all laws that legalize enslavement, the taking of property from people without their consent, or any other form of forcible interference in the life of any human being—no matter in what terms such laws may be couched and no matter what the purported justifications of such laws may be—are immoral. Intellectual honesty therefore compels one to conclude that most laws—federal, state, and local—are immoral.

Politicians preach about respecting the law, but I side with Thoreau, who said, "It is not desirable to cultivate a respect for the law, so much as for the right." Unfortunately, laws are but dictums forced upon people to assure that servitude has a structure. Tyranny can be decorated with impressive-sounding legal language, but that does not change the fact that it is tyranny.

Laws that do protect people from aggression are morally valid. But the reality is that the true purpose of most laws is to protect government from the threat of people becoming free. Even so, a pragmatic person realizes that if one were to challenge every immoral law on the books, he would soon be in jail—or dead.

No matter how much libertarian purists may protest to the contrary, the fact is that you can do nothing to enhance the cause of freedom— neither yours nor the freedom of others—if you are under lock and key. Rightly or wrongly, the legal system is what gives structure to our servitude. No society can exist without a legally enforced code of conduct. While one should do everything within his power to respect the natural rights of others, he should proceed with caution when it comes to matters of government-enforced laws.

Force of Servitude

Finally, we get to the bottom line of control, as expressed so candidly by one of the more infamous mass murderers of modern history, Mao Zedong: "Political power grows out of the barrel of a gun." These are probably the only words Mao ever spoke with which I agree, and it's sad to have to admit that his statement is a harsh reality of life. Gun power is the argument that never fails!

Without the threat of force behind the structure of the law, there would always be people who would commit aggression against others. The intellectual rhetoric, the slogans, the ceremonies, and all the rest of the mind games that government plays are effective; the sanctity of the law is pretty much accepted; but, in the end, it is government's willingness to use force, when and where necessary, which ensures that most citizens will obey the law.

Obviously, it is unwise for power holders to flaunt their gun power. As noted, the most practical (and safest) method of control is psychological. But reality dictates that there must be laws behind mind control, and there must be brute force behind laws. As Machiavelli pointed out, "You cannot have good laws without good arms."

For government force to be effective, it must have a monopoly on its use. At the outset of Chapter 2, I pointed out that one of the two characteristics common to all governments—whether they be democracies or dictatorships—is an institutionalized way of controlling people, backed by a monopoly on the use of force. As John Hospers explains it, if there are two entities competing for the use of force within a nation, then that country is in a state of civil war.

Needless to say, if you were really a free person, no one, including those who work for the government, could use force against you. To the extent government uses force for any reason other than to protect individuals from aggression, such force is immoral and in violation of Natural Law. And because Natural Law is violated not only by the use of force, but also the threat of force, virtually all political action (other than that intended to protect individuals from aggression) is immoral. This is so because all political action carries with it the threat of force.

The fact that people still use force to control the lives of others is the most uncivilized aspect of our twenty-first century civilization. But it's a reality that has always existed and is not likely to go away anytime soon, for it is the ultimate insurance policy for making certain that the system is never challenged. Force is the last resort for keeping the system in place—for ensuring control of the populace should all else fail.

CHAPTER 9

Taking Back America

The time has come. The citizens of this country must draw the line and take back America from the politicians who now control it or they must be prepared to relinquish forever their remaining claims on liberty.

By *taking back America*, I am not implying that the geographical area of the United States should belong to everyone in common. That type of unintelligible nonsense is for the collectivist-minded progressives who have helped raise government to its current omnipotent position.

When I use the phrase *taking back America*, I mean nothing short of restoring the American Dream. Specifically, this means that each individual should be able to regain his right to his life, his liberty, and his pursuit of happiness. It's time for lockstep politicians to get out of our lives—to let go of the reins and allow us to control our own destinies. Self-responsibility was, and is, an integral part of the American Dream.

The fundamental concept of our Founding Fathers was that people have a natural right to sovereignty over their own lives and that governments have no right to interfere with that sovereignty. In that respect, the Declaration of Independence, as a document, was unique in human history. For the first time, men were saying that they were above government, that governments derive "their just powers from the consent of the governed."

"American Government," said Rose Wilder Lane, "is not an Authority; it has no control over individuals and no responsibility for their affairs. American Government is a permission which free individuals grant to certain men to use force in certain necessary and strictly limited ways; a permission which Americans can always withdraw from American Government."

In other words, contrary to what the progressive power holders in Washington would like us to believe, government has nothing whatsoever to do with the American Dream. On the contrary, government has succeeded in nearly destroying that dream. The American Dream is a way of life that can be experienced only by free individuals. Hillary Clinton's infamous reference to "shared prosperity" is abstract nonsense that is but a mask for collectivism.

When you really understand what the American Dream is, you realize that it is not specific to America. The American Dream has to do with the freedom of people to pursue their own happiness without interference from others. It could have originated anywhere in the world, but, fortunately for us, its birth occurred in a geographical area we refer to as the United States of America.

Therefore, when I say I love America, my statement needs clarification. It is true that I like much of the natural beauty of our country, as well as the climates in many of its areas. But what loving America really means to me is loving the American Dream. It means loving freedom and individualism. It means admiring the millions of people who have contributed both to the birth of the American Dream and to its furtherance. It means admiring all people who passionately believe in the cause of human freedom. These people cannot be distinguished by race, religion, ethnicity, occupation, or sex. They can be distinguished only by their common belief that liberty must be accorded the highest of all values.

What I do not love is the fact that an anti-freedom concept has challenged, and nearly destroyed, the American Dream. The proponents of a collectivist, progressive society have succeeded in leading millions of people to believe that the American Dream is outdated. But, in truth, freedom is never outdated. On the contrary, the limitation of the power of man over man is a sign of progress. The reality is that the American Dream was barely in its infancy when its subtle destruction began in 1787.

It is the firmly controlled society, which has been around since the beginning of recorded history, that is outdated. Indeed, it is rare to find a government at any time in history, anywhere in the world, that was not a monarchy or some other form of dictatorship. The attempt to make men free was almost unheard of until 1776.

We must ask ourselves what has worked for the greatest number of people and what has not worked. Our history has made it clear that freedom and self-responsibility (i.e., a lack of government intervention and restraint) have worked best for those who have no desire to commit aggression against others.

The proof? From the moment we undertook our bold experiment in freedom, people began to pour into our country by the millions in search of the American Dream. It was the reasoning behind the Industrial Revolution all over again: People do not travel thousands of miles across oceans, at great risk and expense, leaving familiar surroundings behind, to settle in a new country where the situation is not much better than that which they left behind. The truth about American poverty before the onset of progressive government is that, by comparison to what people left behind in their homelands, America was a dream come true. Most of all, America was the dream of freedom come true.

People who believe that before the advent of government intervention in the economy and business the American Dream was not available to the masses are badly mistaken. The American Dream meant the freedom to pursue a better life, and it was that freedom that inspired millions of people to cross oceans to reach America. Those millions of immigrants were not looking for government handouts. They were looking for opportunity, and the American Dream afforded them that opportunity.

What has not worked is government intervention. The early generations in this country laid the foundation for the greatest advances in the history of mankind—both technological and socioeconomic—prior to the Federal Reserve Act (the key to inflation), the Sixteenth Amendment (the institution of the income tax), and the New Deal and Great Society (which produced today's welfare state), all of which have helped lead to the destruction of a way of life so attractive that people from all over the world yearned to share in it.

We do live in the greatest and freest country on earth, but it is much less great and much less free than it once was. The question is, Do we love living here enough to do something not only about preserving what is left of that greatness and freedom, but also to restore them to their original status?

Those who call others unpatriotic or negative because they point out the realities of our decaying democratic republic have it backward. It is they who are unpatriotic for not having a great enough love of freedom to fight to restore it.

For example, a typical reaction of a blind patriot might be to feel that I should be thankful for living in a country where I am allowed to write books such as this one. But should I? I think not. For if I sincerely believe that human freedom is a natural state, then it follows that it is my natural right to express my ideas openly. I believe it would be improper, as well as contradictory, for me to be thankful to others for allowing me to do something that it is my natural right to do.

I am, however, glad that I do not live in a country that would not allow me to write this book. And therein lies an important point. I am not writing this book because I believe that the United States has the worst form of government in the world. If anything, I am writing it for the opposite reason—the fact that we probably still are the freest country on earth, but that I am concerned we are moving at mach speed in the direction of other liberty-starved nations around the globe. I am writing it because I believe our government, like all governments throughout history, is winning its long-standing tender offer to its citizens: security in exchange for freedom.

In *The Federalist Papers*, James Madison warned, "In framing a government which is to be administered by men over men, the great difficulty lies in this: you must first enable the government to control the governed; and in the next place oblige it to control itself."

Madison's warnings were not heeded. The government did not, and does not, control itself. *Government by the people* now means that government can take a substantial amount of your income, evict you from your home if you refuse to pay the real estate taxes it arbitrarily establishes, close the doors to your business if you do not comply with its regulations and licensing laws, print worthless dollars to help others compete with your hard-earned dollars for the goods and services available in the marketplace, dictate what prices you must charge for your products and what you must pay your employees, and tell you what you can and cannot put into your own body.

Government by the people has come to mean *government by those in power.*

It took many millennia before man was ready to make his way out of the jungle and onto the savannah. But once the Agrarian Revolution began, his life became one of rapid change. The Agrarian Revolution brought with it the advent of government, and, except for a few brief moments in history, men of power have been in control ever since.

The biggest setback to governmental control over people was the American Revolution. Within less than 150 years, however, the government in our country had begun to assert firm control over Americans. While democracy is probably the best form of government ever devised, once the system became firmly entrenched it was only a matter of time before power holders contrived a way to manipulate it to their advantage. The key to the system became majority rule, engineered through the power of the vote. As early as 1857, Thomas Macaulay, the British historian, predicted what the inevitable results of the system would be:

The day will come when [in the United States] a multitude of people will choose the legislature. Is it possible to doubt what sort of a legislature will be chosen? On the one side is a statesman preaching patience, respect for rights, strict observance of public faith. On the other is a demagogue ranting about the tyranny of capitalism and usurers and asking why anybody should be permitted to drink champagne and to ride in a carriage while thousands of honest people are in want of necessaries. Which of the candidates is likely to be preferred by a workman? . . . When Society has entered on this downward progress, either civilization or liberty must perish. Either some Caesar or Napoleon will seize the reins of government with a strong hand, or your Republic will be as fearfully plundered and laid waste by barbarians in the twentieth century as the Roman Empire in the fifth; with this difference, that the Huns and vandals who ravaged the Roman Empire came from without, and that your

Huns and vandals will have been engendered within your country, by your own institutions.

Macaulay's powers of prophecy were incredibly accurate. Our democratic republic has destroyed itself through an excess of democracy. Majority rule has evolved into a free-for-all stampede of citizens appealing to politicians to give them more and more of the plunder. On the horizon is chaos, and just beyond is totalitarian rule. I believe those who don't take this threat seriously will live to regret it. The progressive barbarians have already taken full control of our nation's capitol!

It is time to face the reality that man no longer shapes government to his liking; government shapes man to its liking via the clever use of the vote. *Atlas Shrugged, Brave New World,* and *Nineteen Eighty-Four* can no longer be dismissed as far-out fiction. These books were prophecies, and the prophecies in them are coming true before our very eyes. Indeed, many of the prophecies in books like these not only have come to pass, but are now accepted as a normal way of life. People do, indeed, learn to love their servitude.

Today one feels the ether of these books in the air. Rational people know something is very wrong with America. There is tension and uncertainty. There is ill will. There is fear. Some forty years ago, Eric Hoffer observed that "the feeling of doom is stronger now. There is a widespread feeling that our economic system and our civilization are nearing their end. In the 1930s we still had values, ideals, hopes, illusions, certitudes. In the 1970s many people see life drained of meaning, and there is hardly a certitude left."

Which begs the question: If those were Eric Hoffer's thoughts forty years ago, what would he have to say about today's state of the union? I doubt he'd buy into the notion that the promise of more government control over people's lives equates to restoring the American Dream.

The excitement of living seems to have deserted us. The spirit of adventure and the willingness to take risks have been grossly diminished. Our once-cherished Stoic virtues have been abandoned. We have allowed the power holders to steal from us the joy of life itself. More than 200 years of government-inspired nothink and doublethink have desecrated the American Dream.

The only question that remains is, can it be restored?

Reality

The starting point for solving any problem is reality, and many unpleasant realities stand in the way of restoring the American Dream. Regardless of any pessimism these realities may cause, they cannot be ignored if we are to have any hope of taking back America.

First, of course, is the reality that there have always been, and always will be, people who aspire to power over others. To make matters worse, the envious nature and absolute morality of a great many people fuel this yearning for power. People who desire to see the happiness and success of those more fortunate than them destroyed, or who wish to impose their moral standards on their neighbors, are a politician's dream. Along with the other expedient cravings of virtually all citizens, these two ugly desires are able to tyrannize peace-loving people through the mechanism of the vote. Because of these realities, it is unrealistic to believe that people can ever be completely free (i.e., free of all government control and, in effect, be able to self-govern).

We should also recognize that democracy is a power scheme that few people will ever fully understand. If it operated strictly on the basis of safeguarding the rights of individuals, democracy would work very well. But in its twenty-first century version, it is something quite different. It not only gives the illusion of the consent of those governed, it also creates the illusion of helping the poor. But in reality, as I have explained throughout this book, low-income people are merely used as political pawns.

Another reality of no minor consequence is that most people living today have grown up in an era of increasingly collectivist thinking. They understand neither the realities of collectivism nor that there is a far superior alternative to it. Never having experienced the freedom of the early 1900s, let alone the freedom of our Founding Fathers, they have no way of realizing—especially in view of the well-planned nothink and double-think teachings of our public schools—that what they are experiencing is not freedom, but progressive tyranny.

Then there are those who insist on hiding their heads in the sand and merely tossing it all aside with the attitude that "the world has always had problems." Such people often point to the fact that we survived the Great Depression with flying colors. But, as John Hospers detailed in an article in *Reason* magazine, such people avoid many sobering realities. For one, the federal deficit in 1929 was minuscule by today's standards. Today, the astronomical—and growing—federal deficit is an economic lodestone around the neck of every citizen.

In 1929, the dollar still had substantial gold backing, but today our currency is nothing but paper. Prior to the Great Depression, government benefits were practically unknown. Today government handouts and other government functions have destroyed our incentive and consequently our productive capacity, and people have come to expect them.

The harsh realities that stand between those who cherish liberty and the restoration of the American Dream are considerable in both number and scope. Given these realities, some people have even opted to expatriate, and that exodus will accelerate as the current progressive administration intensifies its war against wealth and success. But there is a sobering reality attached to expatriation: Today there is virtually no place on earth where people do not have the jackboot of government on their necks.

No matter where you go, there will be a government in control. And most, if not all, of them are worse than our own government—at least for now. I myself gave both New Zealand and Australia a try for a number of years, and, although I loved the aura of both countries, I eventually returned to the United States. So, given the slim chances of finding a better place to live, I believe the best hope for the American Dream is to try to resurrect it in America.

Solutions

Unfortunately, as every adult is well aware, there are no perfect solutions in this world. Solutions are created by human beings, and human beings are imperfect creatures. Nevertheless, I believe there are solutions that, if implemented, could begin to turn us in the direction of restoring the American Dream. Perhaps this is a naiveté I will outgrow with age, but I hope not.

I would like you to think of the suggestions I offer in this final chapter as sparks. I hope they will ignite enthusiasm and creativity in other advocates of human freedom and that they in turn will devise more and better ideas for recapturing our lost liberty.

Before I began writing this book, I was fully aware that when one attempts to make people conscious of realities, he is all but assured of being written off by many as a prophet of doom. On the other hand, if one writes only in idealistic terms, few rational people will take him seriously.

Thus, in trying to come up with solutions, my objective has been to link realism and idealism. In other words, given the realities of our situation, what are the most practical actions we can take to begin moving in the direction of a free society once more?

Put another way, what is the best way to deal with the unconstitutional stranglehold our government has on American citizens and improve the prospects of a free America for future generations?

Intellectually, I will always believe that purist libertarianism is the ideal. But from the standpoint of practical solutions (i.e., bringing about libertarian change rather than libertarian discussion), I feel it is a grave mistake to refuse to take the realities of today's world into consideration when searching for solutions. Whether a totally free society is ever possible is an academic question; however, taking the first step toward it is not.

Like my Agrarian Revolution ancestors, I myself question whether civilization can exist without some form of government. Perhaps I have not evolved far enough in my thinking (and in my faith in mankind) to envision a civilized society, in the twenty-first century, devoid of any form of government.

For those who believe in freedom, but share my apprehensions about a society without government, the contradiction will always be there: To preserve freedom, some freedoms must be restricted. While on the one hand I acknowledge the need for protection from forcible interference by others, the reality is that the mere existence of government *is* forcible interference.

The crucial question, then, is where does one draw the line between individual independence and social control? How does one define exactly what constitutes forcible interference? Is pollution of the air (even noise pollution) forcible interference? The law of nonaggression is a good guide, but, admittedly, the answers to many questions about freedom are subjective. Even in a totally libertarian world, there would still be the problem of what to do when one person's freedom interferes with that of another.

Is democracy the best solution we can come up with in an attempt to be as free as possible in a civilized world? At present, it appears to be (although many purist libertarians believe that a world with no government at all would work very well). However, to concede that democracy is probably the best system of government that man has been able to come up with does not rule out the possibility of a better solution at some future date. Our minds should always be open to this possibility if we are sincere about our desire to improve our own well-being and that of our children and grandchildren.

But until that better solution comes along, I believe we would be wise to try to maximize the present system. And maximizing the system means minimizing the problem: government. It means acting on the belief that "that government is best which governs least."

What a nightmarish predicament for a purist libertarian. By conceding even minimal powers to government, he also concedes that certain rights of certain people must be violated. This is so because in order for government to perform any function, it must expropriate assets from others. The purist libertarian's solution to this dilemma, of course, is to make taxation and government control voluntary, and to recognize the right of every individual to self-rule (i.e., if anyone does not wish to subscribe to government protection, he should be left alone to fend for himself).

Morally speaking, what right does the majority have to force anyone to come under government rule? If democratic government is truly by consent of the governed, then it would seem that anyone wishing not to be governed should be allowed to go his own way. For purposes of our discussion, however, I will set aside this argument because it opens areas of debate that, for proper presentation, would require a book unto itself.

In Chapter 1, I said that if a person claims to understand human freedom, yet insists on certain exceptions to it, he is either admitting that he is advocating the violation of Natural Law or demonstrating that he does not really grasp its concept. Thus, I want to emphasize that I am not advocating the violation of Natural Law when I concede minimal functions to government. On the contrary, I am advocating that government control of individuals' lives be reduced to an absolute minimum, as quickly as is practical. More specifically, what I am advocating is the maximization of liberty.

While from a purely philosophical and ideological standpoint it may be distasteful to compromise, I would argue that to decrease current violations of Natural Law by 90 percent or more is an attractive midterm goal. Once accomplished, we could then concentrate on how best to handle the remaining 10 percent (i.e., the remaining government functions) on a wholly consensual basis, without the need for government coercion.

Nevertheless, so long as that 10 percent exists, the same questions will continue to haunt us: Whose rights shall be violated? To what extent? Who shall decide? The hope that these questions can be resolved in a manner reasonably satisfactory to most people rests on an assumption that I made at the outset of this book: that most men and women, when armed with truth, will act honestly and decently; that most men and women are basically good, but misled; that most men and women, once they understand the facts, will act in good faith.

If these assumptions are wrong, then it is doubtful that any solution will work. Remember, we do, indeed, get the government we deserve.

What Won't Work

Before discussing a number of steps that I believe could help restore liberty to our country, it would be instructive to examine a few things that will not work. Too often when people are eager for solutions, they plunge in recklessly and take the same kind of expedient action that has caused the very problems with which we are now confronted. As Bernard Baruch, the great wizard of Wall Street, pointed out, rushing around and taking action just for the sake of action is usually nonproductive:

> *Mankind has always sought to substitute energy for reason, as if running faster will give one a better sense of direction. Periodically, we should stop and ask ourselves if our efforts are focused upon the crux of the problem—the things that must be settled if there is*

to be a manageable solution—or if we are expending our energies on side issues which cannot yield a decision, no matter what their outcome.

Examples of Things that Will Not Work

Listening to or spewing out meaningless patriotic rhetoric, whether in the form of slogans, admonishing statements, or appeals to custom and tradition. Patriotic gibberish will not do anything to move us in the direction of more liberty.

One time, loud and clear: You are not indebted to government (i.e., elected politicians and bureaucrats) for allowing you to exercise your natural rights. You were born with these rights, and government can take them away from you only through the use of force. As Rose Wilder Lane explained:

> *If Americans ever forget that American Government is not permitted to restrain or coerce any peaceful individual without his free consent, if Americans ever regard their use of their natural liberty as granted to them by the men in Washington or in the capitals of the States, then this third attempt (the American Revolution) to establish the exercise of human rights on earth is ended. . . .*
>
> *Everything that an American values, his property, his home, his life, his children's future, depends upon his keeping clear in his mind the revolutionary basis of this Republic.*
>
> *This revolutionary basis is recognition of the fact that human rights are natural rights, born in every human being with his life, and inseparable from his life; not rights and freedoms that can be granted by any power on earth.*

Self-proclaimed patriots profess a love of country; libertarian-centered conservatives profess a love of human freedom.

Continuing to listen to destructive, short-term solutions served up by vote-conscious politicians. From FDR and his New Deal to Barack Obama and his *New* New Deal, devious and corrupt politicians have showered us with instant-gratification programs and policies that have brought our economy to the verge of collapse. When people's emotions run high, they are vulnerable to following a charismatic leader who offers easy solutions. But easy solutions almost always make things worse in the long term.

It's time to start ignoring the political solutions that have been the cause of our problems. Power holders should no longer have your ear when they talk about stimulating the economy through government intervention, prate on about the common good, or espouse the evils of corporate greed. To paraphrase Voltaire, men will stop committing atrocities when men stop believing absurdities.

Looking to government for solutions to your problems. Government cannot solve your problems, because—as Ronald Reagan emphasized—government *is* the problem. When people proclaim that "there ought to be a law" to correct what they deem to be a "social injustice," they are advocating the use of government force to make others conform to their personal desires or moral beliefs.

Government force is something we should strive to minimize. The world is full of problems and purported injustices. If you use your efforts to try to solve these problems through the use of government force (i.e., through new legislation), you are further increasing the problems. On the other hand, if you focus on your own freedom and self-sufficiency, you are contributing to the solution.

Compassion, charity, and concern are good things. Force is not a good thing. The question is not whether man loves his fellow man enough to insist on helping him. The survival question for mankind is whether man loves his fellow man enough to leave him alone! Your neighbor has the right to be left alone to live his life as he so chooses.

As Nobel Prize novelist and poet Anatole France put it, "Those who have given themselves the most concern about the happiness of peoples have made their neighbors very miserable."

Getting hung up on the question of equality. Guaranteed security and equality conflict with freedom. As Will and Ariel Durant put it, "when one prevails the other dies." Efforts toward forcible equality have gained momentum over the past fifty years, and faster than ever under the progressive Obama regime now in power. The American Dream is for all people to have equal *rights*; it does not call for making all people equal. There is a big difference between the two.

Wasting your time arguing with irrational people—those who believe that something for nothing is possible; that transfer of wealth is justified by a worthwhile objective; or that government is a living, omnipotent, omnibenevolent entity that can solve everyone's problems. You do not have enough time in your life to improve your own well-being, enhance the cause of liberty, and also function as a flyswatter.

What You Can Do without Becoming a Crusader

Many people do not have the inclination to become involved in movements or crusades because they believe they are a waste of time, and I generally agree with such a view. But you can help take back America, and thereby regain much of your individual freedom, without becoming a crusader or getting involved in group action.

There are several ways in which this can be accomplished:

Most important, be consistent on the issue of human freedom. In dealing with others, always adhere to the philosophy of nonaggression. I stated in Chapter 1 that the initial premise for the philosophy set forth in this book is that each person owns his own life and therefore has the right to do anything he wishes with that life, so long as he does not use force or fraud against others. I referred to this concept as Natural Law.

I also emphasized that liberty must be given a higher priority than all other objectives, and that one may not, with integrity, abandon his belief in the supremacy of liberty on an emotional whim. This means rejecting any action that involves aggression against others, no matter how worthy you may believe the objective to be.

This unrelenting commitment to liberty requires an understanding of, and belief in, the inseparable connection between freedom and property rights. To take a person's property, regardless of one's justification, is a violation of his human freedom. You should refuse to be a part of any such action in every area possible.

Being adamantly in favor of liberty does not mean you are insensitive to the needs of others, so do not allow anyone to intimidate you with such accusations. Attempting to solve the needs of the poor by the use of force against others is an immoral action and will only succeed in creating worse problems for everyone.

You may wish to contribute to charity voluntarily, and it is certainly your right to do so. Indeed, one of the things that would emerge from a restoration of the American Dream would be an increase in charity. When people are free to keep what they earn, a spirit of charity is much more likely to prevail.

Wage a personal battle against any traces of envy that may have a hold on you. Envy is a negative emotion that not only is counterproductive to your attempts to improve your own well-being, but also has been instrumental in the destruction of the American Dream. Dispense with any notion you may have that your neighbor's material success is somehow a loss to you.

Your success is totally dependent on your own efforts. The opportunity to become as rich as one's talents and efforts could make him was an integral thread that ran through the original concept of the American Dream. As previously stated, America cannot afford not to have rich people, for they are the backbone of productivity, employment, and a better life for all, with or without their enormous charitable contributions.

Demystify and desanctify government, both in your thinking and in your conversations with others. This necessitates developing the habit of challenging basic assumptions. For example, while your peers may wish to debate which government projects or services are a waste of tax dollars or the extent to which people should be taxed, you should have the courage to challenge the basic premise—that confiscation of an individual's property, for *any* reason, is immoral and in violation of Natural Law.

Also, stop thinking of government as a living entity. *Government* is a name given to a group of individuals who seek power over others through the workings of the vote. You are not being disloyal or unpatriotic when you do not go along with their immoral edicts. If our system truly were government of the people and by the people, politicians would have to do what we told them to do. If they did not, then *they* would be guilty of being disloyal and unpatriotic.

Almost without fail, the long-term results of government actions are the exact opposite of what they are purported to be. Among the scores of examples covered in this book, perfect illustrations of this are how minimum-wage laws cause unemployment, wage-and-price controls cause higher prices, and licensing laws make it virtually impossible for those at the bottom of the economic ladder to start a business.

Above all, reject government's use of the mysterious-multiplier concept. As explained in Chapter 3, it has no basis in fact.

When you disrobe government myths and help spread the truth to others in your normal day-to-day conversations, you will be making an important contribution to the cause of liberty without being involved in a crusade.

Never go out of your way to cooperate with the government. Try to avoid all situations that involve your becoming entangled with the government. Many people, due to patriotic rhetoric or the erroneous belief that government is all-good, all-knowing, and all-powerful, mistakenly go out of their way to make it easier for government to interfere in their lives. By all means, obey the law—but nothing more.

For example, don't allow the government to influence your decisions regarding foods, vitamins, and other substances that you wish to ingest into your own body, or decisions regarding sexual matters or any other issues that come under the umbrella of victimless-crime laws. You are not morally obligated to cooperate with government's presumptuous attempts to interfere in your private life. (You may, however, choose to be discreet for personal reasons.)

It goes without saying that investing in government securities would be the biggest of all mistakes in cooperating with government violations of freedom. First, the money raised from the sale of such securities is used to support government functions, almost all of which entail aggression against others. Second, such securities can be repaid only through the sale of new securities or with drastically devalued dollars.

Make an unwavering commitment to become fiercely independent and individualistic. The restoration of the American Dream is the restoration of self-responsibility. Self-actualization is an exhilarating experience that government cannot give you. By minding your own business—by being independent and individualistic—you will be making a great contribution to liberty by eliminating yourself as part of the problem. Thoreau believed that "living one's own life to the full is the best means of helping one's fellow man." I totally agree.

Virtues such as individualism, self-control, self-responsibility, and respect for private property, which made the American Dream come true for millions of people, are in direct contrast to the desire for guaranteed security and dependence on government. "The price of individual liberty," said Rose Wilder Lane, "is individual responsibility and insecurity. . . . When common men were slaves and serfs, they obeyed and they were fed, but they died by thousands in plagues and famines. Free men paid for their freedom by leaving that false and illusory security."

The only way you, as an individual, can ever hope to be free—at least in mind and spirit, if not in body—is to know that you have earned everything you have received. Which brings us to the next point—one of the toughest to adhere to, but perhaps the most important of all.

When at all possible, neither ask for nor accept government favors, handouts, or benefits of any kind. While the realities of monopoly and coercion leave you no practical choice but to use some government services (roads, libraries, postal system, etc.), you should demonstrate your independence, individuality, and self-esteem by refusing to participate in government's redistribution schemes.

Remember, in the final analysis, it's voters who are responsible for deficit spending and inflation because their expediency factors encourage politicians to take politically expedient actions. The problem is therefore perpetuated by the fact that most citizens continue to clamor for their "fair share"—and more.

If you would rather be part of the solution than part of the problem, you should ask only one thing of government: Leave me alone! Every individual who stops asking for and accepting handouts lessens the government's ability to carry out its schemes to increase its power over citizens.

The question that comes to mind, of course, is who will take the first step? Who will be the first to give up his share of government largesse, while millions of others are still benefiting from it? The answer is *you*. If every person who reads this book would start to refuse government benefits, a small ripple would begin to be felt. And if every person who reads this book would state his feelings about government handouts to his friends and acquaintances, it could cause a substantial ripple.

(I realize that it is neither practical nor humane to ask people to give up their Social Security and Medicare benefits cold turkey, and I offer a solution to these entitlement programs later in this chapter.)

The cycle must be broken. Politicians make politically expedient promises to get elected, violate the rights of citizens in order to carry out those promises, and borrow money (which can never be repaid) and inflate the currency (to pay for promises that cannot be covered by direct taxation and borrowing)—all of which help destroy incentive and demoralize the public. The public in turn calls for still more government controls on business in response to politicians who mislead them as to the real source of their problems. The final effect of all this is to destroy production and employment.

The first step toward breaking this cycle is for you, the expediency-minded voter, to stop being fooled by short-term benefits designed only to capture votes. Start thinking long term, which means being concerned about a total economic collapse and a resulting loss of freedom.

As former U.S. Comptroller General David Walker has been preaching for years, if the economy continues on its present course, it is guaranteed to self-destruct. And that would mean that you would be working not only long after the time you had planned to retire, but also at a job that the government chooses for you, during the working hours it dictates, and for the wages it believes you should be paid.

Everyone who receives a government check of any kind—which includes citizens and noncitizens—is contributing to the further destruction of the American Dream. What each of us should ask ourselves is, Is my piece of the government pie worth it to me if it means that my children and grandchildren will live in a police state brought about by the financial collapse of our economy?

If you now work for the government, the biggest contribution you can make to America is to quit your job and find work in the private sector. If you are responsible and conscientious, the marketplace is full of opportunities for you. And when you put your efforts into private industry, you will be producing wealth (i.e., products and services that people actually want, not services they are forced to use).

And, speaking for myself, I certainly do not want government protecting me from myself, whether such protection involves foods, medications, or safety devices. I decline government help in all these areas, maintaining a staunch conviction that I am quite capable of making all decisions regarding my own well-being.

Americans must grow up. We must become wary of anyone—especially politicians—who implies that people can live without producing. Government favors, services, and handouts are paid for by *we, the people*, which is why they must be refused whenever and wherever circumstances permit us to do so. Intellectually, the morality of spreading the wealth must be refuted at all times.

Do not think of yourself as part of a group. Groups are grist for the politician's mill. By aligning yourself with others on the basis of sex, race, religion, profession, or any other factor, you play into the hands of those who seek your vote. The result is the creation of voting blocs—labor against business, blacks against whites, rich against poor, men against women, and so on—blocs to which politicians excel at making expedient promises. Grouping is an expediency-factor trap laid by government.

If you're an African-American, Mexican-American, senior citizen, or a member of any other minority, refuse to allow government to use you as a political pawn. Politicians are not your friends; they merely exploit you to win elections. You have a valid right to be individualistic. Government can use force against citizens, but it has no power to change their thoughts. Self-respect and the respect of others cannot be given to you by politicians. They are commodities that must be earned.

Think of yourself as an individual. To live in a free society, individuals must be free.

Ignore self-styled consumer advocates and other publicity-hungry crusaders who have set themselves up as civilian protectors of the public. Even before the advent of Ralph Nader, consumer advocates helped accelerate government intervention in the economy, which has played a major role in its destruction. No self-styled crusader has a right to speak on your behalf.

If I am dissatisfied with a product or service, I am quite capable of complaining to the company from whom I purchased it. If the company refuses to give me satisfaction, I have the option of either not dealing with that company in the future or taking the dispute to court (charging fraud or violation of an implied contractual obligation).

If you are a businessperson, stop running to the government for special favors, monopoly protection, price fixing, and other forms of intervention. The effects of such action have already been discussed at length. To the extent you seek special favors from the government, you are contributing to the problem. To the extent you refuse to be a party to such government intervention, you are contributing to the solution.

In addition, stop appeasing free-enterprise antagonists. Have the courage to stand up for, and openly defend, the economic system that made the American Dream possible.

Take a rational, well-thought-out approach to the question of voting. Because of the Four Great Political Realities discussed in Chapter 2, coupled with the fact that voting seems to represent nothing but a validation of the system, voting for the wrong reasons can actually be an immoral act.

When it comes to voting, you should always ask yourself the following question: Am I voting for someone because I genuinely want him to govern me or because I believe him to be the lesser of two evils? With just a few exceptions, over the past 50 years this has brought mostly less-evil men into the Oval Office to rule over us. Never forget that the lesser of two evils is still evil.

It could be legitimately argued that the person who votes for a candidate simply because he is not as bad as any of the other candidates is unpatriotic. That's because he is, in effect, acting as an enabler to a politician he considers to be unworthy, encouraging him to believe that "the people have chosen."

Since the day he was inaugurated, Barack Obama has hammered his subjects over the head with his insistence that the American people gave him a mandate—even though, as pointed out earlier, slightly less than 30 percent of the 231 million eligible voters actually voted for him. Thus, the millions of people who voted for Obama only because they viewed him as the lesser of two evils (read, John McCain) unwittingly became his enablers by helping to create the illusion in his mind that he had a mandate of the people.

The sad truth is that in most elections (though not all), it doesn't matter who wins. When Democrats are in office, they move aggressively to the left. When most Republicans gain office, they meekly accept the Democrats' agenda and merely slow things down a bit—but they still move to the left!

It's time that we wake up and face the reality that government does not represent us. Candidates are elected by an elite group of men and women who have managed to finesse their way through the political maze that leads to the inner circle of the establishment. The lesser-of-two-evils voting philosophy merely validates the right of government to perpetuate the mandate ruse.

If the ballot does not provide you with the opportunity to vote for a candidate who places liberty above all other objectives, the only way you can exercise your so-called freedom is to not vote—which, in reality, is a protest vote. I appreciate that this is anathema to many well-meaning, patriotic Americans, but when someone chastises you for not voting, isn't he really saying that you have no right to exercise a "no" vote?

I am not presumptuous enough to advise you whether to vote in any given election. I am simply encouraging you to take the issue of voting very seriously. Before casting, or not casting, any ballot, you should consider your decision from an intellectual, moral, and practical viewpoint.

Above all, if you do vote, you owe it to yourself, your family, and future generations to work hard to make certain that people you believe will uphold the Constitution are on the ballot—whether they be Democrats, Republicans, Libertarians, or members of any other party. Party affiliation is not nearly as important as ideological beliefs. If you believe in the true meaning of the American Dream, you already are a libertarian-centered conservative—regardless of whether you call yourself a Republican, Democrat, Libertarian, or nonvoter.

The greatest challenge of liberty-loving people in this country is how we can get men and women elected to high office on a platform that does not promise more government benefits to expediency-minded voters. This is why I am such a strong proponent of educating the public. In the end, the public does, indeed, get the government it deserves.

I leave you with one word of caution: Never forget that the government is armed and dangerous and therefore has the means to change the rules of the game at any time. It does, in fact, do so continually—and has accelerated its "fundamental change of America" considerably since the last presidential election. That puts you, me, and everyone else at a decided disadvantage, no matter how much we may wish to help the cause of freedom. Government can change anything and everything overnight simply by passing a new law. And today, major changes are being made without Congress even having the opportunity to vote on them.

Major Solutions on a Political Level

If you are inclined to become more involved (i.e., help bring about change on a scale that goes beyond making sure that your own day-to-day actions are consistent with the ideals of liberty), there are many ways you can contribute. Because most of today's laws violate human rights, campaigning for the repeal of such laws is a worthwhile endeavor.

An important note of caution: Do not get lulled into the trap of trying to make everyone in our society financially equal. That is precisely what expediency-minded politicians have been doing for years. To restore the American Dream, the objective must be to return to a system whereby everyone has an equal *opportunity* to improve his well-being—an equal opportunity to pursue his life, liberty, and happiness without interference from others.

Our overall objective should be to bring about a drastic reduction in the power of man over man and a maximization of liberty. And that in turn translates into minimizing both the size and scope of government. Plain and simple, minimizing government means reducing it to its only legitimate functions:

- Providing protection for the lives and property of citizens.
- Providing a system of arbitrating contractual disputes.
- Providing for a national defense.

On at least one point, all libertarians, conservatives, and libertarian-centered conservatives are united: It is not government's function to help people fulfill their desires. Such help translates into fueling expediency factors and inevitable violations of human rights. In short, the more government is minimized, the more it becomes government of the people, by the people, and for the people.

There are several ways in which minimization of government can be accomplished:

- *All office holders, especially the president, should serve only one term.* This one step would remove a great deal of corruption from the system. While it may be true that politicians would still have to lie to get elected, at least they would not feel as obliged to deliver on their promises of aggression once in office.

  We should do away with professional politicians once and for all. Some people might argue that this would not give politicians time to develop their political skills, but that would be a *good* thing. Political skills give politicians the expertise to manipulate us to their benefit, particularly for the purpose of getting reelected. The professional politician should become an extinct species. After one term, all politicians should be required to return to the real world and earn a living just like everyone else.

- *Most taxes should be phased out as swiftly as is practical.* When I say *practical*, what I am referring to is avoiding the chaos that would ensue if government were to suddenly have no source of revenue. I am an advocate for peaceful, positive change.

  The taxation burden was brought about in a gradual manner, and I believe it should be phased out in the same way. Perhaps a twenty-five-year plan of cutting back on the income tax, at the rate of

4 percent a year, would be realistic. The ultimate objective, of course, should be to repeal the Sixteenth Amendment so that the government would never again have the right to tax people's incomes. Eventually, only voluntary user charges on government services might remain as a way to cover government's minimal expenditures.

Two other alternatives are also worth exploring. One is the flat tax—taxing everyone the same low percentage of their incomes so that taxation becomes a fairer proposition. And, as a huge bonus, dealing with taxes would not require the massive amount of paperwork that it does today.

The other alternative is the fair tax—a national sales tax on goods and services purchased, which would eliminate the need for filing tax returns altogether. It would also eliminate a hugely expensive and intrusive bureaucracy. Interestingly, more than one highly respected politician and economist has said that some IRS officials have told them they would actually favor such simplification measures.

The inflation tax, of course, should be repealed immediately, meaning that government should not be allowed to print new money at all, except to replace money that is damaged or worn out. If there were no budget deficits, there would be no need to print money. As previously explained, if production increased without a corresponding increase in the supply of money, prices would drop. Each dollar would be worth more because there would be fewer of them.

There is no other way to deal with inflation. So-called hedging against inflation creates a society of speculators and further weakens production. As Henry Hazlitt cautioned, "There is no safe hedge against inflation except to stop it." Longer term, after people have had an opportunity to see the wonders that a decrease in the printing of paper money can bring, the goal should be to get government completely out of the money business. This means repealing the legal tender laws and abolishing the engine of the inflation fraud— the Federal Reserve System. The ultimate solution, of course, is a 100 percent gold-backed money system of privately issued receipts.

■ *The redistribution-of-wealth functions of government should be phased out, which means cutting government spending to the bone.* This, of course, is the corollary to phasing out taxes. Government spending would simply decline at the same rate as the decline in taxes.

Within a matter of a few years, this cutback would begin to turn our whole economy around. Those at the low end of the economic ladder would start to see the benefits within a short time because they are hurt most by government spending and taxation. The worse the economy, the worse it is for the poor. Presently, most of these people have no way of understanding the facts underlying this truth, so they keep right on voting for redistribution-of-wealth programs.

These less fortunate people do not understand the inherent contradiction in the welfare-state philosophy, a contradiction that must inevitably lead to collapse. Simply put, to have wealth to redistribute, you need a high level of production; redistribution programs, however, destroy incentive and productivity, so there is less and less to redistribute.

While some programs, such as unemployment benefits and various other forms of welfare, should be phased out over shorter periods of time, others, particularly the Social Security scheme, should be phased out over much longer periods. Because a large majority of citizens have been victims of the Social Security swindle, the fairest approach would be to decrease benefits over, say, a forty-year period so people who have been counting on Social Security for their retirement years would not be financially devastated.

In other words, people becoming eligible for Social Security during the first year that such a plan went into effect would receive 100 percent of their promised benefits; people eligible the next year would receive only 97.5 percent; those eligible the third year would receive 95 percent; and so on.

■ *Government services, and thus government employees, should be gradually eliminated.* Again, it would be important here to make the phase-out period reasonable enough so that government employees could be absorbed into the private sector. Employees who have been at their jobs twenty or thirty years obviously should not be thrown out of work. In most cases, such employees have innocently invested their lives in government job security, with perfectly good intentions.

The smoothest way to effect a transition would be over a long period of time, with those who have been on government payrolls the least number of years being terminated first. As older employees die off, their jobs should simply be eliminated. Eventually, what we would end up with would be more people gainfully employed in the private sector, producing the goods and services that consumers actually want. For reasons that have been repeated throughout this book, this makes for a healthy economy and improves everyone's well-being.

Longer term, there would still be postal workers, firefighters, and other kinds of civil servants, except they would no longer work for the government. They would be employees of private companies performing the same functions as before—only better, less expensively, and more efficiently than in the old government-employment days.

■ *The law of supply and demand should be allowed to operate freely.* This can be accomplished only by abolishing virtually all governmental regulatory agencies and repealing virtually all laws regulating business. Among those that should be repealed immediately are minimum-wage laws, so-called antitrust and anti-monopoly laws (which actually establish and protect monopolies), fair-pricing laws, and rent-control laws. It goes without saying that all business subsidies of any kind should be outlawed.

All regulatory agencies should be eliminated over a period of no more than ten years, but the most useless and harmful ones should be dismantled at once so that business could get back to producing wealth, increasing employment, and making life better for everyone.

Among the agencies that should be abolished immediately are the SEC, FCC, and FTC. I had originally planned to include the EPA and the Occupational Safety and Health Administration (OSHA) in this list of agencies to be immediately abolished, but, on reflection, I feel they should be dismantled over a period of two to three years. This would give those who have legitimate concerns regarding worker safety and the quality of our environment confidence that the heavy hand of government is not needed to safeguard these areas. I wish to make it clear, however, that I believe EPA and OSHA to be among the most destructive of governmental agencies, if for no other reason than the fact that they cripple productivity, which actually *endangers* people's lives.

■ *In the same vein, so-called consumer advocates, environmentalists, and other self-proclaimed protectors of the people should be held civilly and criminally liable for their actions.* If such people use coercion or force to interfere with the freedom of others, including the freedom of businesspeople, they should be vigorously prosecuted. And, needless to say, they should not be handed tax dollars to carry out their self-righteous crusades. Like everyone else, they should have to work for a living or suffer the consequences of unemployment.

■ *Most government property and businesses should be sold.* Not being an individual or privately run company, the government has no right to own land or operate businesses and refer to them by the abstract term *public ownership*. Public ownership simply means that those in power control certain property. Incredibly, the federal government owns some 657 million acres of land, or nearly 30 percent of all land in this country. In Alaska alone it owns about 98 percent of the land, while in Nevada the figure is about 86 percent.

As Lysander Spooner pointed out more than a century ago, for government to claim that it owns vast tracts of land lying between the Atlantic and Pacific Oceans is absurd. Government is supposed to protect the lives and property of individuals. How in the world did it get into the business of owning land?

By selling off most of its land, buildings, and businesses, government would be able to pay off the entire national debt and probably have trillions of dollars left over to rebate to citizens. As a bonus, the absurd notion of public property would cease to exist, which would eliminate many areas of argument about what that term really means.

- *All victimless-crime laws should be repealed, and all people imprisoned for violations of such laws should immediately be granted a full pardon.* These include not only the traditional victimless-crime laws, but also rarely discussed victimless-crime laws relating to compulsory education, home schooling, and affirmative action.

- *All laws that invade the privacy of individuals should be repealed, and no new laws to make such invasion easier for government should be enacted.*

The millions of files the government now holds on American citizens—for example, FBI and CIA files that contain material of a strictly private nature—should be destroyed. It sounds great to ramble on about how these agencies protect our lives from domestic and foreign threats, but the reality is that these agencies spend too much of their time snooping on private citizens.

I realize this is a sensitive subject, but it's one that needs to be thoroughly examined. How did we get along so nicely without these agencies throughout most of our country's history? It's true that the world is a more dangerous place today than it once was, but keep in mind that these agencies did nothing to prevent 9/11. And, of course, they also got it wrong about weapons of mass destruction (WMD) in Iraq. Those two failures alone have cost thousands of American lives and hundreds of billions of dollars.

Intellectual honesty compels us to ask ourselves if there isn't a better way to protect Americans from both foreign and domestic threats. If the FBI and CIA are to continue, their focus should be 100 percent on those whose aims are to do harm to America and zero percent on American citizens who pose no such threat.

I'm open to debate on this one, but only serious, factual debate. No talking points, please.

- *Our counterproductive interference in the affairs of other nations, including foreign aid, should immediately be brought to a halt.* I purposely avoided discussing foreign policy in this book, primarily because it, too, is a book unto itself. But the mess of our so-called foreign policy has gotten so out of hand that it would be inappropriate not to at least mention it here.

First, along with the decline of other moral virtues, groveling has been the dominant characteristic of our foreign policy for years. We grovel at the feet of third-world nations that demand we give them handouts under the threat of allying themselves with our enemies. Yet, the more we give them, the more they seem to hate us. There is nothing in the Constitution that compels American citizens to give part of their earnings to support people in other countries.

"To be a liberal American today," said Irving Kristol, "is to be infused with instant guilt . . . especially toward poor and distant nations to whom we have never done any harm." The Western world, and the United States in particular, has gradually become the blackmail victim of underdeveloped countries. Much of this has been motivated by our politicians' irrational desire to race around the globe competing with Russia, China, and other perceived enemies and competitors for allies. Had all the billions of taxpayer dollars we've given away bought us the friendship and goodwill of people in other countries, perhaps one could make a practical argument (though not a moral one) that it was worthwhile. But such is not the case.

Our continued interventionist actions in the face of hatred toward America are those of a panicked nation. Our strength from within is decaying, so we comb the earth trying to buy support and friendship to reassure ourselves that we are a worthy people. This, I believe, is the neurosis behind our current president's apology tours.

The same panic and lack of character is reflected in our policy of continuing to enter into political partnerships with totalitarian regimes. It is doublespeak when politicians say that by restoring diplomatic relations with bloody regimes we are taking a step toward understanding them. Who wants to understand criminals?

It is preposterous and weak for the United States to sit in the United Nations and negotiate with dictatorships such as Cuba, North Korea, and Venezuela, whose leaders hold their citizens in bondage. We should withdraw from the United Nations immediately and demand that its headquarters be removed from our soil.

We do not need to spread our shaky dollars around the world frantically begging for friends. We do not need to make political agreements with inhumane dictatorships in order to feel safe. Instead of flooding foreign countries with armaments and free handouts in an effort to buy goodwill, what we should do is set an exemplary domestic example for the rest of the world. Indeed, that is exactly what we did in bygone days when (legal) immigrants came by the millions to our shores to share in the American Dream.

All of us, or our ancestors, were immigrants at one time or another. And, ironically, newly arrived immigrants are the people most endowed with the American spirit because they are thankful for the freedom to accept or reject any job offer. I again emphasize that I am referring here only to legal immigrants.

■ *We should always keep more ambitious goals in mind for the long term when it comes to decreasing the size of government and increasing the liberty of the individual.* Perhaps some day we will figure out a way to maintain an orderly society without the tyranny of majority rule. That is a worthwhile goal for young libertarians, conservatives, and libertarian-centered conservatives at universities to be thinking about—how to make people completely free from the desires of the majority.

Another long-term, ambitious goal should be the attainment of the world's first totally laissez-faire business environment. While it is hard to imagine such freedom at this time, who knows what the future holds if we can succeed at taking back America from the corrupt power holders in Washington and allow individuals to be free to pursue their own well-being? Even if we should never attain a pure laissez-faire society, every step toward it is a step closer to freedom and a better way of life for everyone who is willing to work.

Thinking long term, the goal should be to find a way to completely eliminate government. That is the premier question for young libertarian-centered conservative scholars: Can civilization and order prevail without at least a skeletal form of government to protect people from aggression? Perhaps the dream of a society without government is as unrealistic as Karl Marx's dream of a society where everything would belong to the people in common.

But, who knows? On the scale of a cosmic calendar, modern man has existed for only about 30 seconds out of a one-year period, so perhaps it's just a matter of the evolution of our ability to think in a different dimension. In the meantime, we should always keep in mind the words of Henry David Thoreau: "'That government is best which governs not at all'; and when men are prepared for it, that will be the kind of government which they will have."

You and I will not live to see a nation totally devoid of government, but it is possible that we may live to see an America in which government is relegated primarily to the role of protecting our lives and property—in the words of John Hospers, an America in which we would scarcely be aware of the existence of government.

Restoring the American Dream

Is it too late? Is the system too entrenched to permit the rescue of the bold experiment undertaken by our libertarian founders in Philadelphia in 1776? Is the world so saturated with problems that our only alternatives are world control or world destruction?

If there is to be any hope for mankind, I believe that Americans must succeed in restoring the American Dream. As America has declined at an accelerating pace over the past fifty years, the rest of the world has declined along with it. I do not believe this has been a coincidence. America once represented a shining hope for all mankind—the living proof that freedom was attainable. As that hope has diminished, so too have the aspirations of enslaved peoples throughout the world. And the U.S. government's increasing willingness to negotiate with totalitarian regimes has succeeded in further dampening those aspirations.

If the destructive cycle of politically expedient promises, deficit spending, taxation, borrowing, and inflation is not halted and then drastically reduced, politicians will increasingly use free enterprise as the scapegoat. And as taxation and regulation of business increase, motivation to produce will die, leading to a further nationalization of our industries. That is the step that will take America from its present stage of decay to its final demise. It happened in Greece; it happened in Rome; it's happened in every civilization that has tried to buy off its citizens with government benefits and then blame businesspeople for its financial collapse.

If we are to stop the momentum of repeating the errors of past civilizations, the people of this country must come to understand that wealth without work is an illusion. They must come to understand that if they do not give up government benefits voluntarily, they ultimately will lose them, along with their freedom, through government force.

As I began to write the final chapter of the original edition of this book, I received a piece of literature in the mail that most people would have thrown in the wastebasket. But I kept it because this seemingly unimportant piece of junk mail epitomized the twisted moral standards that are even more prevalent today. It was an advertisement for a book titled *Encyclopedia of U.S. Government Benefits*, and I reprint here some of the advertising copy:

> *Here at last is the only complete guide to government payments and services ever published. You will find . . . how to get Social Security and Medicare benefits, scholarships and loans, a government mortgage . . . what are the eligibility requirements for all benefits; and much more.*

In other words, it was a guide on how to outmaneuver your neighbor for a bigger share of government largesse!

The choice is ours. We can keep our expediency factors in high gear, thus cutting off our left arm and ignoring the fact that we are, in the process, killing our right arm as well. Or we can use our intellect and reasoning power to think long term and start living like civilized people of goodwill.

One of the biggest roadblocks to restoring the American Dream is that each succeeding generation has grown up under increasing government intervention and restraint, thus being conditioned to accept the welfare state and an all-controlling control as normal.

When freedom and free-enterprise advocates of the 1930s tried to warn our parents and grandparents that FDR's folly of false prosperity would be paid for by their children and grandchildren, not many of them took heed. Most were caught up in blind patriotism and thought of FDR as a patron saint. But their patriotism was misguided. They were patriotic to politicians—to men of power—instead of to the cause of liberty. Shall we continue to make the same mistake and destroy what is left of the American Dream?

I was greatly disturbed by a conversation I had many years ago with a friend. I said to him, "Just think, at the rate we're going, people living in the United States fifty years from now will be virtual slaves of a totalitarian regime. Isn't that depressing?"

In response, my friend said that fifty years ago people were sitting around a room just like we were, talking about the same thing. The tyranny they envisioned has turned out to be far worse, but the average person today does not think of it as tyranny because he has grown accustomed to this way of life. Therefore, even though people in this country probably will be living under pure totalitarianism fifty years from now, they will have learned to cope with it and will not think of it as being as bad as we do.

What a depressing thought, particularly in view of recent events in Washington. It was right out of *Brave New World*, when Mustapha Mond assured the Savage that eight-ninths of the people were happier "below the water line." In other words, what one doesn't know won't hurt him. The point is that if a person grows up never having experienced freedom, he has nothing to which he may compare his way of life.

I think about this often as I watch the people of this country hooked on their "somas"—NFL football, reality TV, dining out, and a general attitude of letting the good times roll. Until the recent economic collapse, their minds were so tuned in to enjoying their false prosperity that their general response to our current crisis was, "I just can't believe things are as bad as some of those doomsayers claim they are. The world has always had problems, but the government has a way of muddling through."

Of course, they were entirely wrong. The world has never before been confronted with the problems of today, except on a smaller scale in such places as ancient Greece and Rome, and in those cases, things did not work out. Those civilizations died. (Ironically, modern Greece is dying once again, and for pretty much the same reasons.) And it is absolutely impossible for things to work out for us unless William Simon's statement becomes a reality: "I am confident that the American people would demand massive reforms *if they understood the situation*." [Italics added.]

Our Best Hope

To understand just how serious our plight is and what needs to be done, people—young people, in particular—need to become informed. Unless a massive dissemination of truth occurs, most people will continue to not understand the situation, which virtually assures they will continue to make the situation worse.

The majority of people in this country certainly will never read this book or any other book that unmasks the realities of government. That is why I believe that the best hope for America lies in educating the young. And because government-controlled primary and secondary schools will never willingly teach children the truth, the job must be done by parents and those of us who are willing to put forth the effort to spread the cause of liberty. It is this belief that motivated me to start the Liberty Education Interview Series (www.robertringer.com), which gives people the opportunity to listen to libertarian, conservative, and libertarian-centered conservative leaders discuss the merits of liberty.

Finally, when the original edition of this book was published, it contained a letter to the *Los Angeles Times* from a woman by the name of Linda Timmons. The letter gave me hope that people were beginning to understand the situation and that the American Dream could still be restored.

I've got the paycheck blues again, and it made me start thinking about America, land of the free.

I had always interpreted that phrase to mean I was free to live my life the way I chose. I believed I had the right to make all decisions affecting my life as long as I didn't harm anyone or break any laws. I believed that the laws were there to protect me, and that people who broke them were criminals.

These concepts always sounded fine to me. I was sure I could live a happy, productive life within their framework, because I knew I was an honest, conscientious person responsible for my actions. I was proud to be an American.

I lived with this fantasy until I was 19 years old. That was when my husband received his draft notice, on our first wedding anniversary. Within days, the boy I had loved since I was 13 was gone. The government, which made the laws to "protect" me, said that he had to go where it sent him, and that he had to do what it ordered. If he didn't, he would be a criminal and could go to jail. And so they sent him to Vietnam. They risked his life without his consent. I didn't understand.

My husband came back safely after 11 months, and was honorably discharged from the service. We started a family, saved our money and bought a small house in Hermosa Beach, where we'd grown up. We were careful not to get into debt. Each year the property taxes on our small house increased; in 1976 they doubled, and then last year they doubled again. We couldn't afford the $2,400 that the government wanted—but this was our home, this was the town where we grew up. What were we to do? The government, which made laws to protect us, said that we had to pay if we wanted to stay. I didn't understand.

Proposition 13 lowered our property taxes, so that we could keep our home. But now the court is suggesting that soon my children may not be able to attend the school at the end of our street; they might have to ride a school bus for up to 40 minutes each way, to go to school in someone else's town. We chose to live in this town because we grew up here. It is a small community, with lots of involved citizens. We wanted our children to have pride in their neighborhood, and in its school. The government, which makes rules to protect us, says that this is not important; something called integration (not education) is more important.

Receiving what's left after taxes of my first few paychecks of 1979 has prompted me to reflect on my life. I believe that I finally understand: I am not free at all; it is the government that's free to do what it wants. The laws are not designed to protect my family and me; they are designed to protect the government. And we, the people, support this system with our money, our children—our very lives. If we don't, we risk breaking the law.

Yes, now I understand, and I am not so sure how I feel anymore about being an honest, conscientious person responsible for my actions. America, land of the free—it rings hollow. I'm still proud to be an American, and I wouldn't want to live anywhere else, but I am not as naive as I once was.

Because this letter was written so long ago, I had intended to leave it out of the new edition of this book. But when I reread it, I realized that the essence of what this woman said is probably even more relevant today than it was in 1979. And I realized it even more when Glenn Beck read an "open letter to our nation's leadership" on his show from a fifty-three-year-old Arizona woman by the name of Janet Contreras. Following is an abridged version of that letter.

I'm a home grown American citizen, 53, registered Democrat all my life. Before the last presidential election I registered as a Republican because I no longer felt the Democratic Party represents my views or works to pursue issues important to me. Now I no longer feel the Republican Party represents my views or works to pursue issues important to me.

The fact is I no longer feel any political party or representative in Washington represents my views or works to pursue the issues important to me. There must be someone. Please tell me who you are. Please stand up and tell me that you are there and that you're willing to fight for our Constitution as it was written. . . .

I am not an activist. I am not a community organizer. Nor am I a terrorist, a militant or a violent person. I am a parent and a grandparent. . . .

I thought we elected competent people to take care of the business of government so that we could work, raise our families, pay our bills, have a little recreation, complain about taxes, endure our hardships, pursue our personal goals, cut our lawns, wash our cars on the weekends and be responsible contributing members of society and teach our children to be the same all while living in the home of the free and land of the brave.

I entrusted you with upholding the Constitution. I believed in the checks and balances to keep from getting far off course. What happened? You are very far off course. Do you really think I find humor in the hiring of a speed reader to unintelligently ramble all through a bill that you signed into law without knowing what it contained? . . .

I also know that I am far from alone in these feelings. Do you honestly feel that your current pursuits have merit to patriotic Americans? We want it to stop. We want to put the brakes on everything that is being rushed by us and forced upon us. We want our voice back.

You have forced us to put our lives on hold to straighten out the mess that you are making. We will have to give up our vacations, our time spent with our children, any relaxation time we may have had and money we cannot afford to spend on you to bring our concerns to Washington. . . .

We want all of you to stop focusing on your reelection and do the job we want done, not the job you want done or the job your party wants done. You work for us and at this rate I guarantee you not for long because we are coming. We will be heard and we will be represented.

You think we're so busy with our lives that we will never come for you? We are the formerly silent majority, all of us who quietly work, pay taxes, obey the law, vote, save money, keep our noses to the grindstone and we are now looking up at you.

You have awakened us, the patriotic spirit so strong and so powerful that it had been sleeping too long. You have pushed us too far. Our numbers are great. They may surprise you. For every one of us who will be there, there will be hundreds more that could not come. Unlike you, we have their trust. We will represent them honestly, rest assured. They will be at the polls on voting day to usher you out of office. We have cancelled vacations. We will use our last few dollars saved. We will find the representation among us and a grassroots campaign will flourish.

We didn't ask for this fight. But the gloves are coming off. We do not come in violence, but we are angry. You will represent us or you will be replaced with someone who will. . . . Democrat, Republican, independent, libertarian. Understand this. We don't care. Political parties are meaningless to us.

Patriotic Americans are willing to do right by us and our Constitution and that is all that matters to us now. We are going to fire all of you who abuse power and seek more. It is not your power. It is ours and we want it back. We entrusted you with it and you abused it. You are dishonorable. You are dishonest. As Americans we are ashamed of you. You have brought shame to us.

If you are not representing the wants and needs of your constituency loudly and consistently, in spite of the objections of your party, you will be fired. Did you hear? We no longer care about your political parties. You need to be loyal to us, not to them. Because we will get you fired and they will not save you. If you do or can represent me, my issues, my views, please stand up. Make your identity known. You need to make some noise about it. Speak up. I need to know who you are.

If you do not speak up, you will be herded out with the rest of the sheep and we will replace the whole damn congress if need be one by one. We are coming. Are we coming for you? Who do you represent? What do you represent? Listen. Because we are coming. We the people are coming.[9]

I am tempted to say that the more things change, the more they stay the same, but this letter pretty clearly spells out just how much worse things are today than they were back in 1979 when Linda Timmons wrote her letter to the *Los Angeles Times*.

Though our universities still teem with Marxist professors intent on twisting the minds of impressionable youths, I am pleased to see so many young men and women speaking out against the evils of a collectivist, anti-capitalist, anti-wealth society in which government seeks to control all aspects of every citizen's life. They are starting to challenge the logic and morality of heretofore unchallenged assumptions. More and more young people are rejecting the notion that it is legitimate to violate people's rights so long as it is for a cause deemed to be worthy by self-anointed moralists.

The first thing young people need to be taught is the morality inherent in Natural Law. Once that is understood, freedom and free enterprise fall naturally into place. They must learn that property rights and human rights cannot be separated. They must learn that capitalism has not failed, that what has failed is our mixed economy (i.e., capitalism burdened by government intervention in the marketplace). They also must learn that the gold standard did not fail, that it was government's immoral and irresponsible inflation of our currency that failed.

They must learn that forced equality means a loss of freedom, and that in all countries where it has been tried, the citizens of those countries have experienced only equal misery. They must learn that socialist countries have been totally unsuccessful in their attempts to improve the well-being of the masses.

Above all, they must learn the destructive ramifications of the sinister political equation: Expediency Factors + The Vote = Government Functions.

Once understood, they will also realize that government functions must be drastically reduced, for it is that part of the equation that spells a loss of liberty for all.

Time Is Running Out

Perhaps the American Dream will never again flourish on this planet. Perhaps its next appearance will be in a world in a far-off galaxy unknown to us. If so, you and I certainly will not be a part of it. The nearest star to us lies 30 trillion miles beyond Pluto, and most stars in our own galaxy are a thousand times more distant. For you and me, the picture is pretty clear: We either restore the American Dream, right here and now, or we most certainly will never live to experience it again.

To restore the American Dream, we have to recapture the spirit that exemplified it—the spirit of individualism, self-reliance, and risk taking—the spirit described by Rose Wilder Lane in *Give Me Liberty*:

> *It was the Americans who lived and kept their fighting spirit through the hard and bitter times that followed every surge of prosperity, it was men and women who cared enough for their own personal freedom to take the risks of self-reliance and starve if they could not feed themselves, who created our country, the free country, the richest and the happiest country in the world.*

Time is running out on the United States and other Western democracies. Freedom and equality cannot coexist. We have tried it, and, like others before us who attempted it, the results have been disastrous. It is time for us to come to grips with the reality that if we continue to allow the corrupt parasites in Washington to dole out favors to us, we cannot expect to live in a free society.

In simple terms, it's time to face the reality that the party is over. We must let go of our false-prosperity past. For more than seventy years, we have acted like naughty, irresponsible children, grabbing possessions from others without their permission. The sooner we admit our errors and begin accepting our punishment (in the form of a massive deflation to adjust wages and prices to their true levels), the sooner we can get back to enjoying the liberty that has escaped us. Either we pay for our false prosperity voluntarily or we will pay for it through a loss of our remaining freedoms.

In the original edition of this book, I said that the final turning point in the decay of the American Dream was Lyndon Johnson's Great Society, which represented false prosperity—false prosperity made possible only through tyranny. Thanks, however, to Ronald Reagan and the unrelenting entrepreneurial spirit of tens of millions of Americans, we managed to nudge, ever so slightly, the liberty-tyranny pendulum back toward liberty.

But because of our lack of vigilance, the barbarians are no longer at the gates; *they are in control of our government.* The decades-long dream of arrogant, power-hungry progressives has come true: control of the House, Senate, and executive branches in Washington. And they are one death or retirement away from taking control of the judiciary, which, as Judge Sonia Sotomayor reminded us in a mocking, flip manner, illegally makes, rather than enforces, the law.

The American Dream is not to be found in the New Deal, the Great Society, or, worst of all, the *New* New Deal. The American Dream represents true prosperity, which is possible only in a free society. The heart of the American Dream is freedom; the lifeblood of the American Dream is free enterprise.

A free individual is someone not under the control or power of another. A free individual is free to govern himself. I do not want to relate to you as a competitor for government favors and largesse. I want to relate to you as a neighbor, with both of us acting in a spirit of goodwill. I want to relate to you as a free individual.

Remember, the fight against totalitarianism is a generational struggle, and it is our turn to be vigilant. Freedom or free lunch—which will it be? Ultimately, freedom must be achieved, or it must be forever lost in the pursuit.

Source Notes

Chapter 2: The System

Page 14   "The question . . . is not whether the system works . . ." Sy Leon, with Diane Hunter, *None of the Above: The Lesser of Two Evils . . . Is Evil* (Santa Ana, California: Fabian Publishing Company, 1976), pp. 204–205.

Page 21   "You pool your life and property with those of other citizens . . ." Jim Davidson, "Why Voting Isn't Necessarily the Most Patriotic Act You Can Perform," *Playgirl* (November 1976), p. 18.

Page 21   "The crowd so loves flattery . . ." Will Durant, *The Story of Philosophy: The Lives and Opinions of the Great Philosophers of the Western World* (New York: Simon and Schuster, 1961), p. 20.

Page 25   "Yet from the very beginning it [representative government] fell far short of its promise." Alvin Toffler, *The Third Wave* (William Morrow and Company, Inc., 1980), p. 91.

Page 29   "In politics we presume that everyone . . ." Will Durant, *The Story of Philosophy: The Lives and Opinions of the Great Philosophers of the Western World* (New York: Simon and Schuster, 1961), p. 20.

Page 30   "There seems to be but one remedy for acute Politicoholics." Sy Leon, with Diane Hunter, *None of the Above: The Lesser of Two Evils . . . Is Evil* (Santa Ana, California: Fabian Publishing Company, 1976), p. 170.

Chapter 3: How People Get the Things They Want

Page 42   "The function of profits . . ." Henry Hazlitt, *Economics in One Lesson* (New York: Harper & Brothers Publishers, 1946), p. 171.

Page 46   "A major source of objection to a free economy is precisely that . . ." Milton Friedman, *Capitalism and Freedom* (Chicago: The University of Chicago Press, 1962), p. 15.

Page 51   "When the capitalist is gone," she asked . . . Rose Wilder Lane, *Give Me Liberty* (Mansfield, Missouri: Laura Ingalls Wilder-Rose Wilder Lane Home Association, reprinted by *Libertarian Review*, 1977), p. 4.

Chapter 4: The Gourmet Banquet

Page 64   "A member of the committee will say, for instance, 'Here's an appropria-
tion for such-and-such.'" S.I. Hayakawa, "Mr. Hayakawa Goes to Washington,"
Harper's, January 1978, p. 39.

Page 64   "The institutionalization of the 'political means' of acquiring wealth."
Walter E. Grinder, "Introduction" in *Our Enemy, the State*, Albert Jay Nock
(New York: Tree Life Editions, 1973), p. xviii.

Page 65   ". . . violent revolutions do not so much redistribute wealth as destroy
it." Will Durant and Ariel Durant, *The Lessons of History* (New York: Simon
and Schuster, 1968), p. 72.

Page 68   "If a man grows up believing that trespass is all right . . ." Robert
LeFevre, "Fundamentals of Liberty; Lesson 41: Protection—II" (Santa Ana,
California: Rampart College), p. 6.

Page 72   "The next revolution in this country will be . . ." James Brown,
"Newsman Paul Harvey—He Reigns on His Parade," *Los Angeles Times*,
October 8, 1978, Calendar, p. 3.

Page 74   "No involuntary unemployment can exist . . ." Robert LeFevre,
"Fundamentals of Liberty; Lesson 22: Prices and Unemployment—II" (Santa
Ana, California: Rampart College), p. 7.

Page 76   "People hired by government know who is their benefactor." Milton
Friedman, "Humphrey-Hawkins," *Newsweek*, August 2, 1976, p. 55.

Page 78   "*Social Security is not a system under which nine out of ten working
people . . .*" Milton Friedman, "Tax Shenanigans," *Newsweek*, December 19,
1977, p. 55.

Page 83   "There are now more people employed by government than by manufacturing and construction combined." Data 360, http://www.data360.org/dsg
.aspx?Data_Set_Group_Id=228.

Page 85   ". . . *when it is no longer worth the producers' while to produce . . .*" John
Hospers, "The Two Classes: Producers and Parasites," *Reason* (September
1975), p. 13.

Page 90   "if everybody is rewarded just for being alive . . ." S.I. Hayakawa, "Mr.
Hayakawa Goes to Washington," *Harper's*, January 1978, pp. 42–43.

Page 91   ". . . *periodically wealth is redistributed . . .*" Will Durant, *Our Oriental
Heritage* (New York: Simon and Schuster, 1954), footnote, p. 19.

Chapter 5: Taking the *Free* out of Free Enterprise

Page 99   "An exclusive grant or franchise" Robert LeFevre, "Fundamentals of
Liberty; Lesson 18: Competition and Monopoly" (Santa Ana, California:
Rampart College), p. 5.

Page 107   "Every increase in the minimum-wage rate . . ." Milton Mueller,
"Affirmative Action: Quota to End All Quotas?" *The Libertarian Review*
(January 1979), p. 38.

Chapter 6: Promoting the General Welfare

Page 116   "It is plainly not in the interest . . ." Anne Wortham, "Individualism: For Whites Only?" *Reason* (February 1979), p. 33.

Page 117   "Our results suggest that the effect . . ." Thomas Sowell, "Are Quotas Good for Blacks?" *Commentary* (June 1978): footnote, p. 40.

Page 123   *"The good, bad, or indifferent consequences . . ."* Murray N. Rothbard, *For a New Liberty* (New York: Macmillan Publishing Co., 1973), p. 116.

Chapter 7: How the Bill Is Paid

Page 131   "The average American worker pays . . ." Jim Davidson, "Tired of Being Pushed Around Every April 15? Punch Out the IRS!" *Playboy*, April 1976, pp. 84, 86.

Page 136   "Each generation and country . . ." Henry Hazlitt, *Economics in One Lesson* (New York: Harper & Brothers Publishers, 1946), p. 182.

Page 139   "Karl Marx, in *The Communist Manifesto* . . ." Robert LeFevre, "Fundamentals of Liberty; Lesson 27: Banking," p. 6.

Page 149   "Inflation, then, encourages the free-for-all spirit . . ." Henry Hazlitt, *The Inflation Crisis, and How to Resolve It* (New Rochelle, New York: Arlington House, Publishers, 1978), p. 76.

Page 150   "The self-destruction Hazlitt described . . ." Ibid., pp. 57, 121.

Page 156   *"Doesn't everybody know, in his personal life . . ."* Henry Hazlitt, *Economics in One Lesson* (New York: Harper & Brothers Publishers, 1946), p. 4.

Chapter 8: Keeping It All in Place

Page 158   "It is incredible how as soon . . ." Etienne de la Boetie, *The Politics of Obedience: The Discourse of Voluntary Servitude*, translated by Harry Kurz (Montreal, Canada: Black Rose Books, 1975), p. 60.

Page 161   "My paramount object in this struggle . . ." Robert Froman, *Racism* (New York: Delacorte Press, 1972), pp. 53–54.

Page 161   "I am not nor ever have been in favor . . ." Ibid., pp. 53, 54.

Page 161   "I don't go so far as to think that the only good . . ." Lewis H. Carlson and George A. Colburn, *In Their Place: White America Defines Her Minorities, 1850–1890* (New York: John Wiley & Sons, 1972), p. 1.

Page 162   "To make a contented slave, it is necessary to make . . ." Anne Wortham, "Individualism: For Whites Only?" *Reason* (February 1979) p. 31.

Page 164   *"Men fear thought as they fear nothing else on earth . . ."* Giles St. Aubyn, *The Art of Argument* (Buchanan, New York: Emerson Books, 1962), p. 28.

Page 169   *"When faith and the power to persuade . . ."* Eric Hoffer, *The True Believer* (New York: Harper & Row, Publishers, 1951), p. 67.

Page 170   *"Time sanctifies everything . . ."* Will Durant, *Our Oriental Heritage* (New York: Simon and Schuster, 1954), p. 24.

Chapter 9: Taking Back America

Page 175   "American Government . . . is not an Authority." Rose Wilder Lane, *The Discovery of Freedom: Man's Struggle Against Authority*, Foreword by Robert LeFevre, Introduction by Roger Lea McBride (New York: Arno Press and The New York Times, 1972), p. 190.

Page 179   "Today one feels the ether of these books . . ." Eric Hoffer, *Before the Sabbath* (New York: Harper & Row, Publishers, 1979), p. 53.

Pages 183–84   *"Mankind has always sought to substitute energy for reason . . ."* Morgan Maxfield, *1929 Revisited* (Kansas City, Missouri: National Youth Foundation, 1977), p. 155.

Page 184   "If Americans ever forget that American Government . . ." Rose Wilder Lane, *The Discovery of Freedom: Man's Struggle Against Authority*, Foreword by Robert LeFevre, Introduction by Roger Lea McBride (New York: Arno Press and The New York Times, 1972), pp. 189–190.

Page 188   "The price of individual liberty . . ." Rose Wilder Lane, *Give Me Liberty* (Mansfield, Missouri: Laura Ingalls Wilder-Rose Wilder Lane Home Association, reprinted by *Libertarian Review*, 1977), pp. 21, 44.

Page 196   "Incredibly, the federal government owns . . ." http://findarticles.com/ p/articles/mi_m0HIC/is_2_17/ai_98543759/; WorldNetDaily, "The Fight against Government Land Ownership," www.wnd.com/news/article.asp?ARTICLE_ ID=43824; Lighthouse Patriot Journal, http://lighthousepatriotjournal .wordpress.com/2009/ 08/09/myth-blaster-woman-in-arizona-writes-letter-to-glenn-beck/.

About the Author

Robert Ringer is the author of three #1 best sellers and publisher of the pro-liberty e-letter *A Voice of Sanity in an Insane World*, in which he shares his analyses of today's economic, sociological, and political environment from a pro-free-market point of view. He is also a regular columnist for *WorldNetDaily*.

Through the publication of his classic *New York Times* best seller *Restoring the American Dream*, he became an outspoken advocate for the cause of freedom and free enterprise long before it was popular to do so. His friend and close ally, former Secretary of the Treasury William E. Simon (who wrote the Foreword to the original edition of *Restoring the American Dream*), summed up Ringer's impact on America when he passionately stated:

> *"[You are] a courageous, dedicated, and brilliant American patriot who supports and, more importantly, fights to preserve the fundamental principles and ideas that built our beautiful country. My deep gratitude for all your support and assistance, and everything you are doing to preserve my children's freedom."*

Unwavering in his belief that liberty must be given a higher priority than all other objectives, Ringer is openly committed to stemming the tide of socialism in America and getting the country back on the right path.

To this end, he hosts the highly acclaimed *Liberty Education Interview Series* (www.robertringer.com), which features interviews with today's top political, economic, and social leaders. In these powerful sessions, he focuses on the most vital and controversial issues of the day in an effort to give listeners the information they need to help promote the cause of liberty.

Ringer has appeared on numerous national talk shows, including *The Tonight Show, Today, Good Morning America, ABC News Nightline*, and *The Charlie Rose Show*. In addition, he has been the subject of feature articles in such major publications as *Time, People, The Wall Street Journal, Fortune, Barron's*, and *The New York Times*.

Index